THE LAB

ALLISON CONWAY

Thank you to my mom and dad, and to Mrs. Weimer my art teacher, who told me to "just finish it."

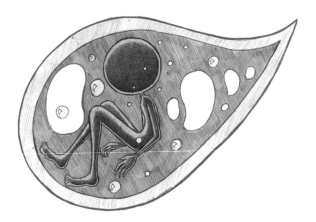

The Lab © 2020 Allison Conway

Published by Top Shelf Productions, PO Box 1282, Marietta, GA 30061-1282, USA. Top Shelf Productions is an imprint of IDW Publishing, a division of Idea and Design Works, LLC. Offices: 2765 Truxtun Road, San Diego, CA 92106. Top Shelf Productions®, the Top Shelf logo, Idea and Design Works®, and the IDW logo are registered trademarks of Idea and Design Works, LLC. All Rights Reserved. With the exception of small excerpts of artwork used for review purposes, none of the contents of this publication may be reprinted without the permission of IDW Publishing. IDW Publishing does not read or accept unsolicited submissions of ideas, stories, or artwork.

Editor-in-Chief Chris Staros.
Edited by Chris Staros.
Designed by Allison Conway & Gilberto Lazcano.

Visit our online catalog at www.topshelfcomix.com

ISBN 978-1-60309-461-0

Printed in Korea.

24 23 22 21 20   1 2 3 4 5

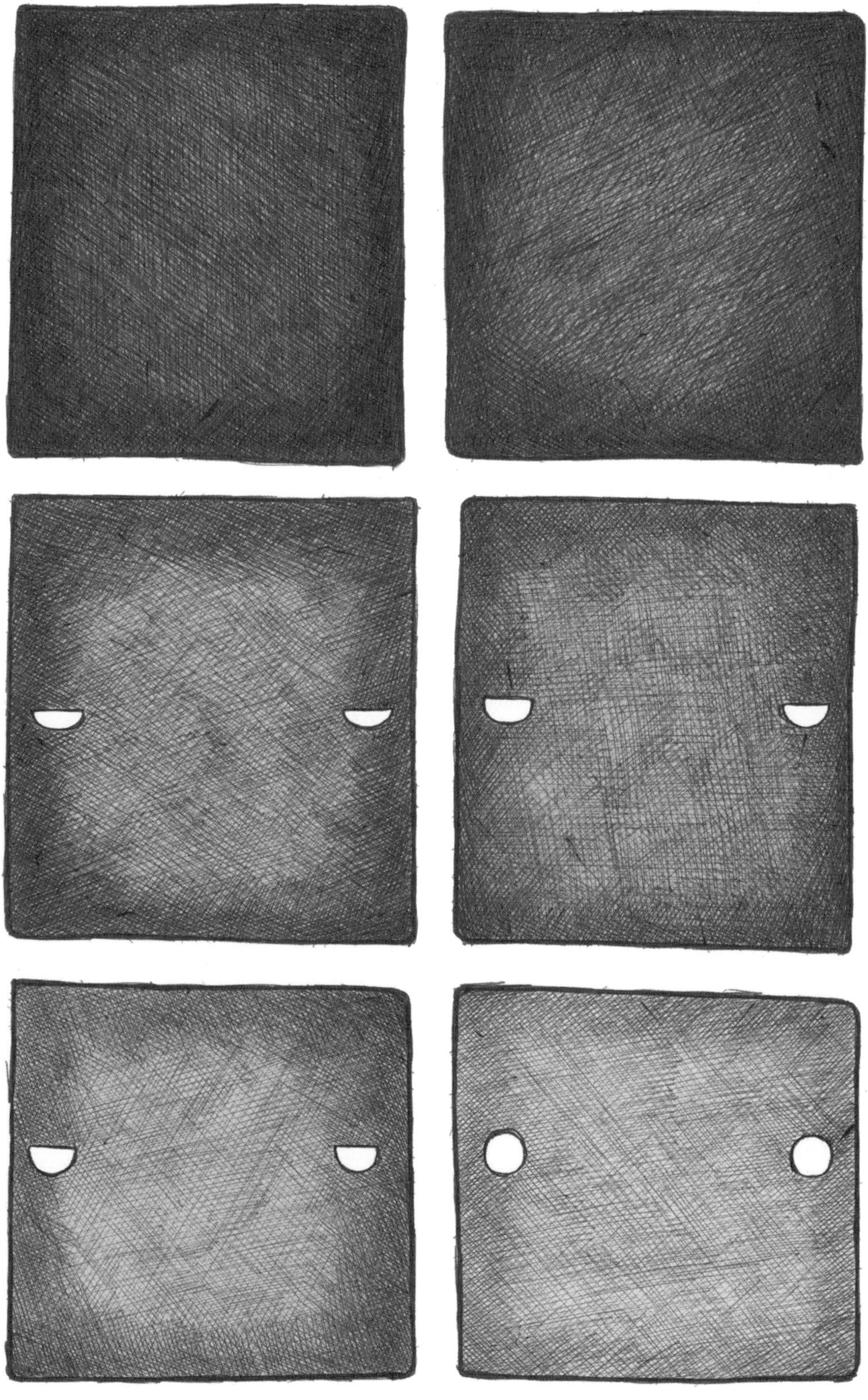

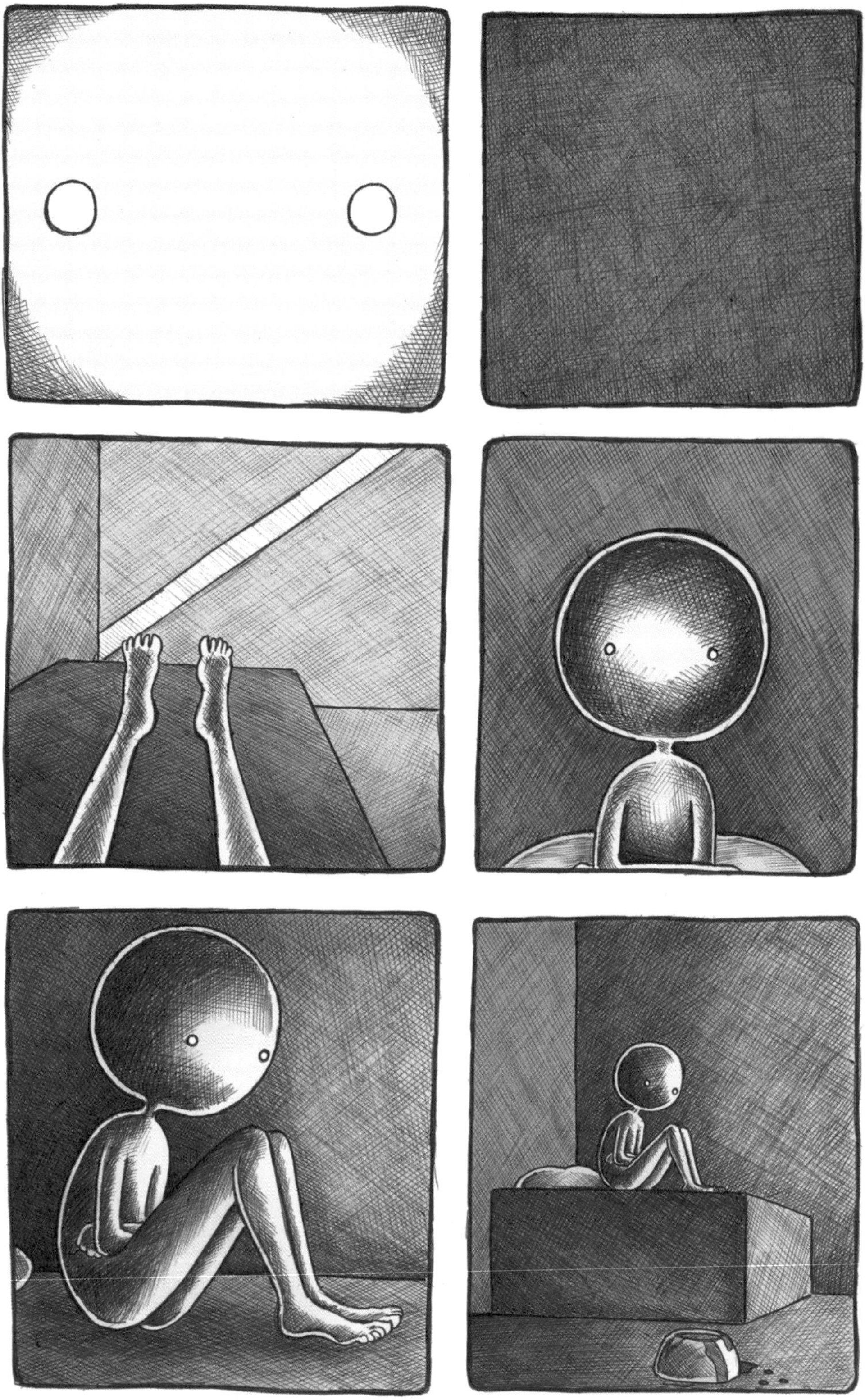

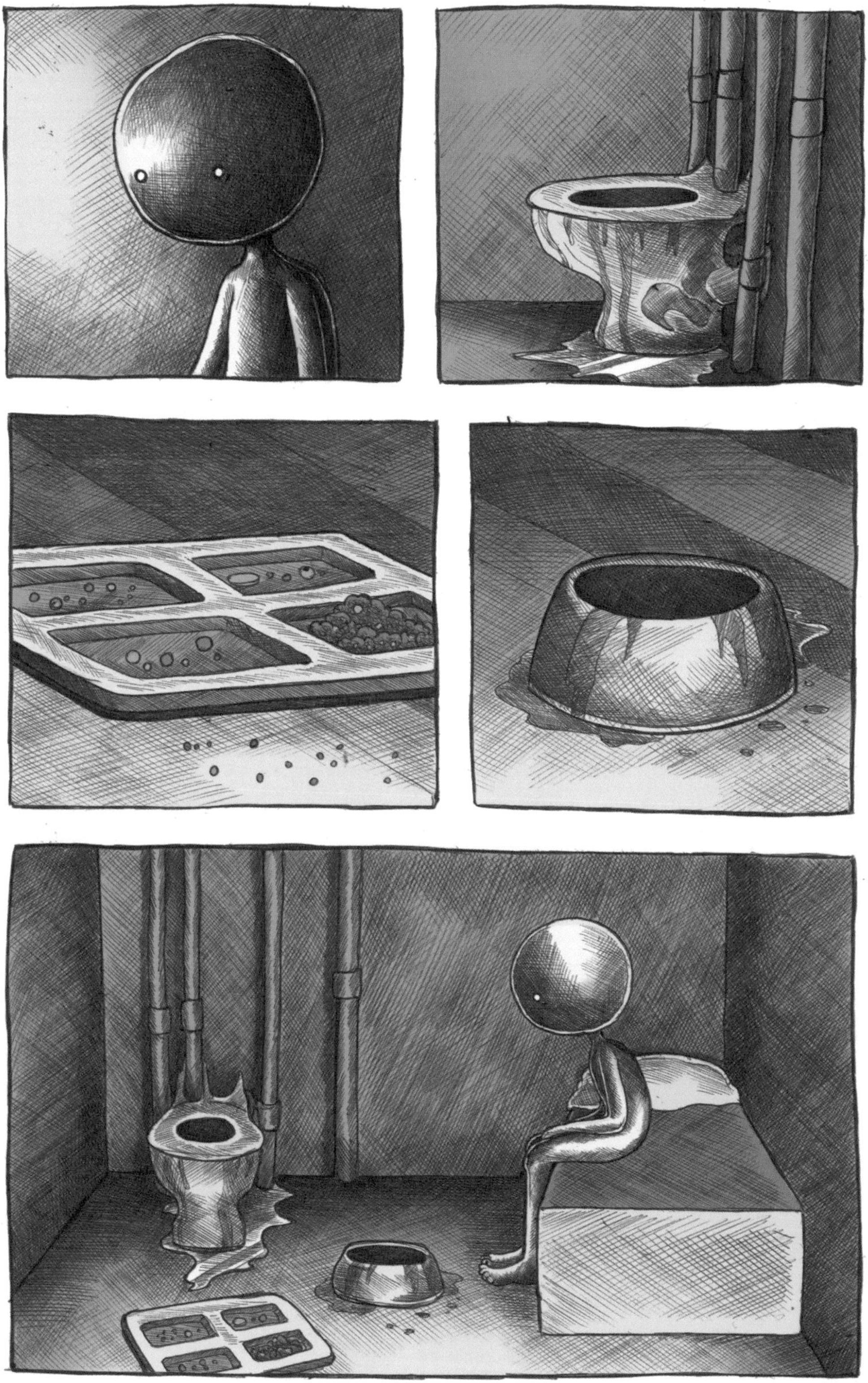

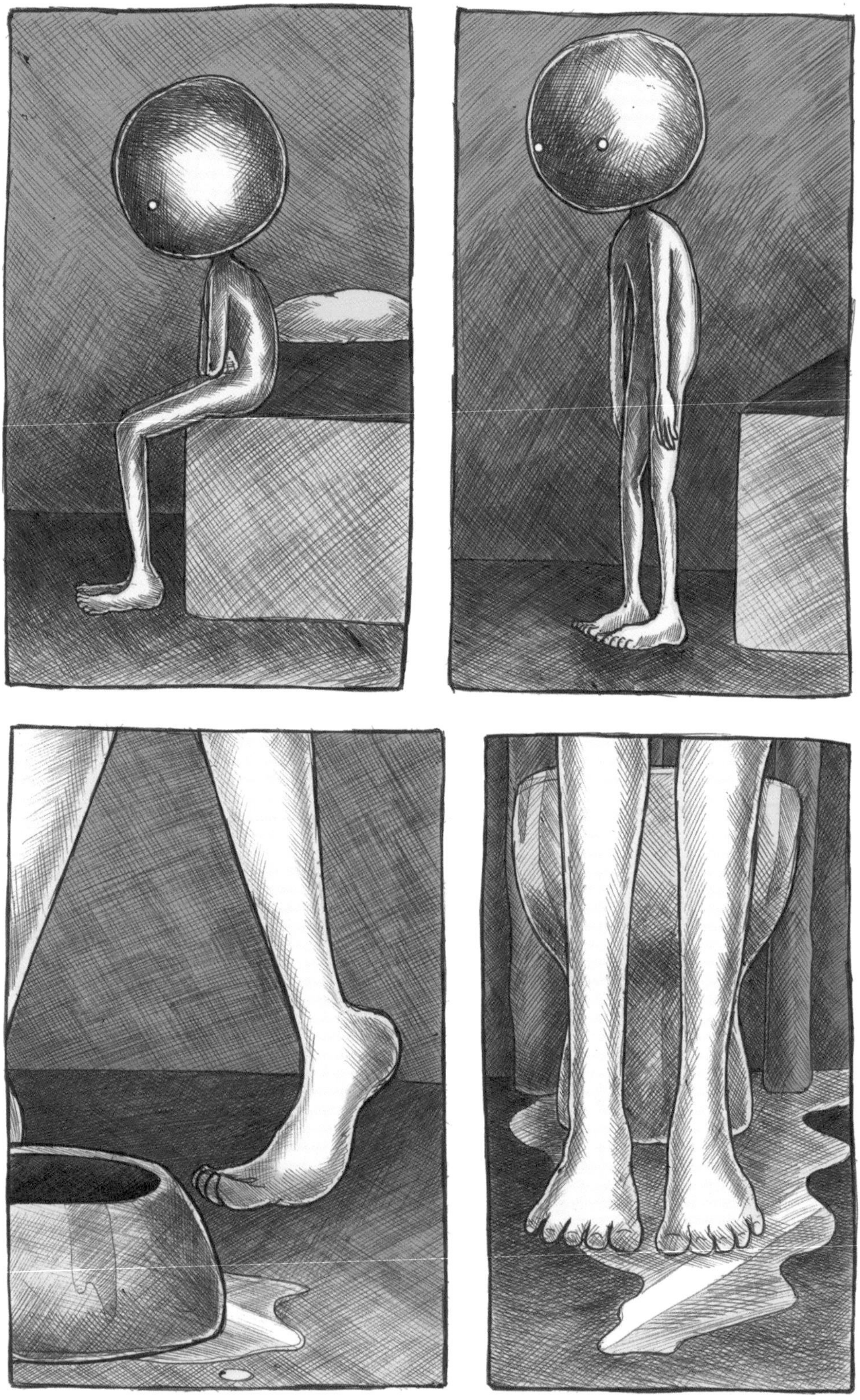

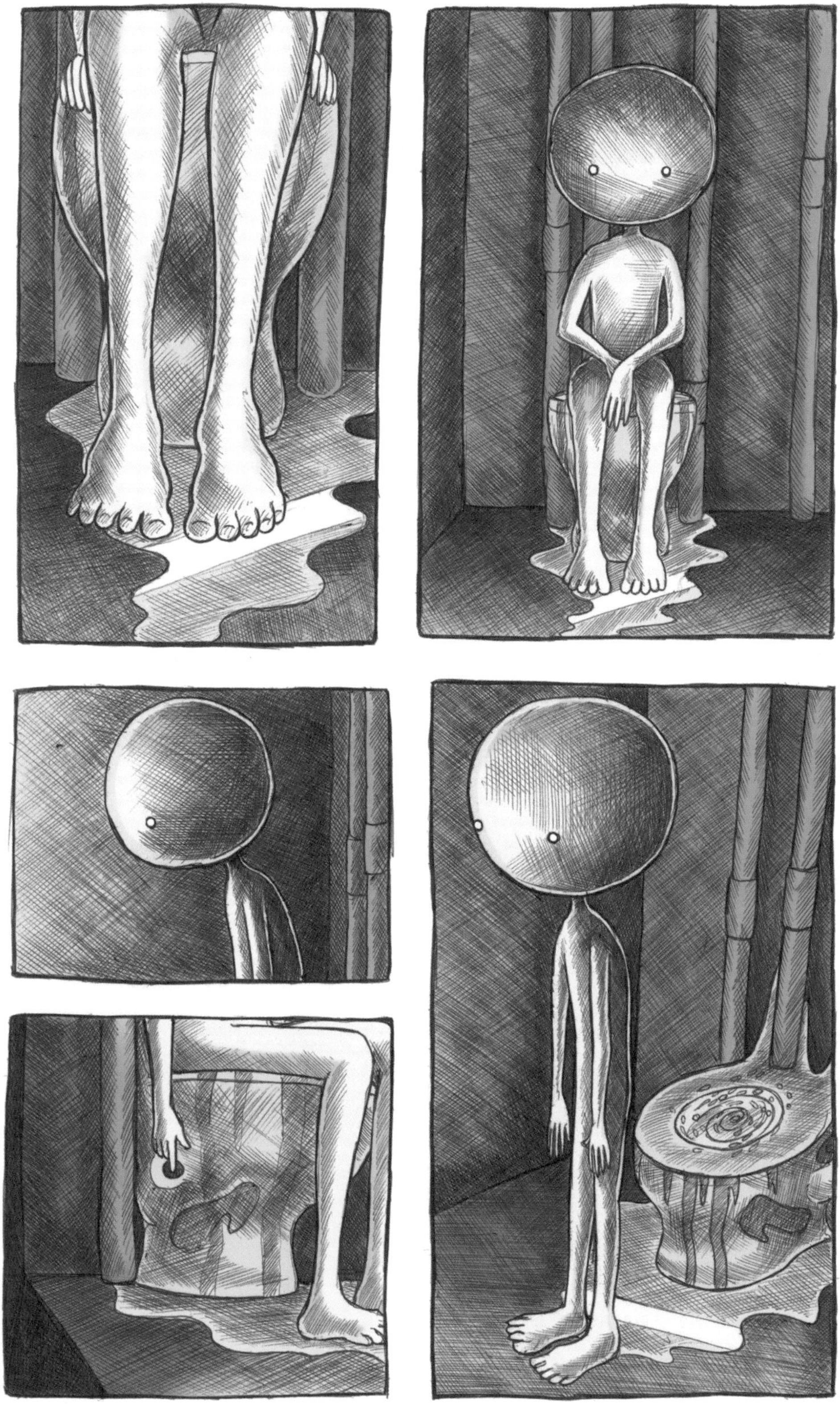

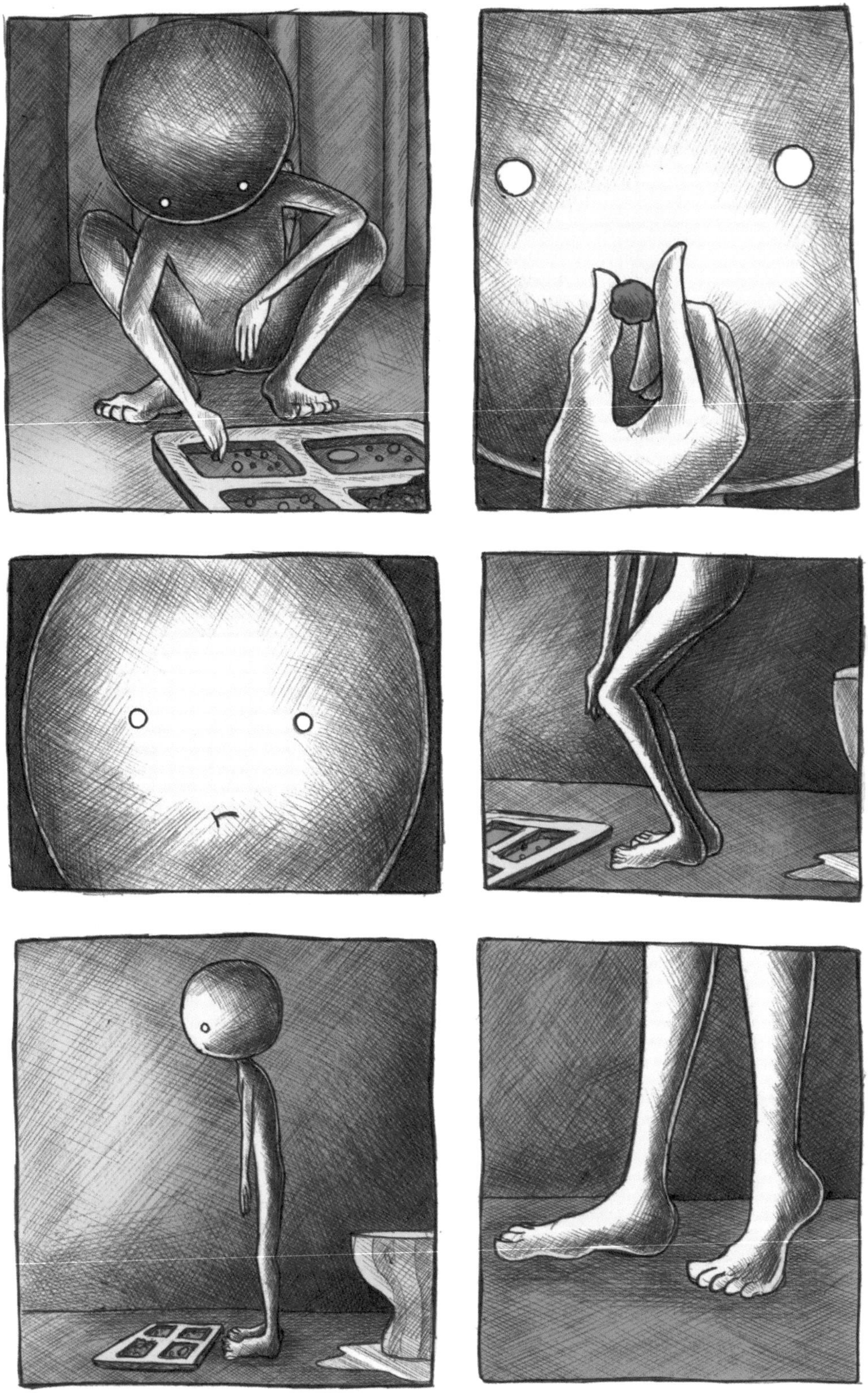

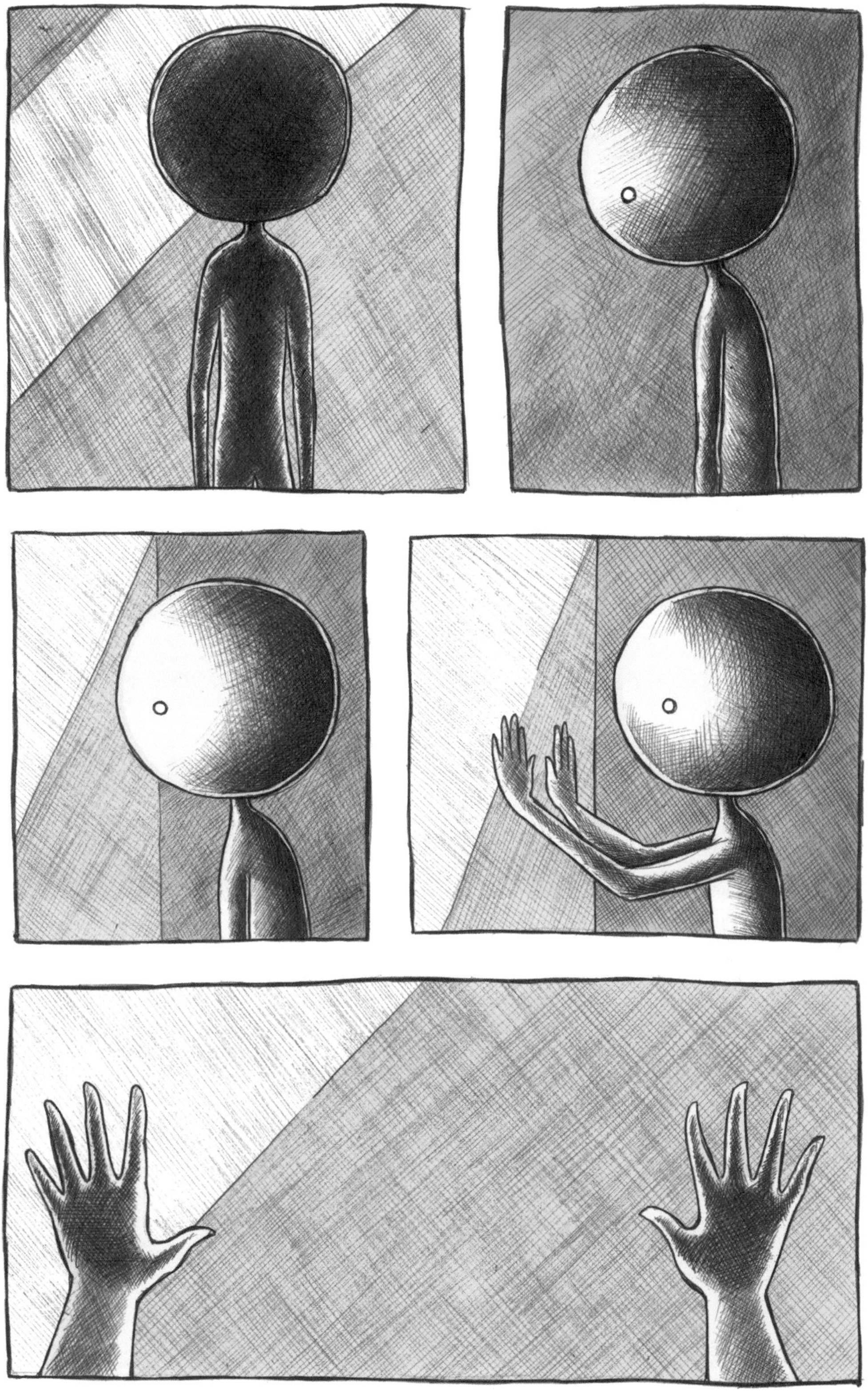

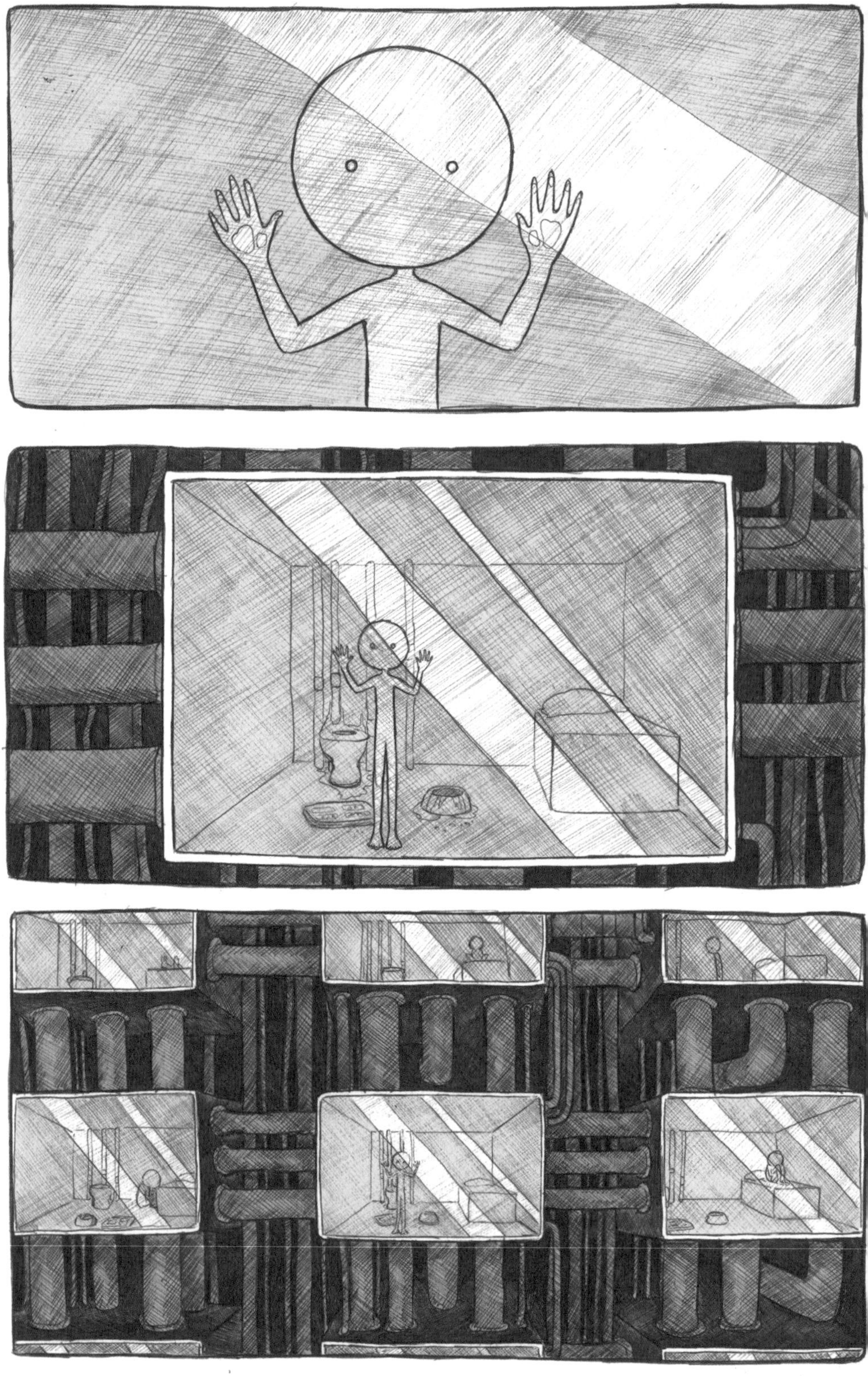

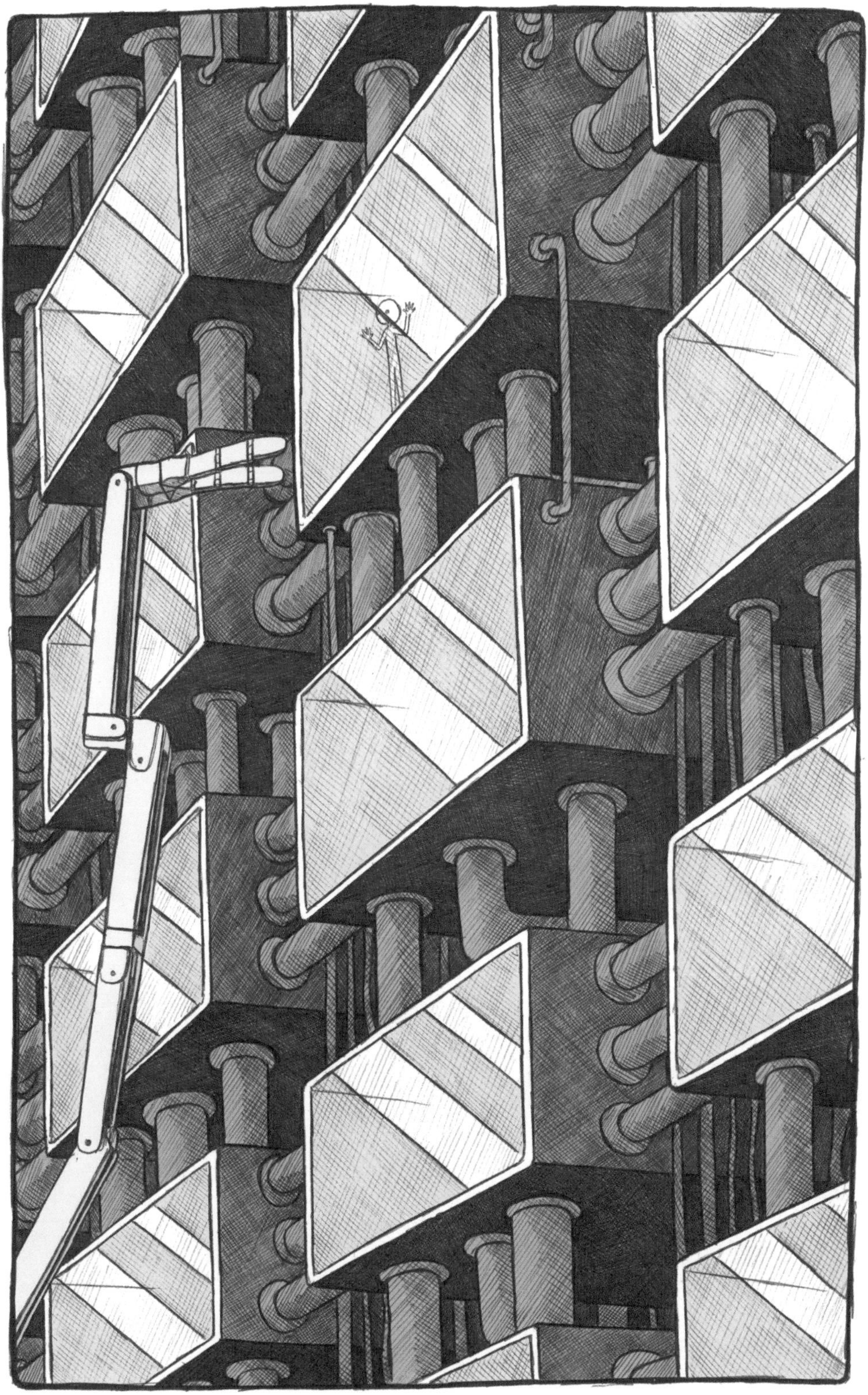

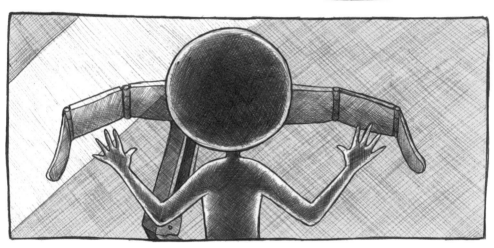

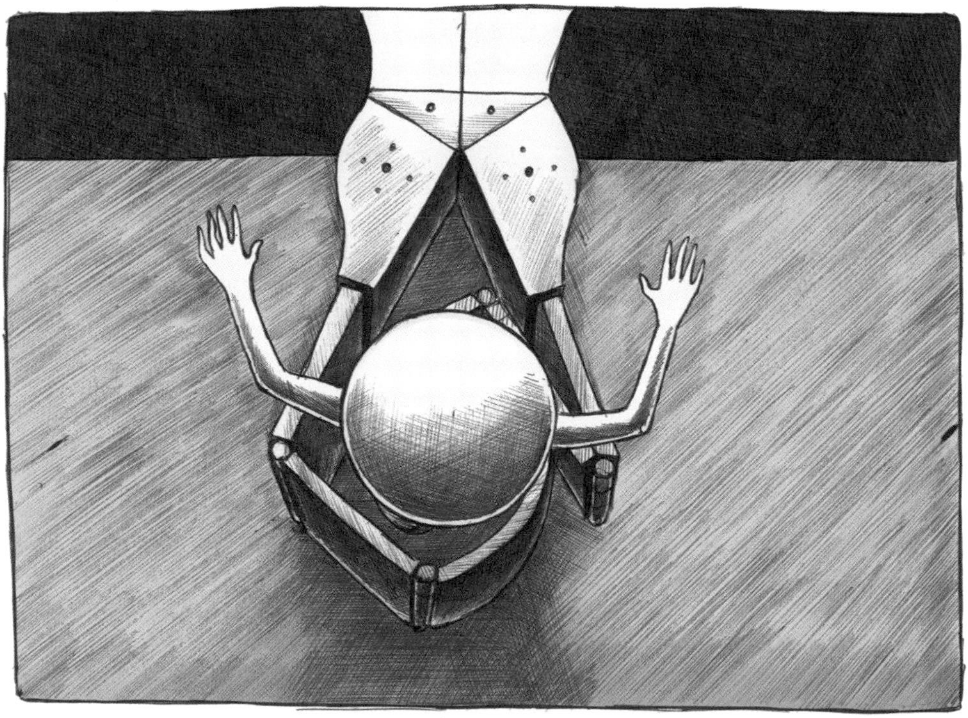

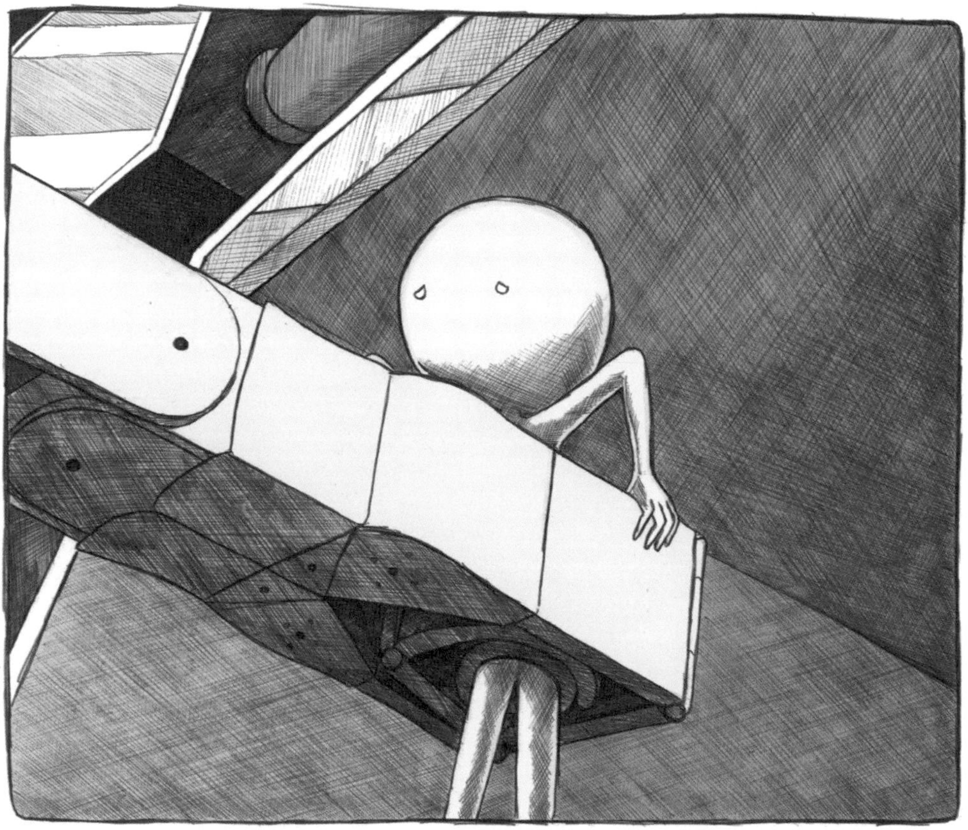

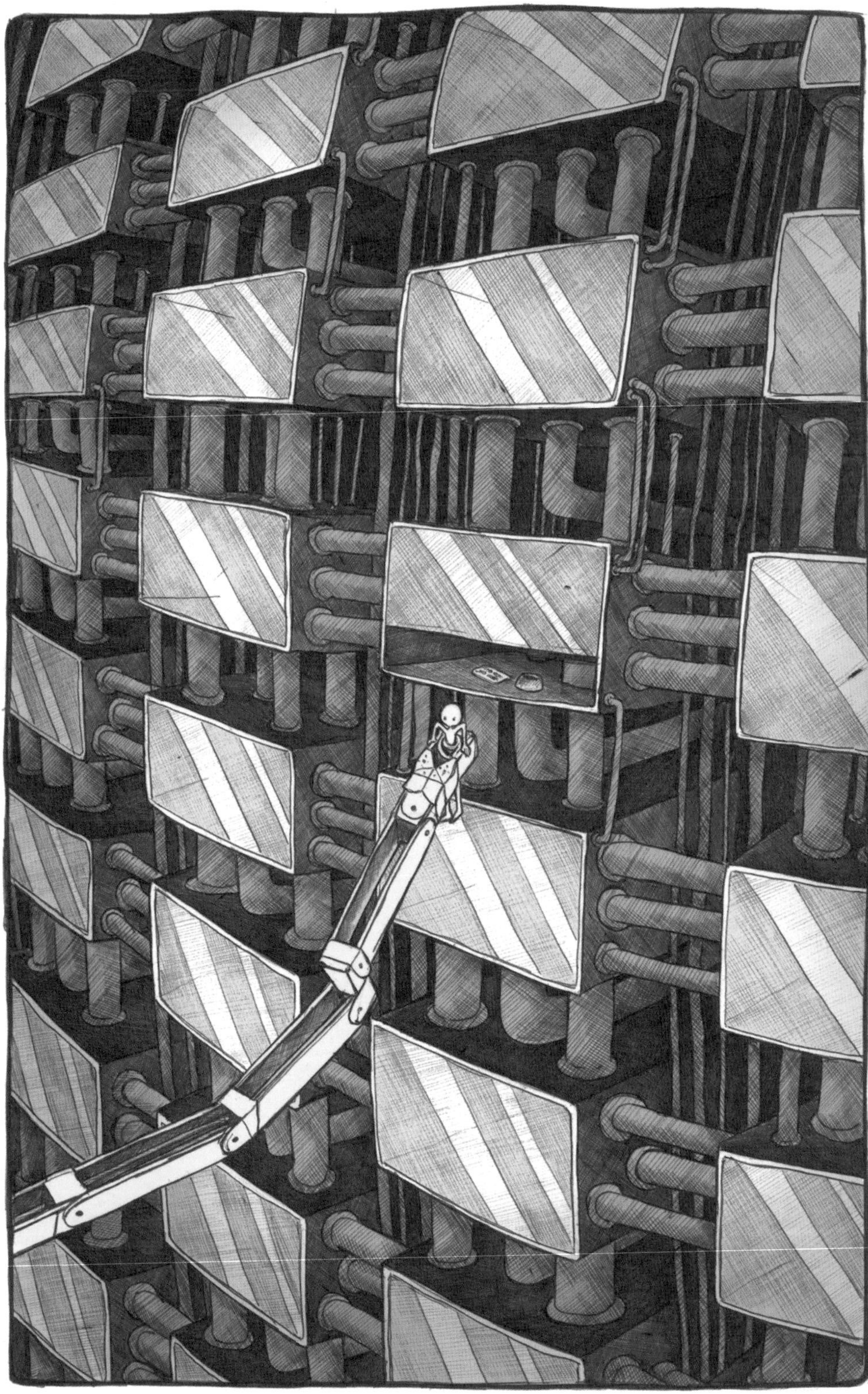

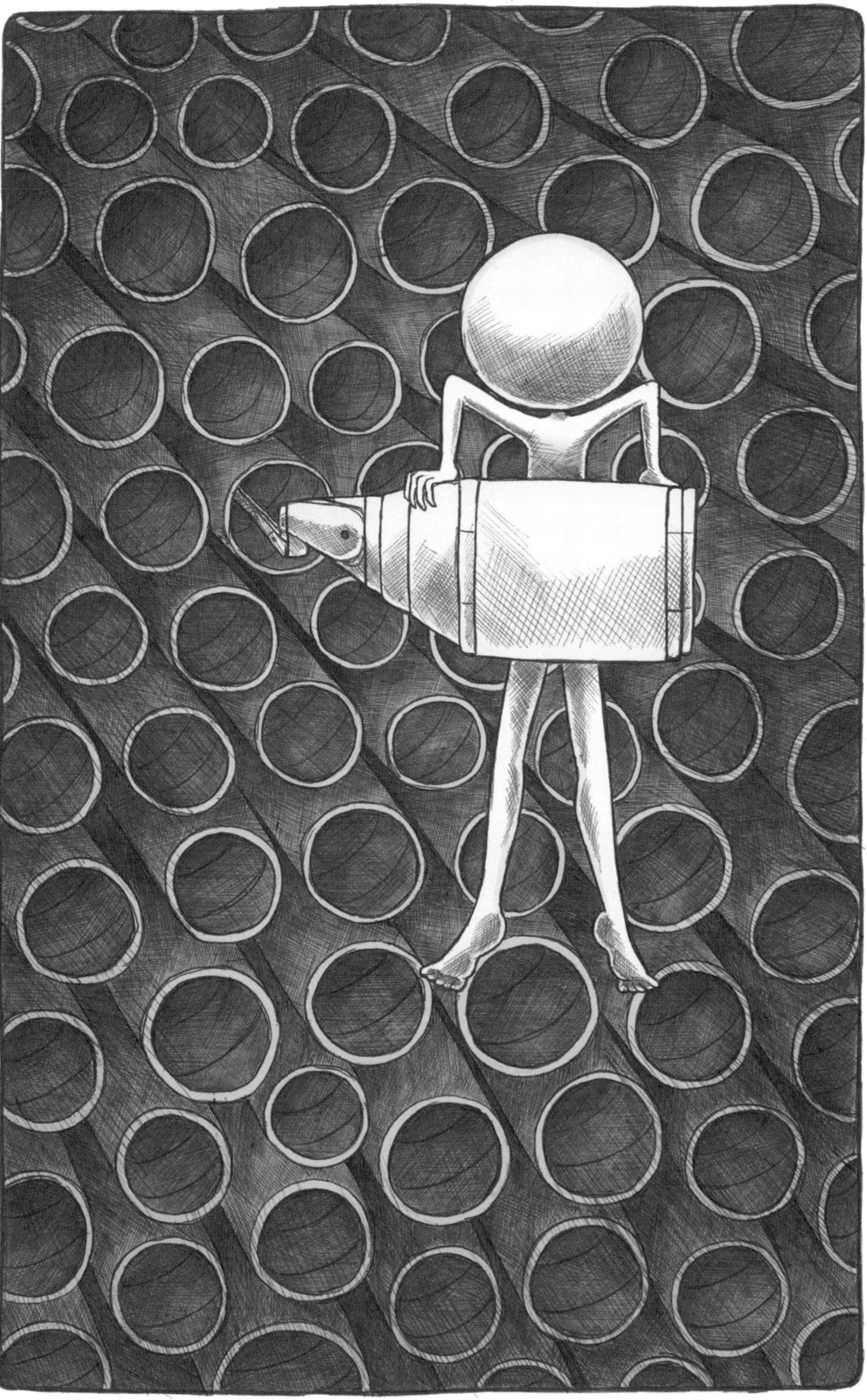

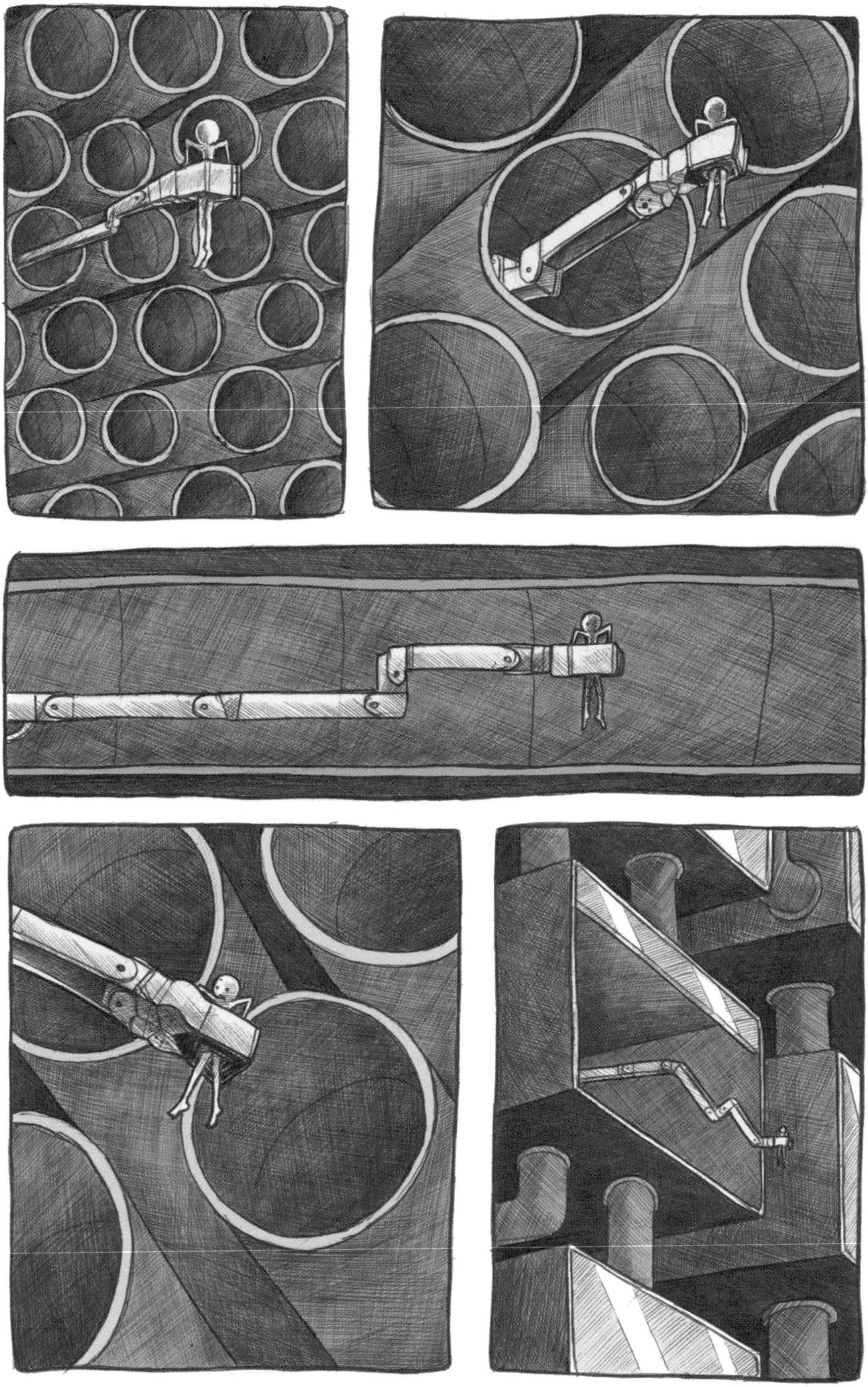

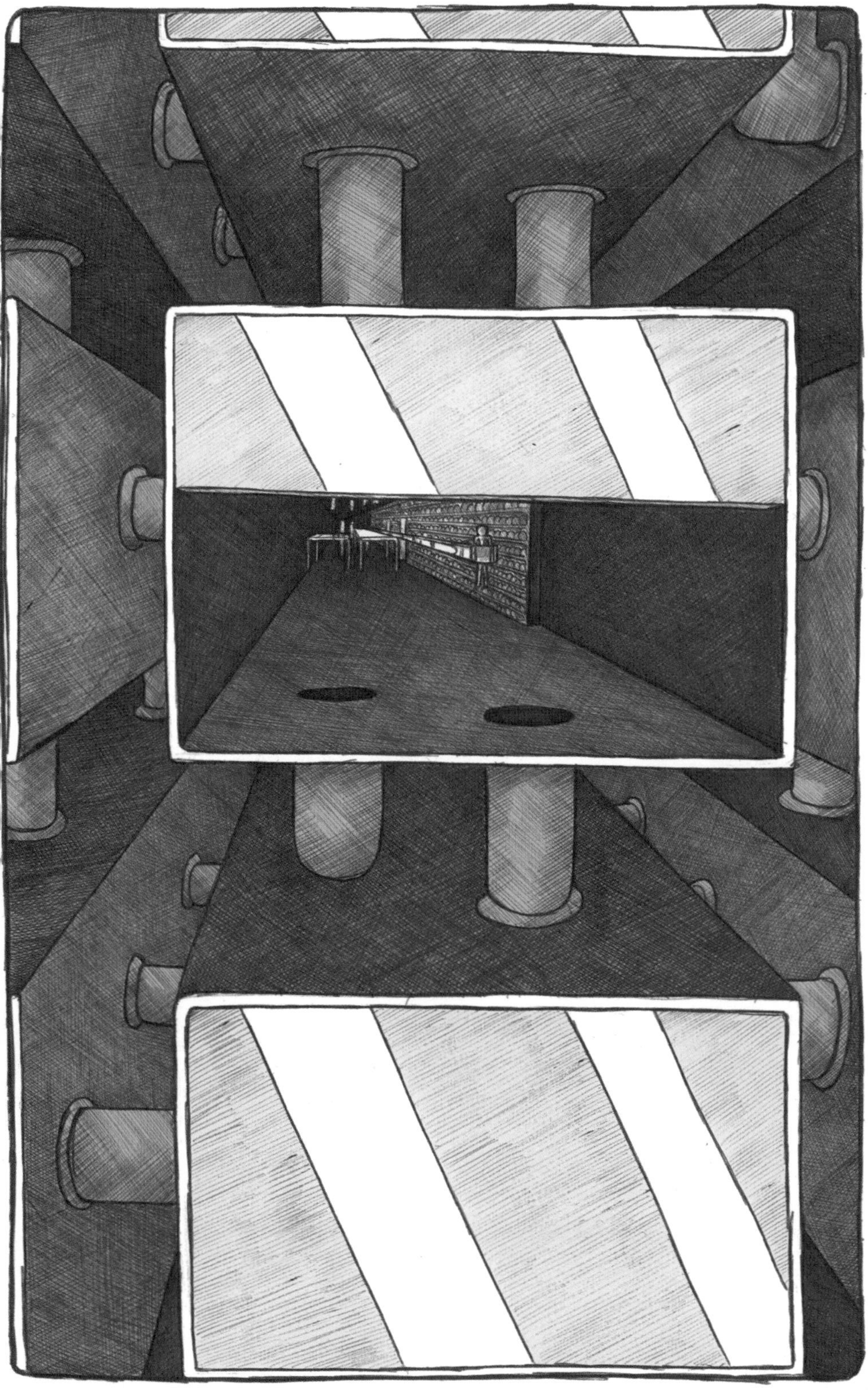

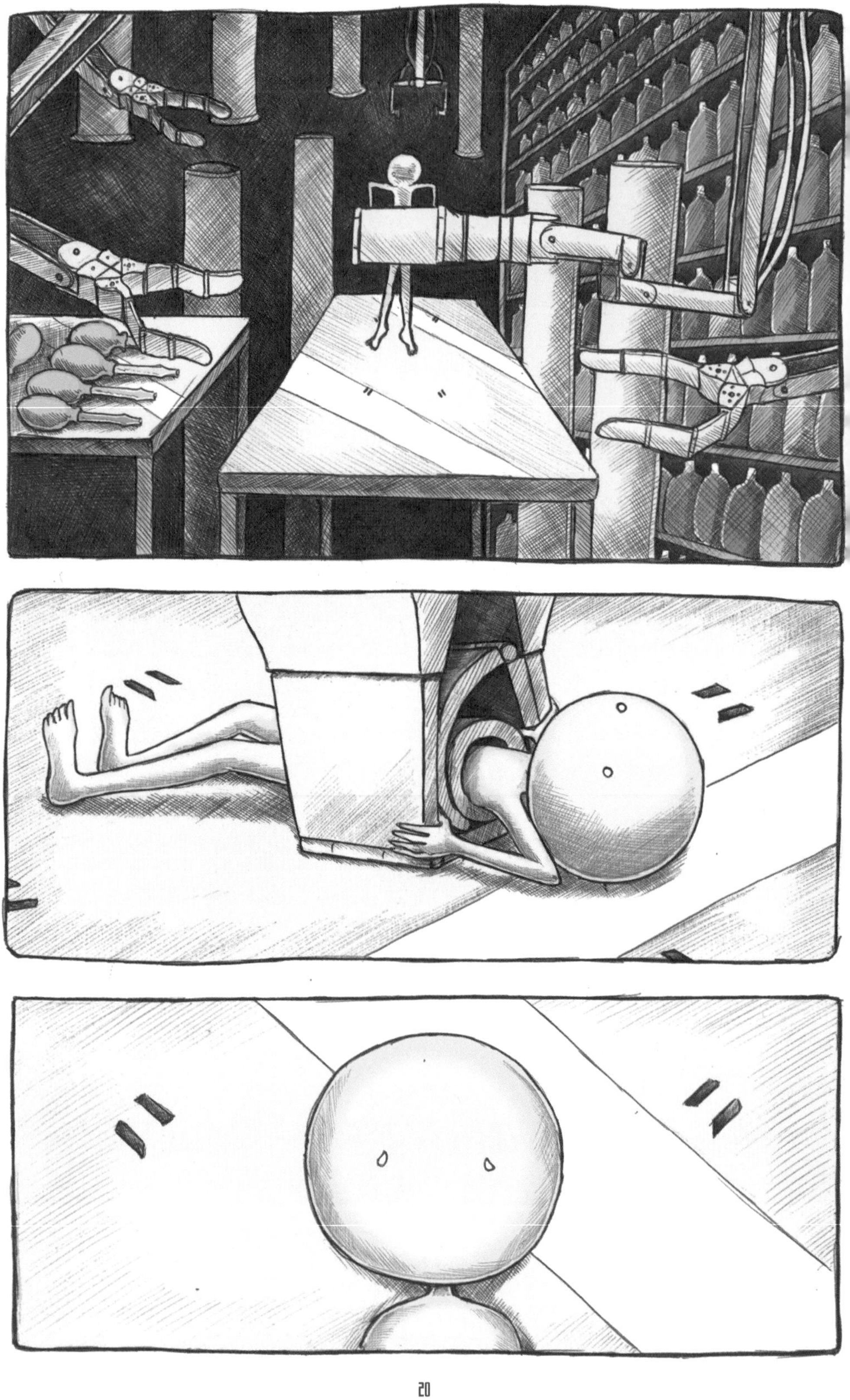

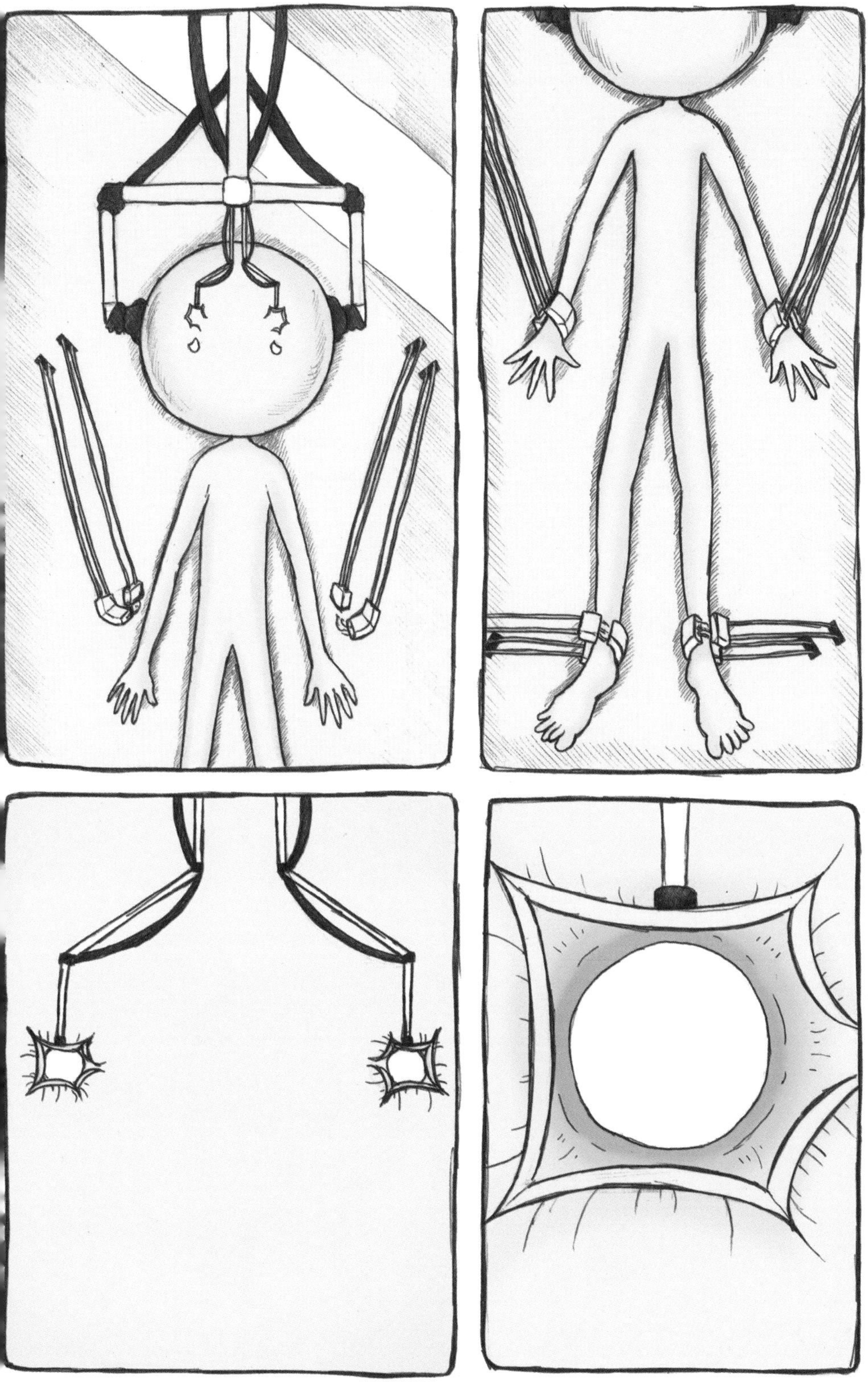

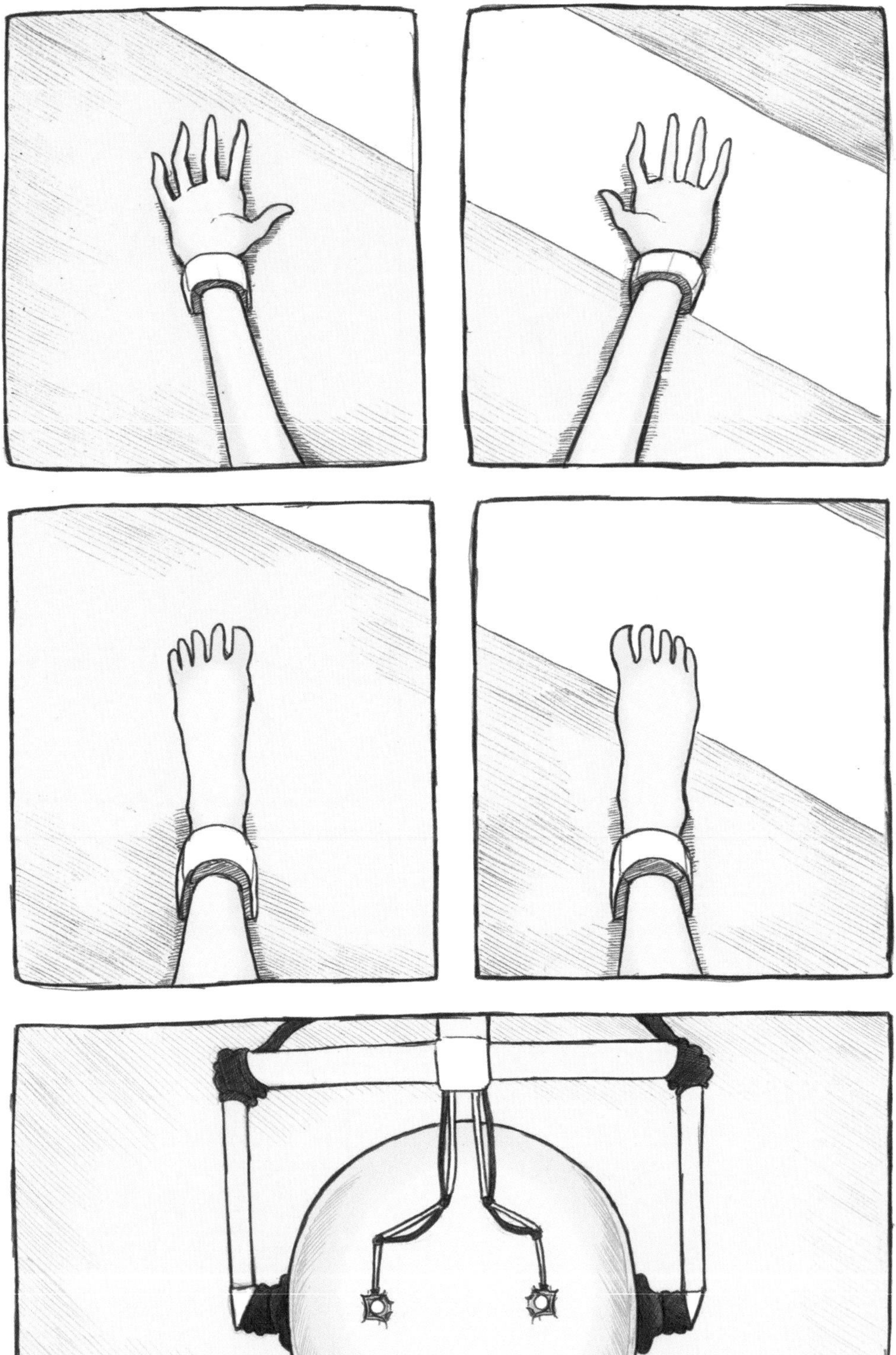

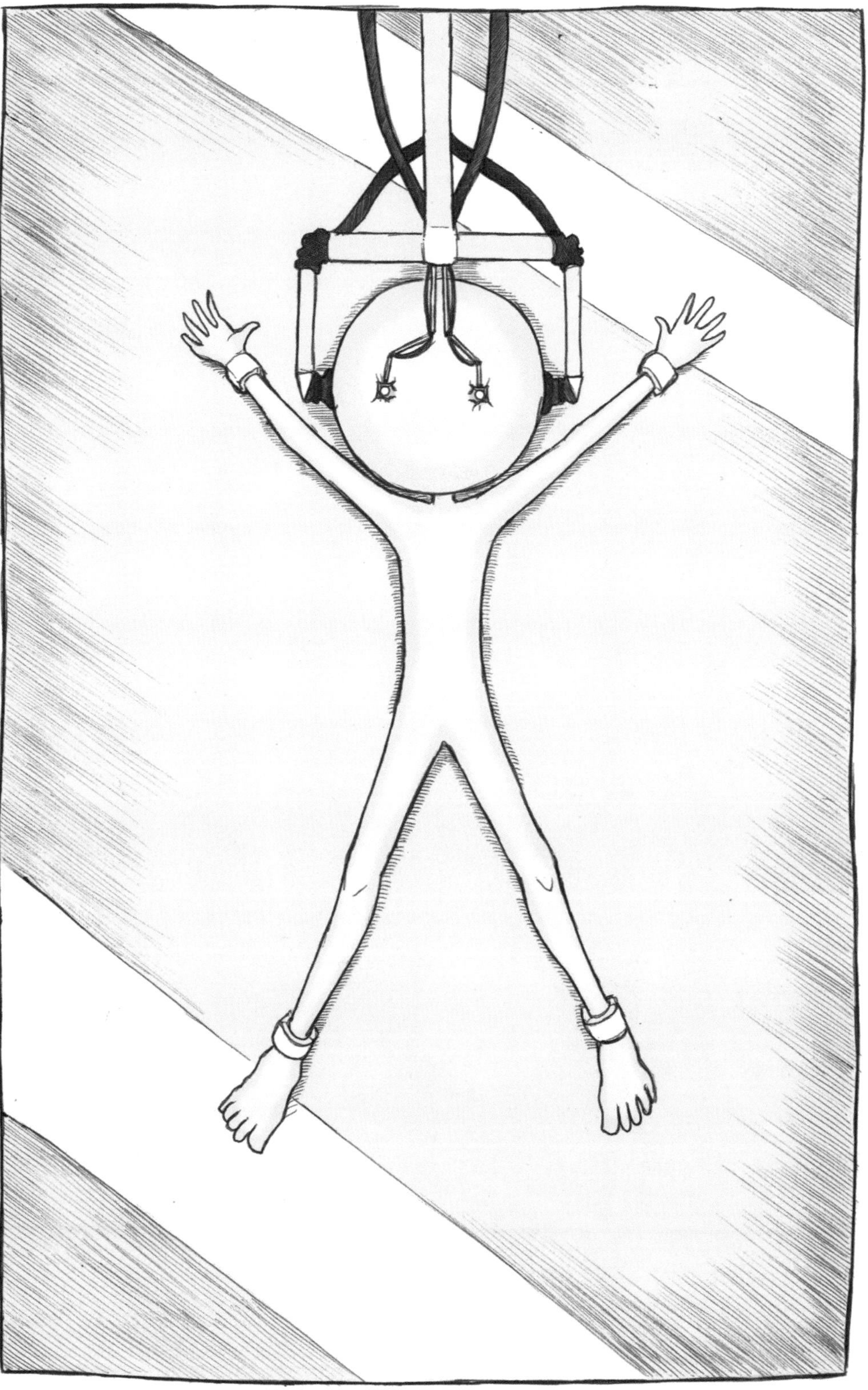

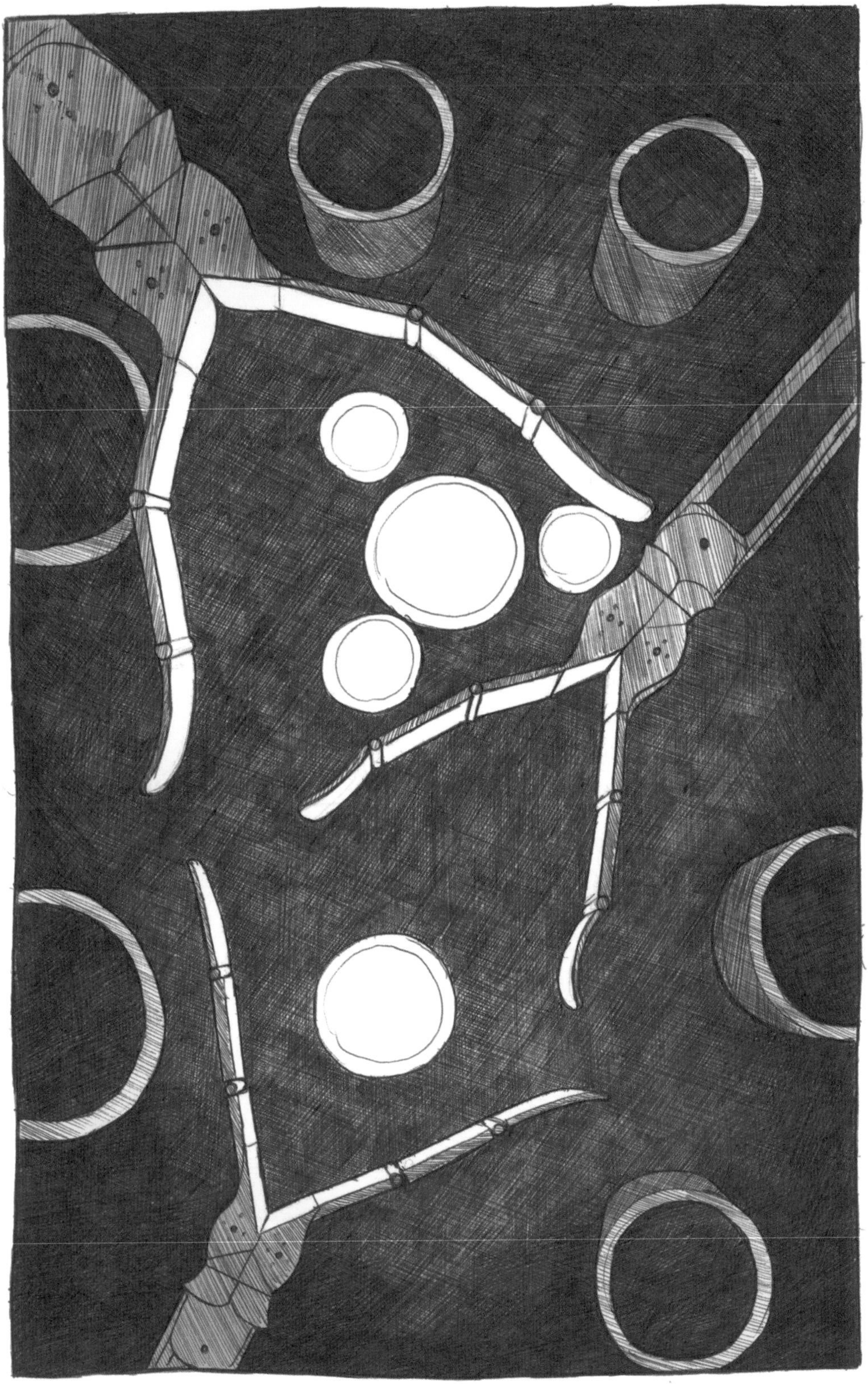

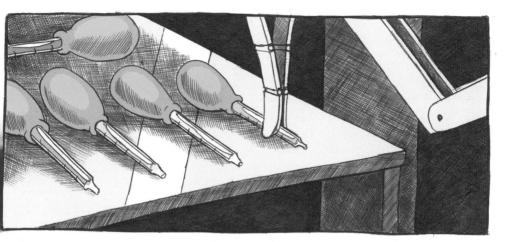

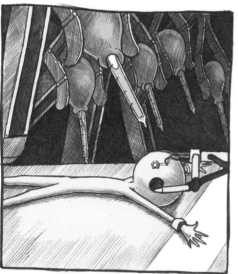
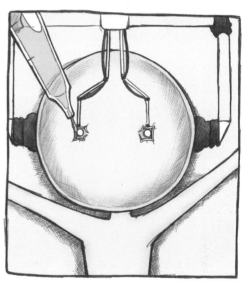

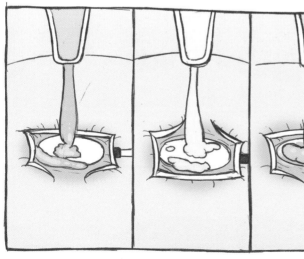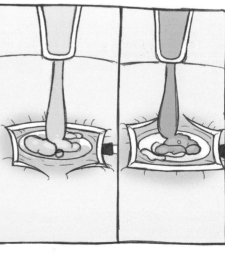

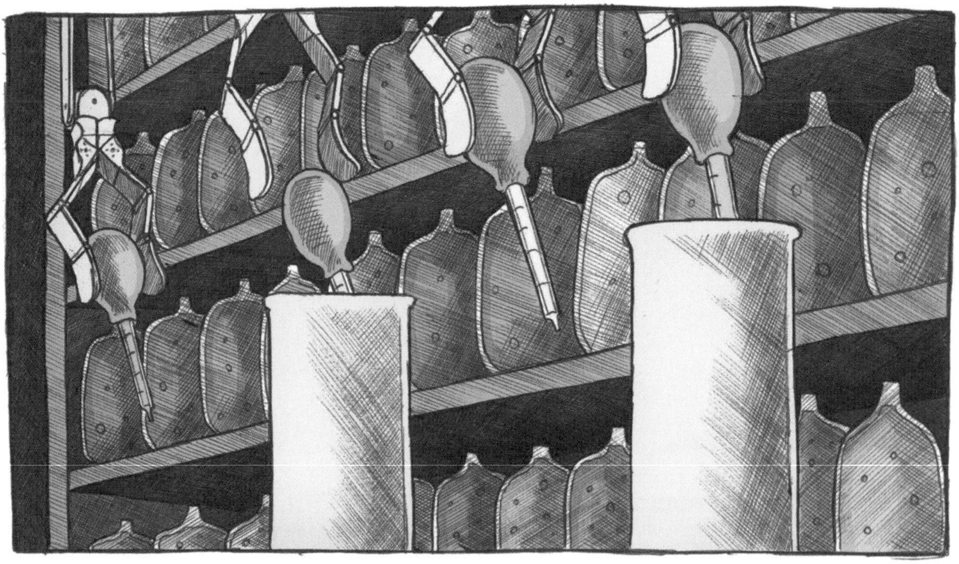

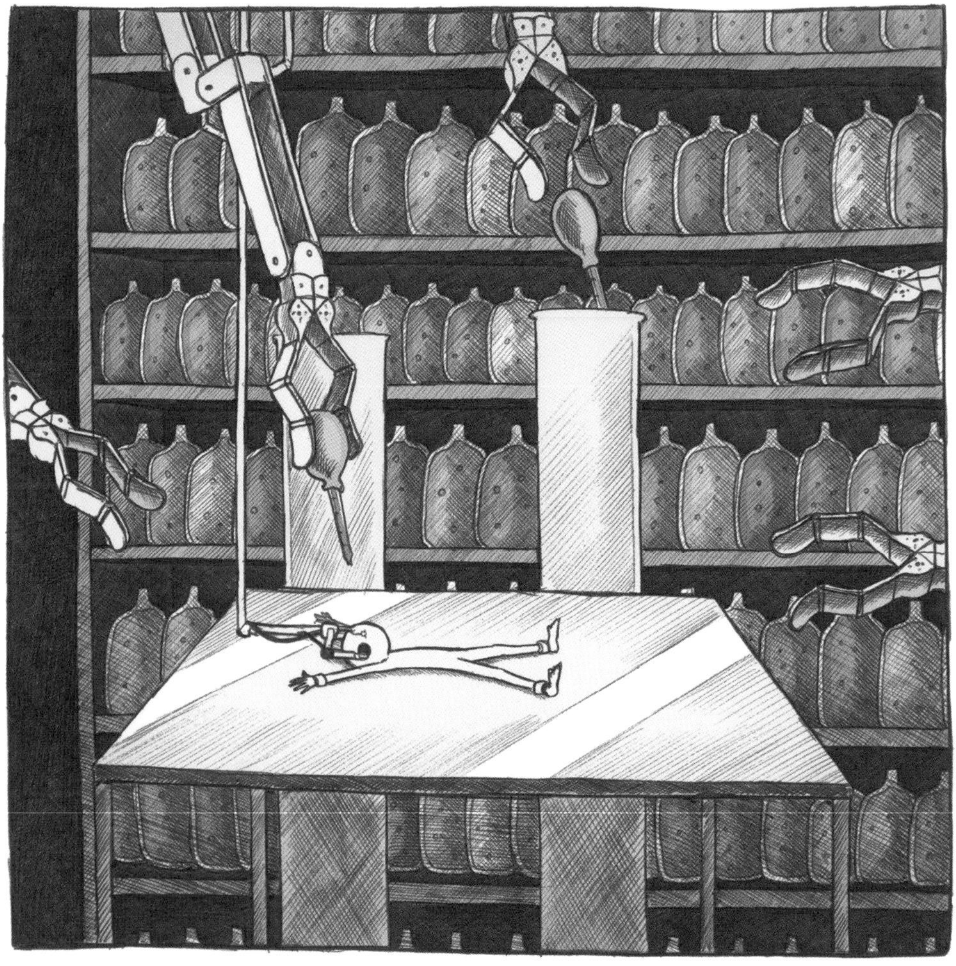

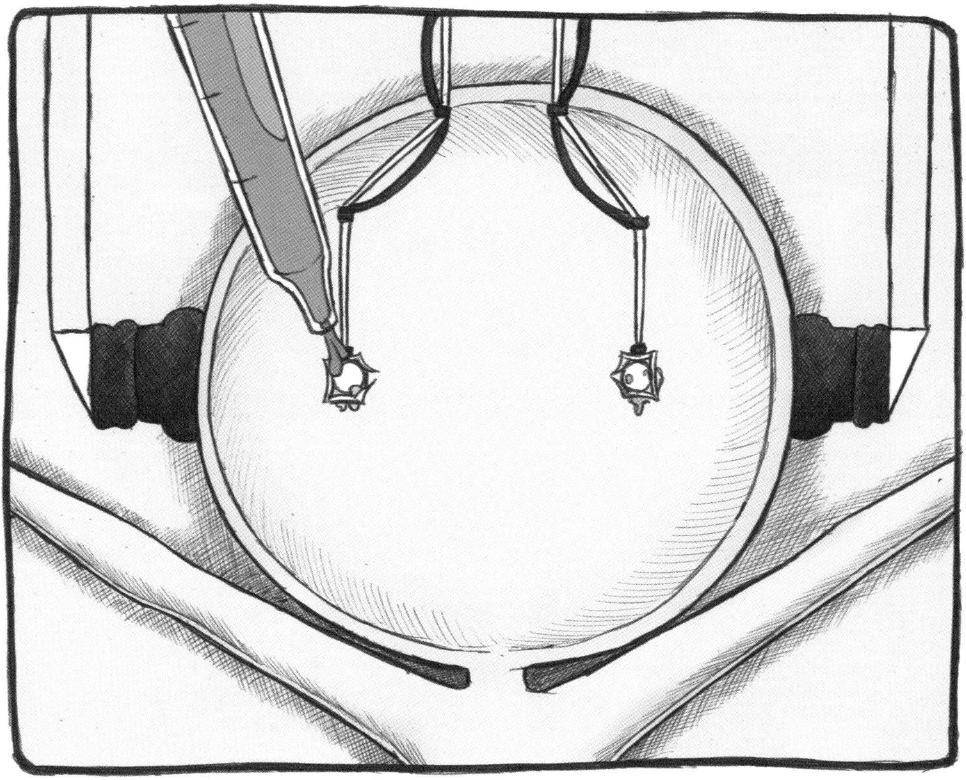

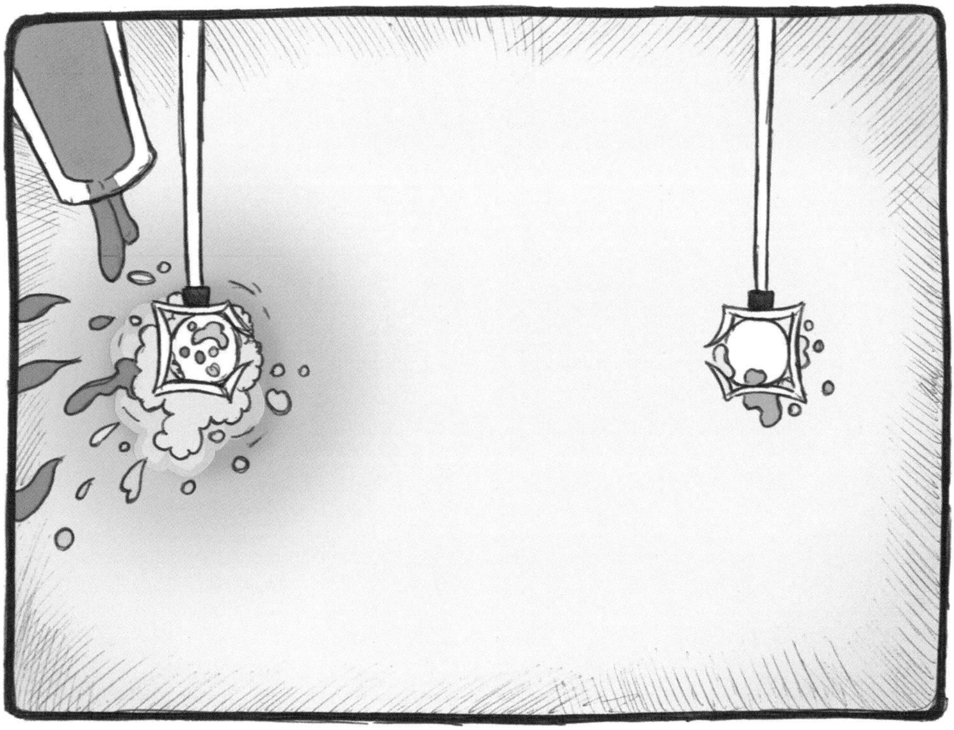

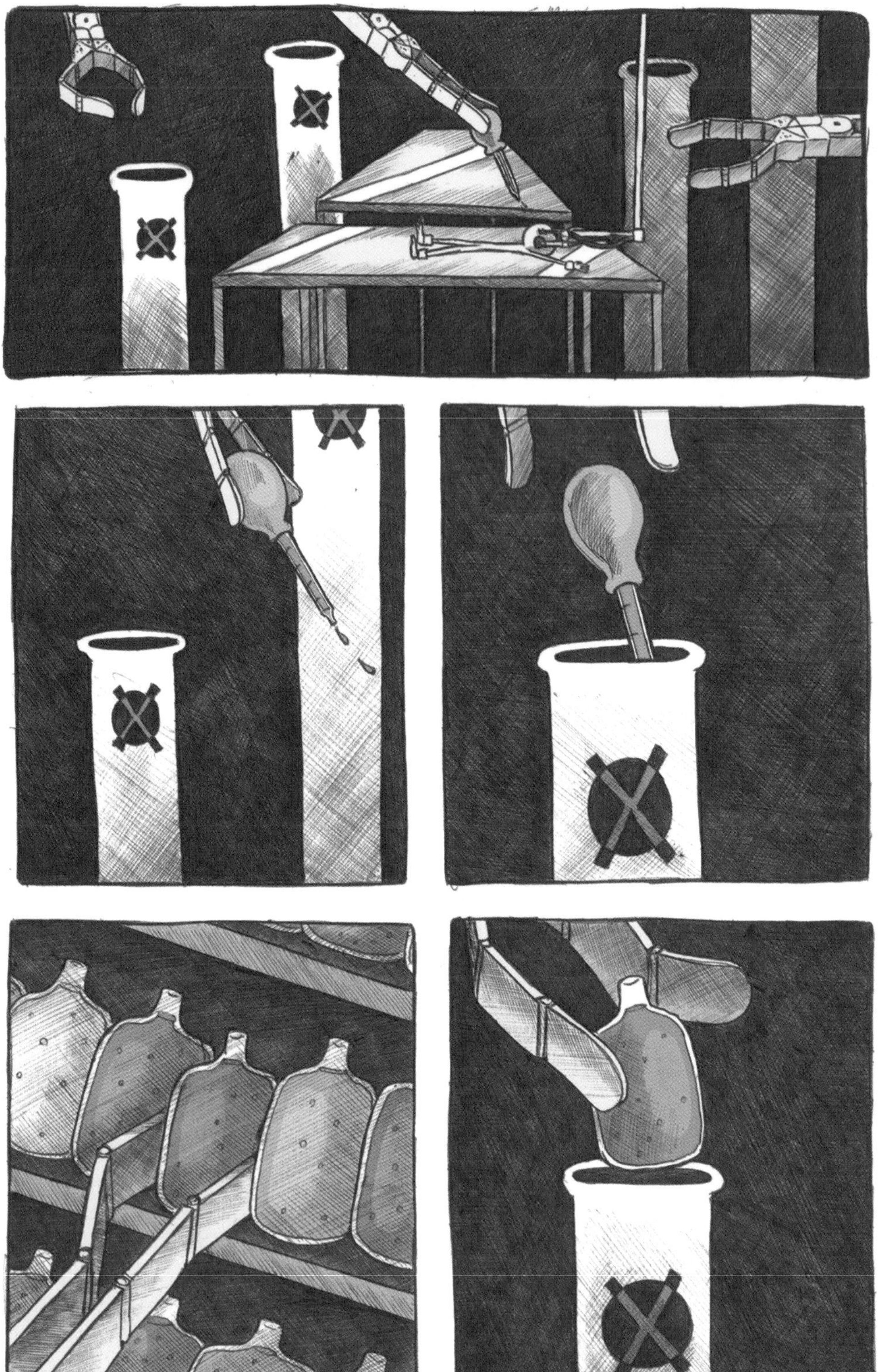

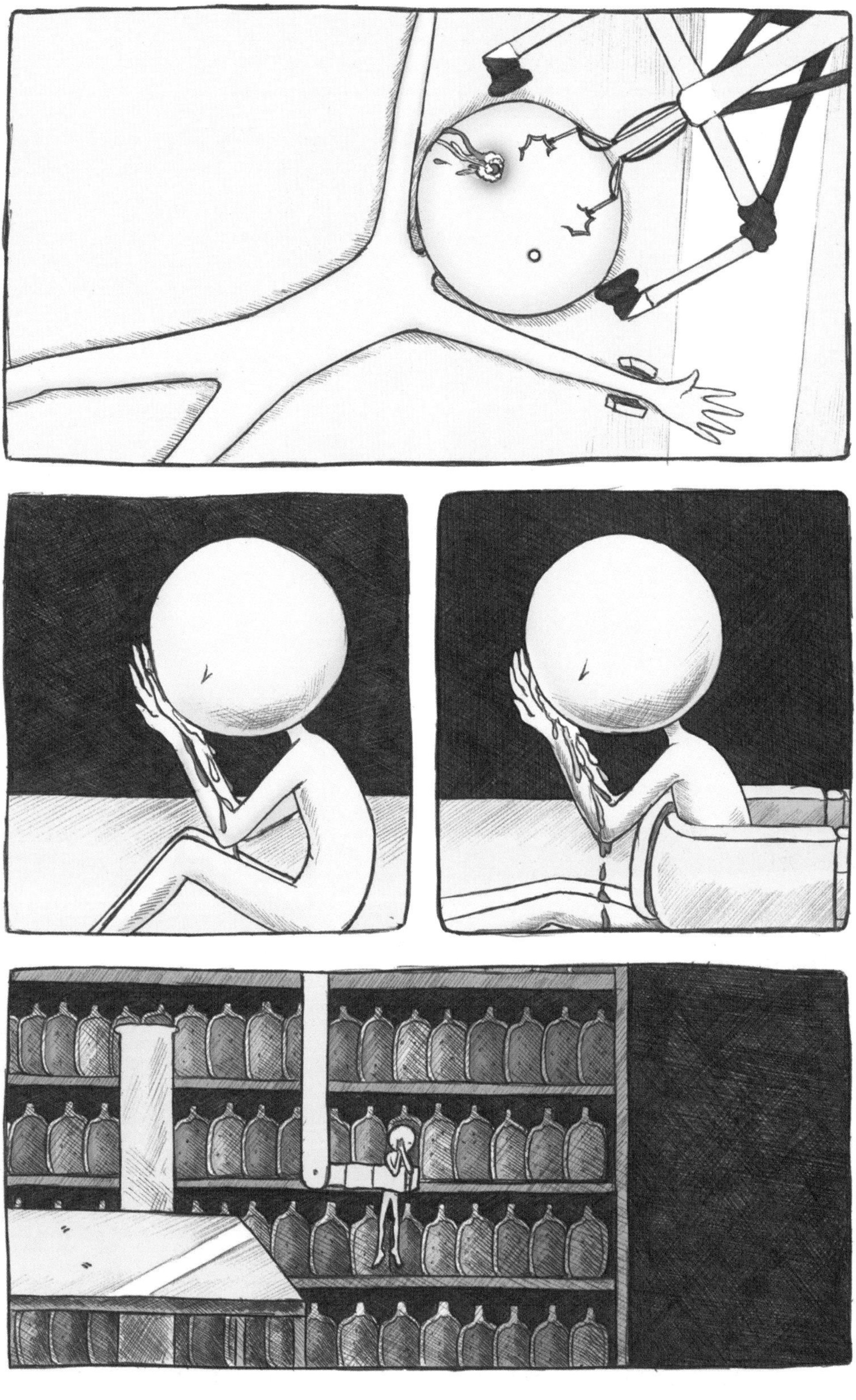

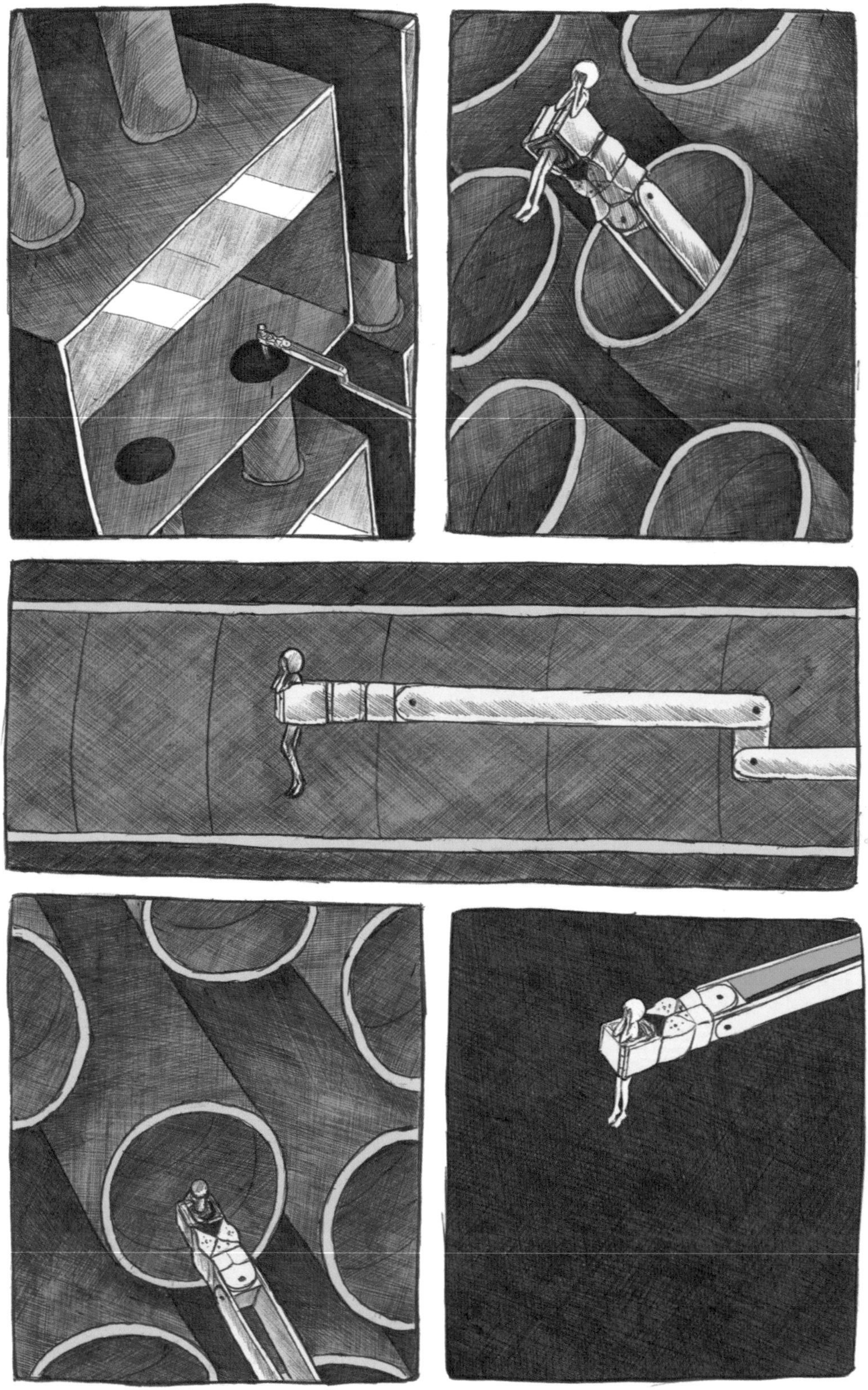

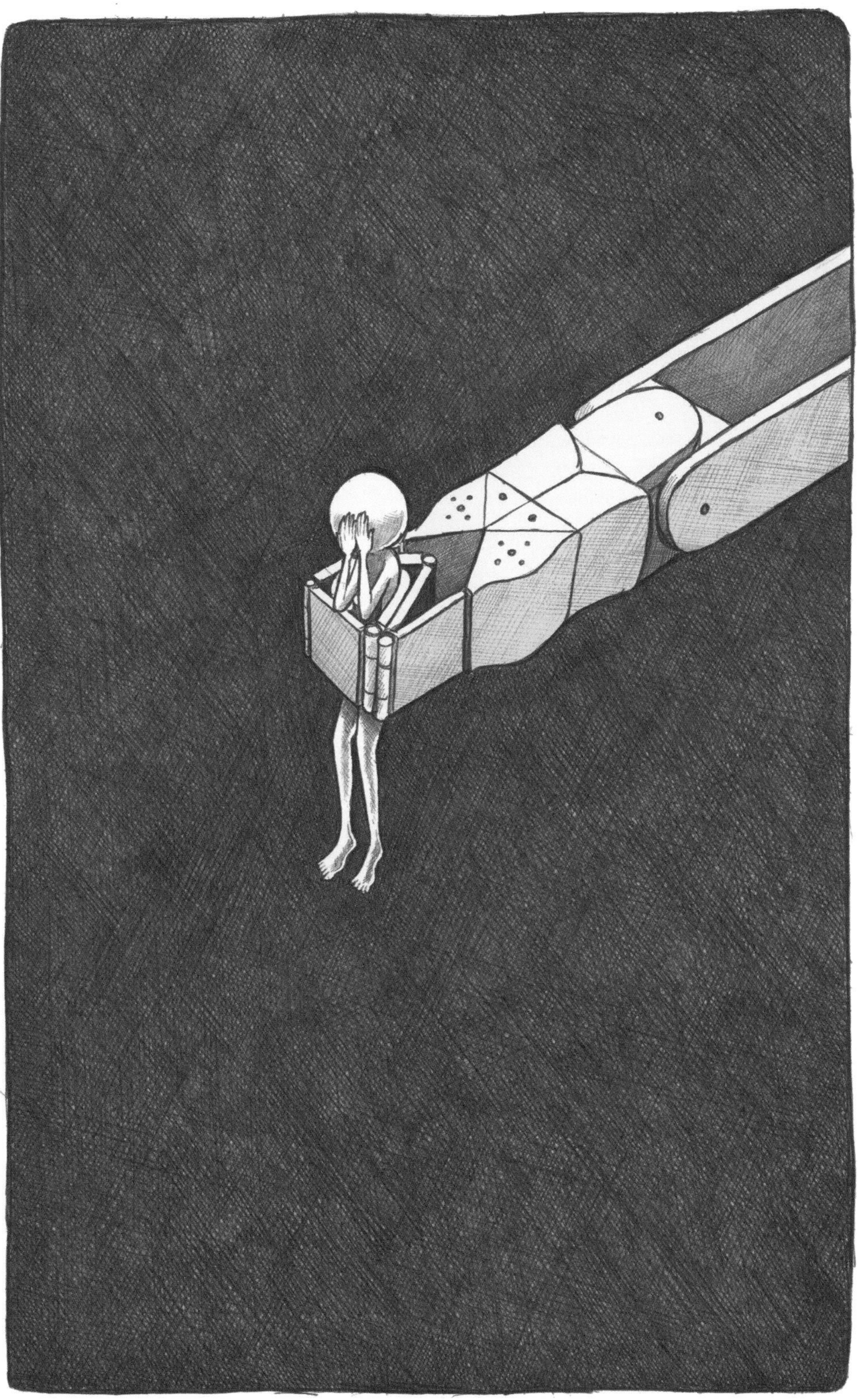

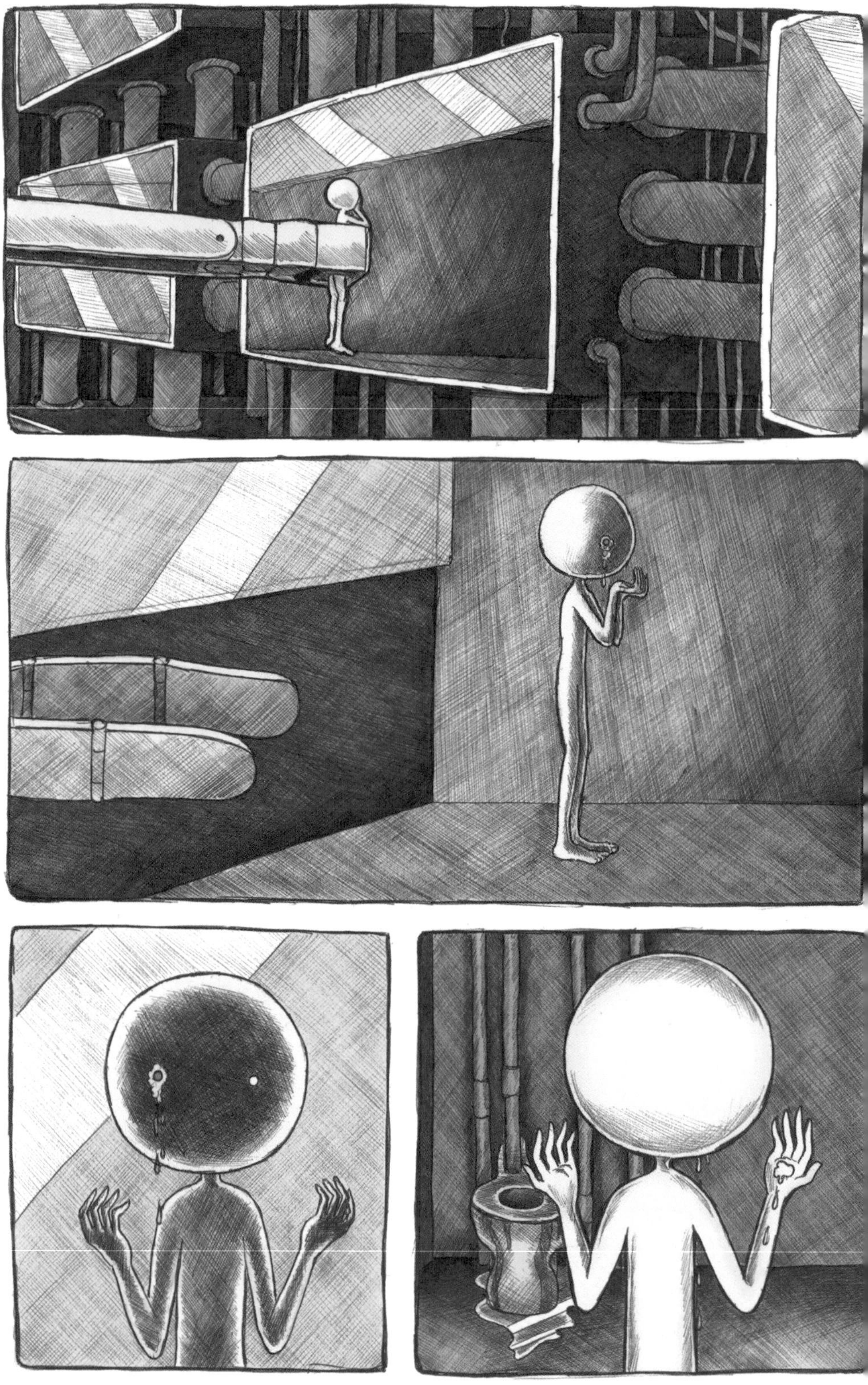

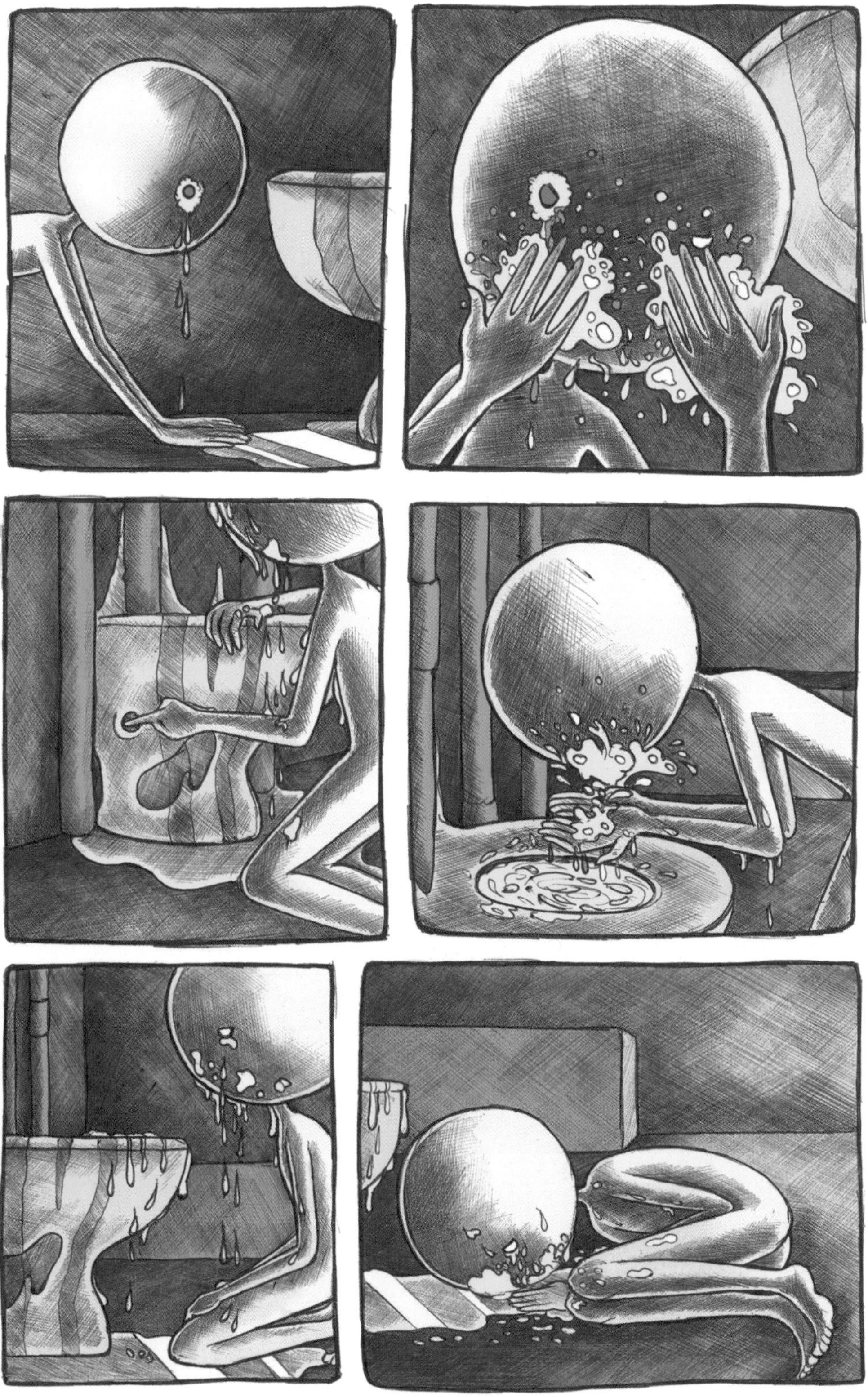

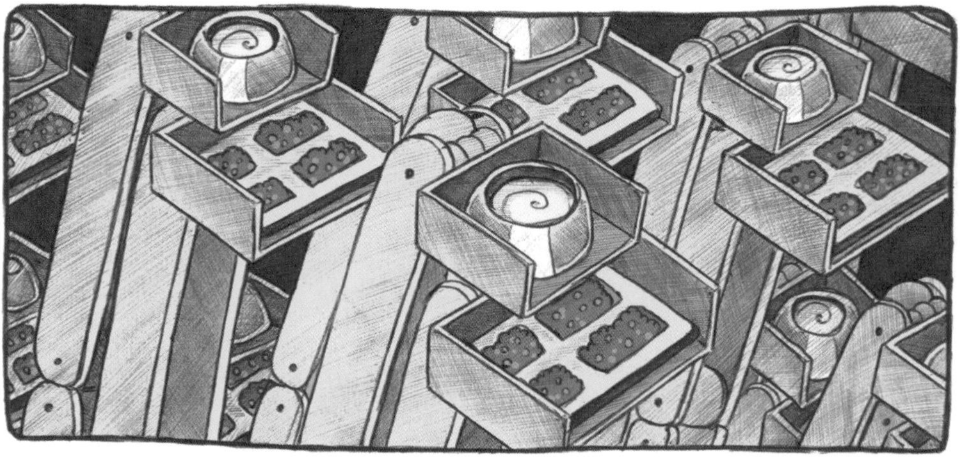

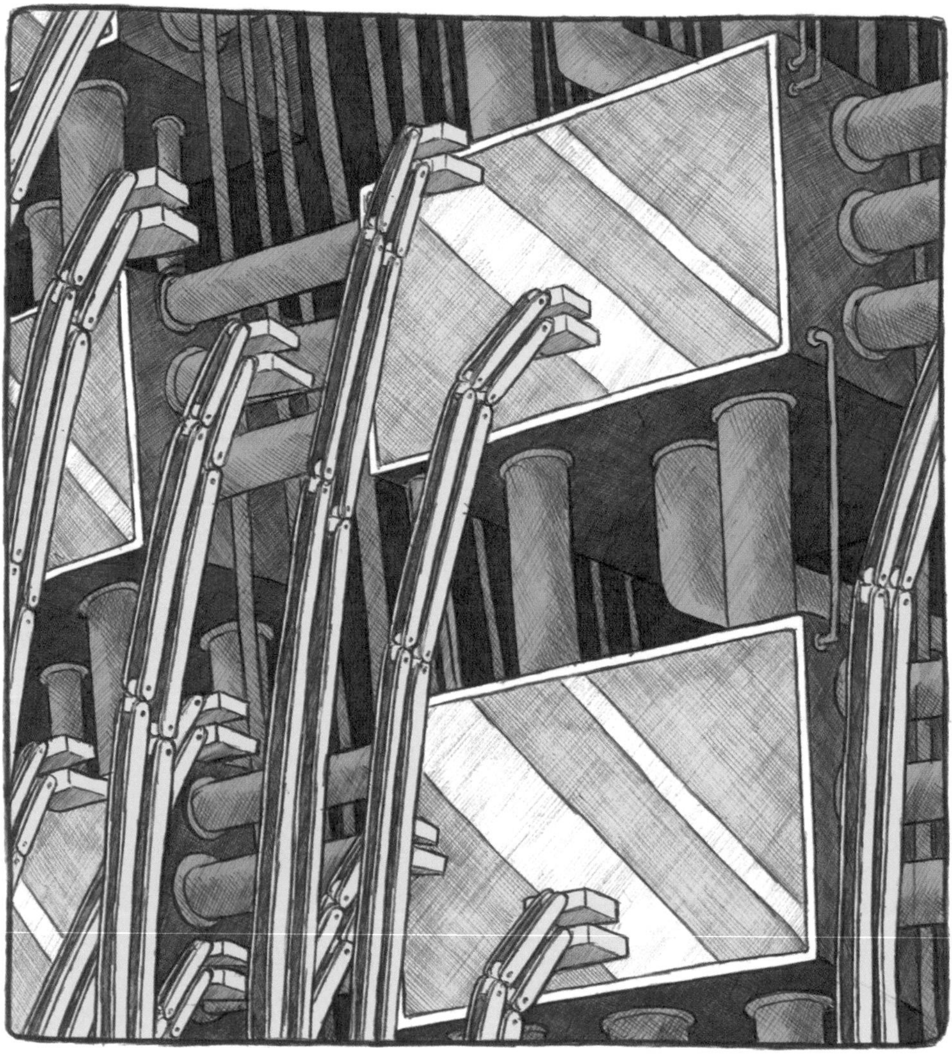

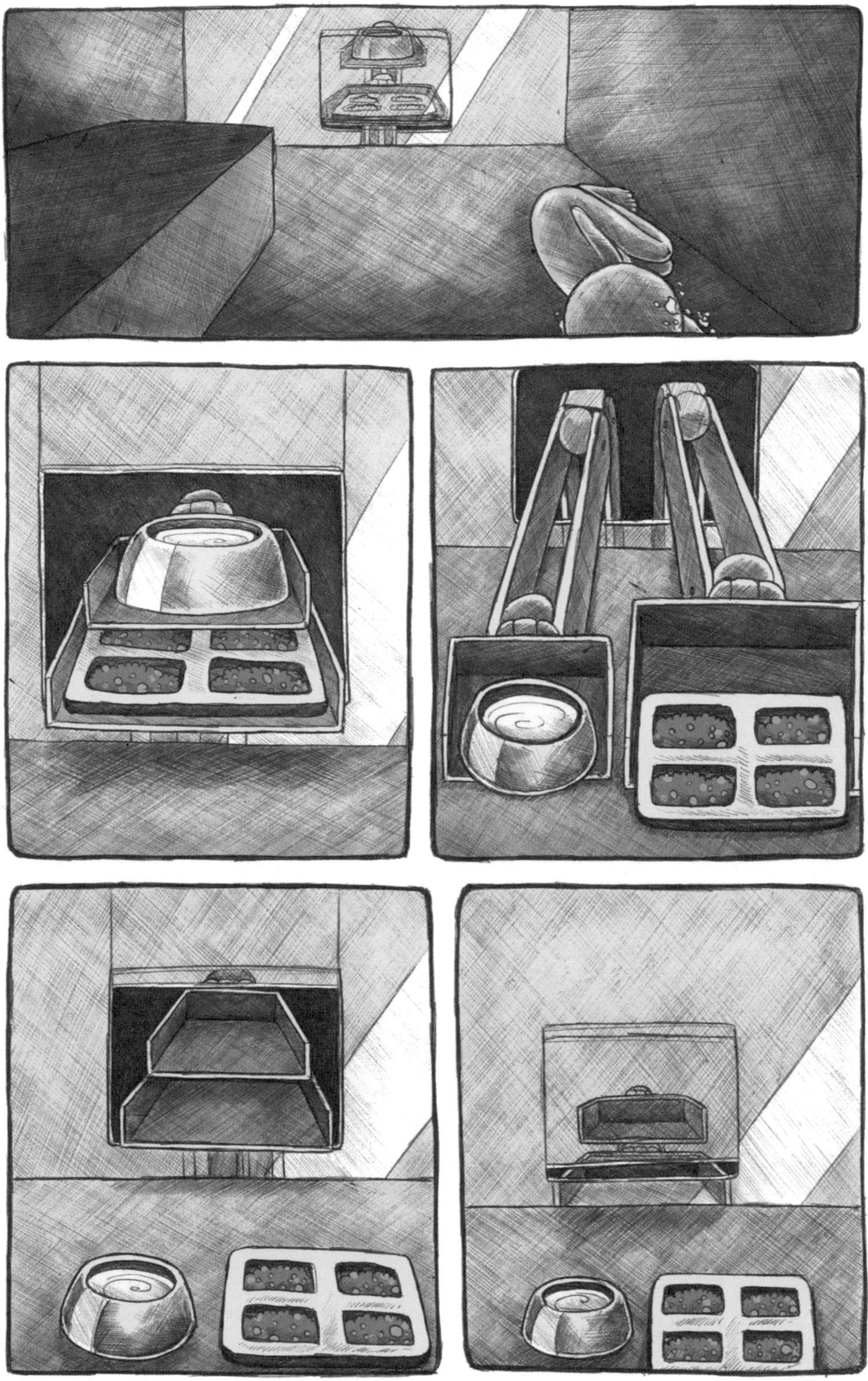

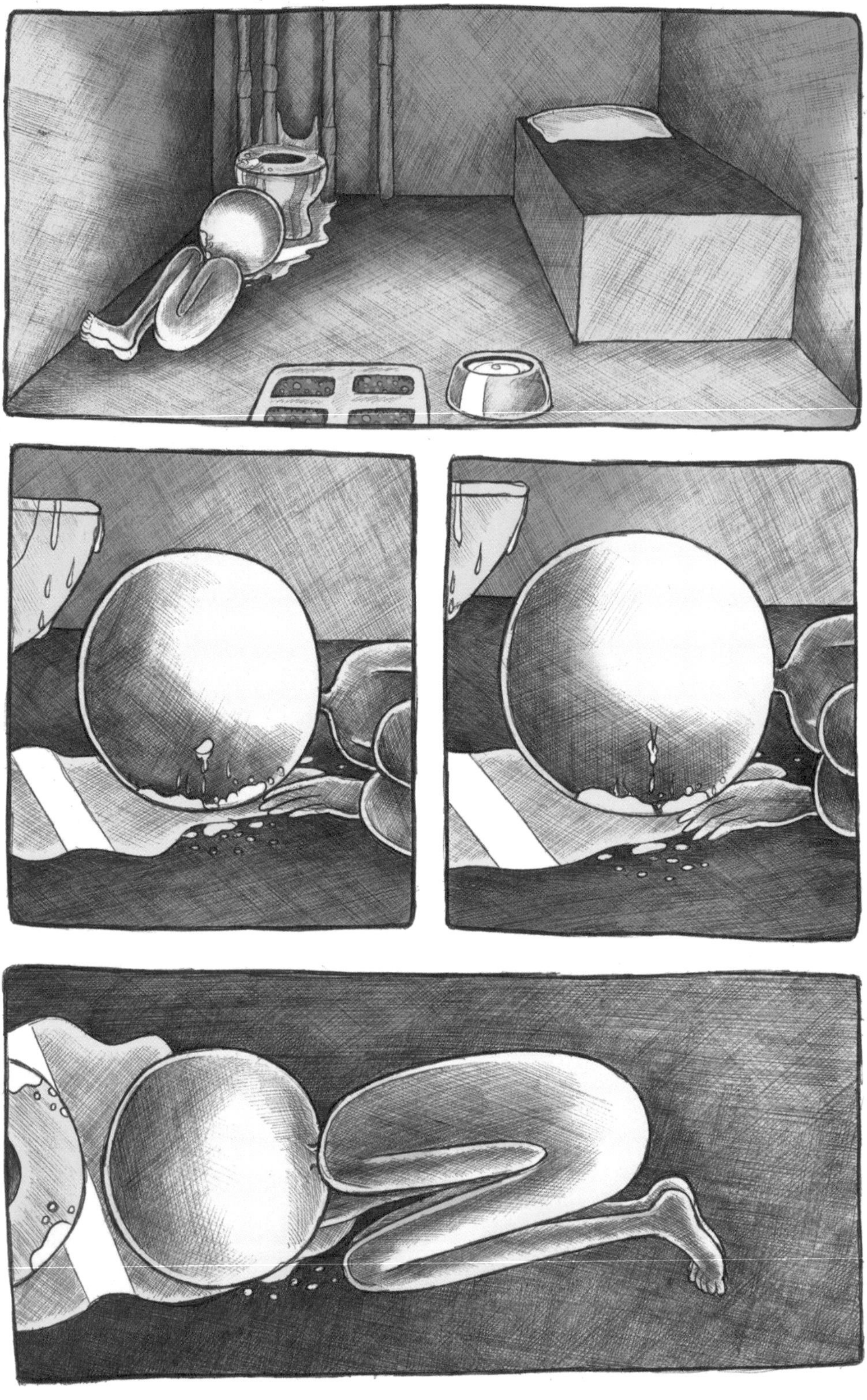

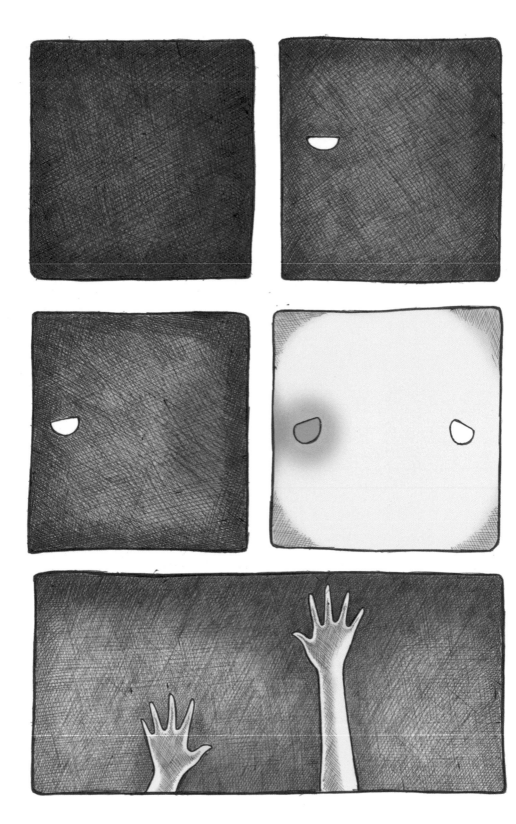

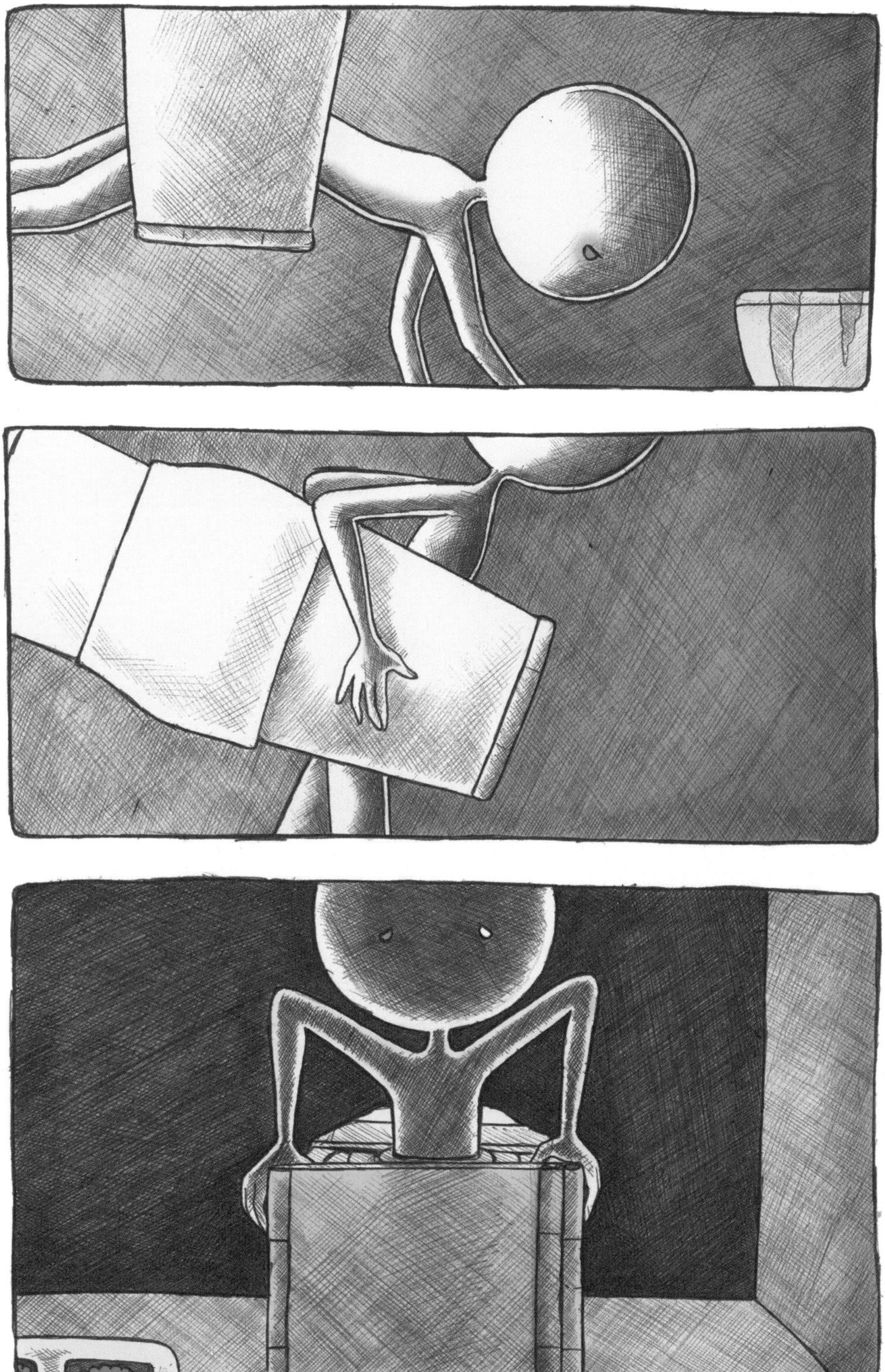

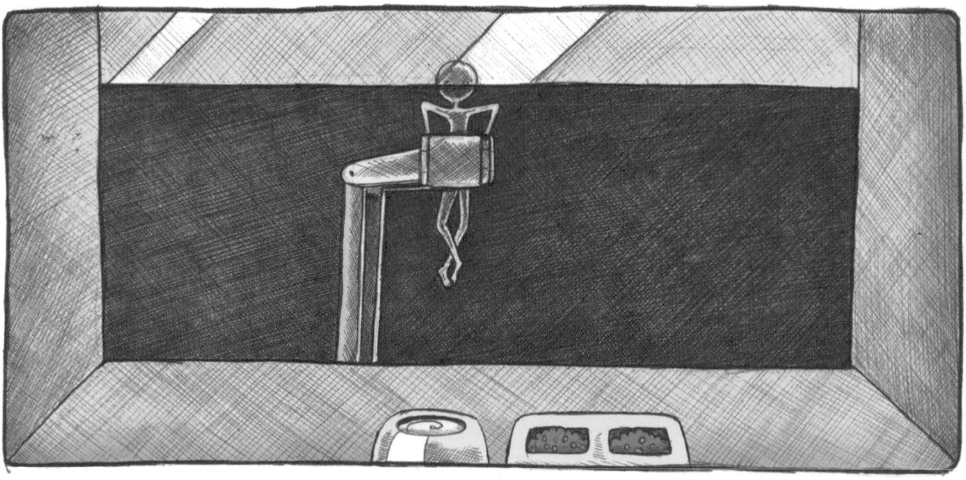

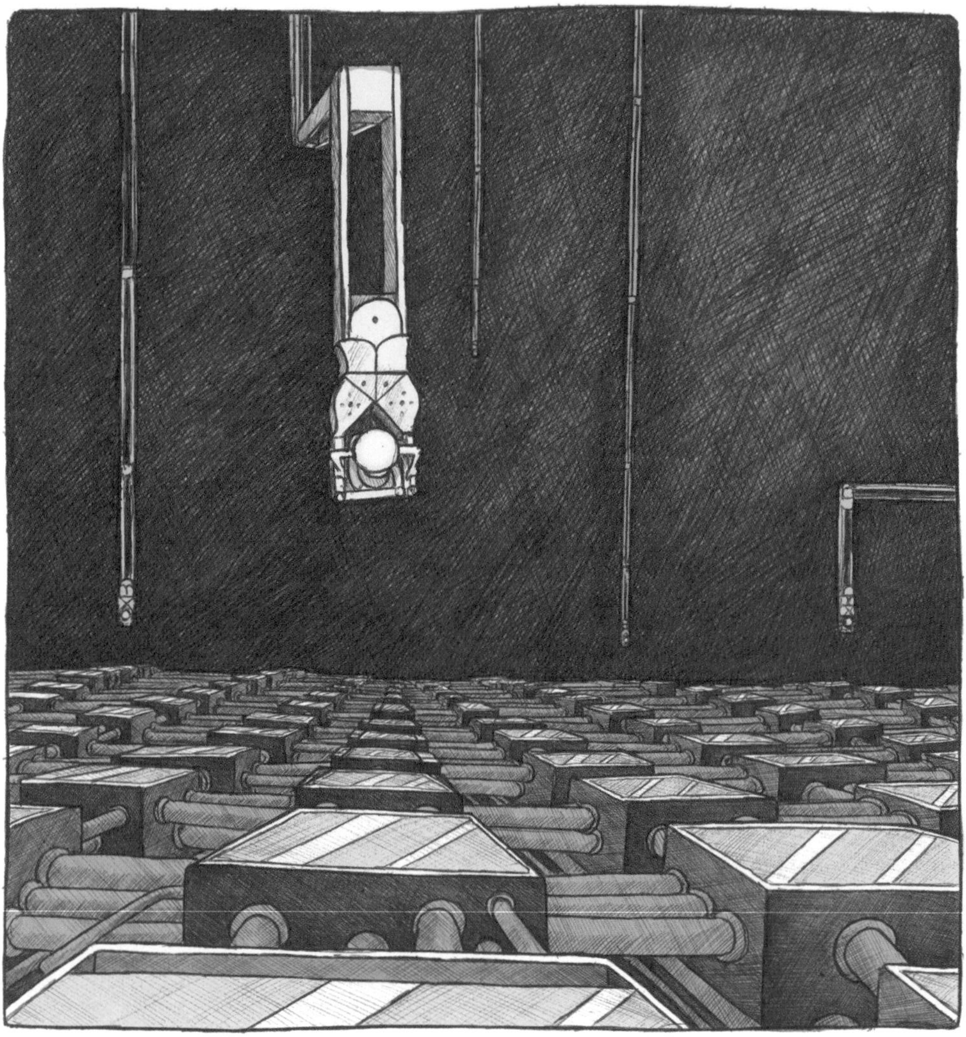

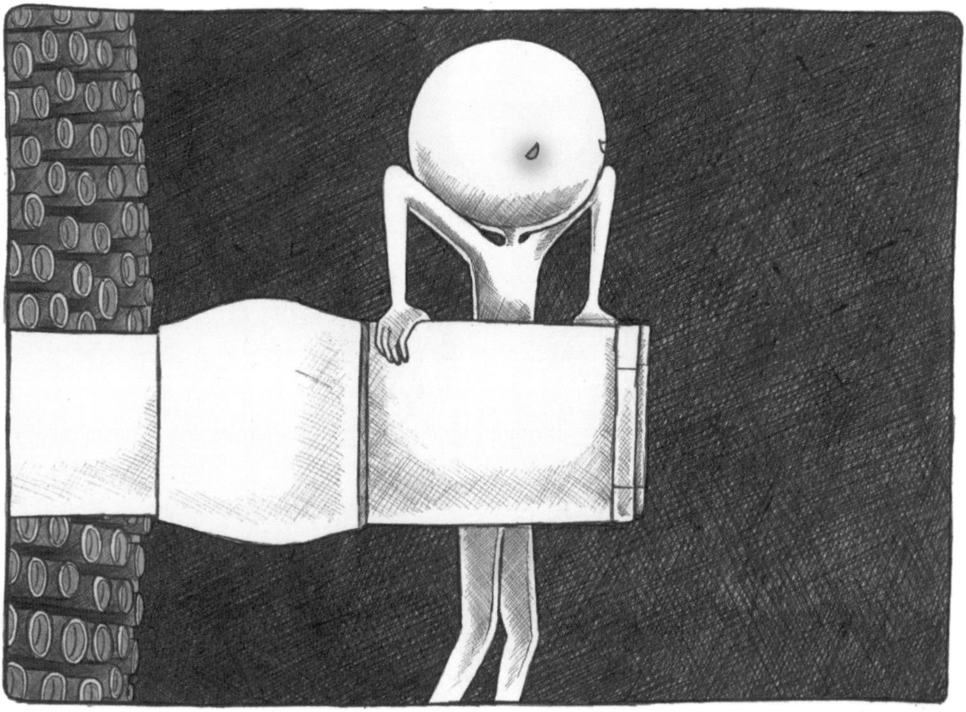

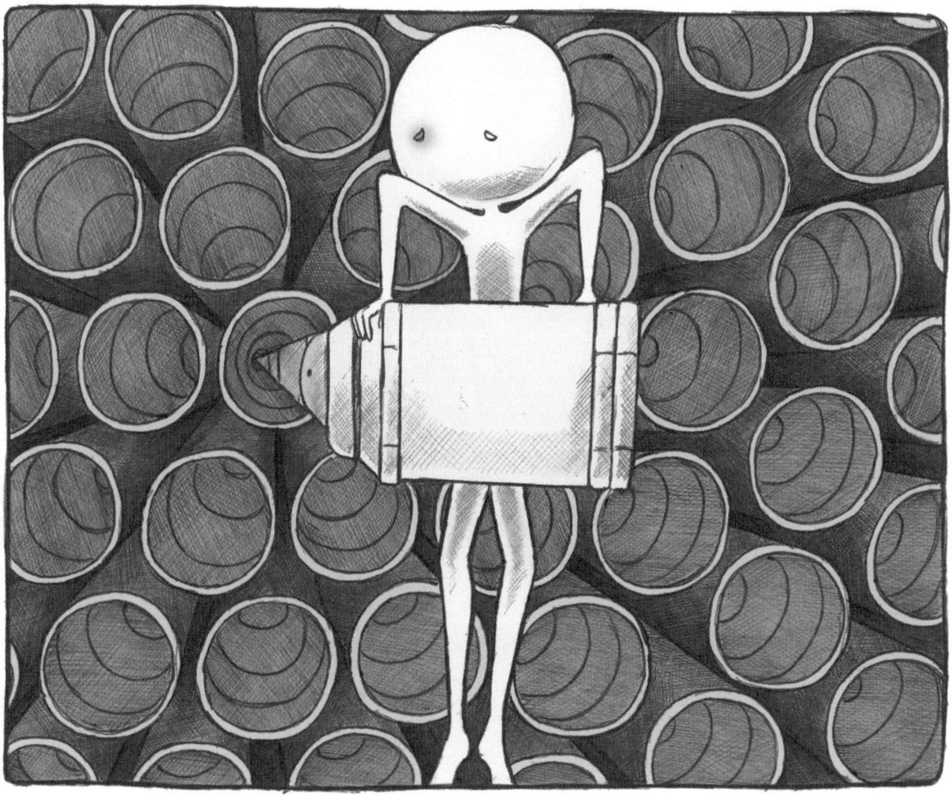

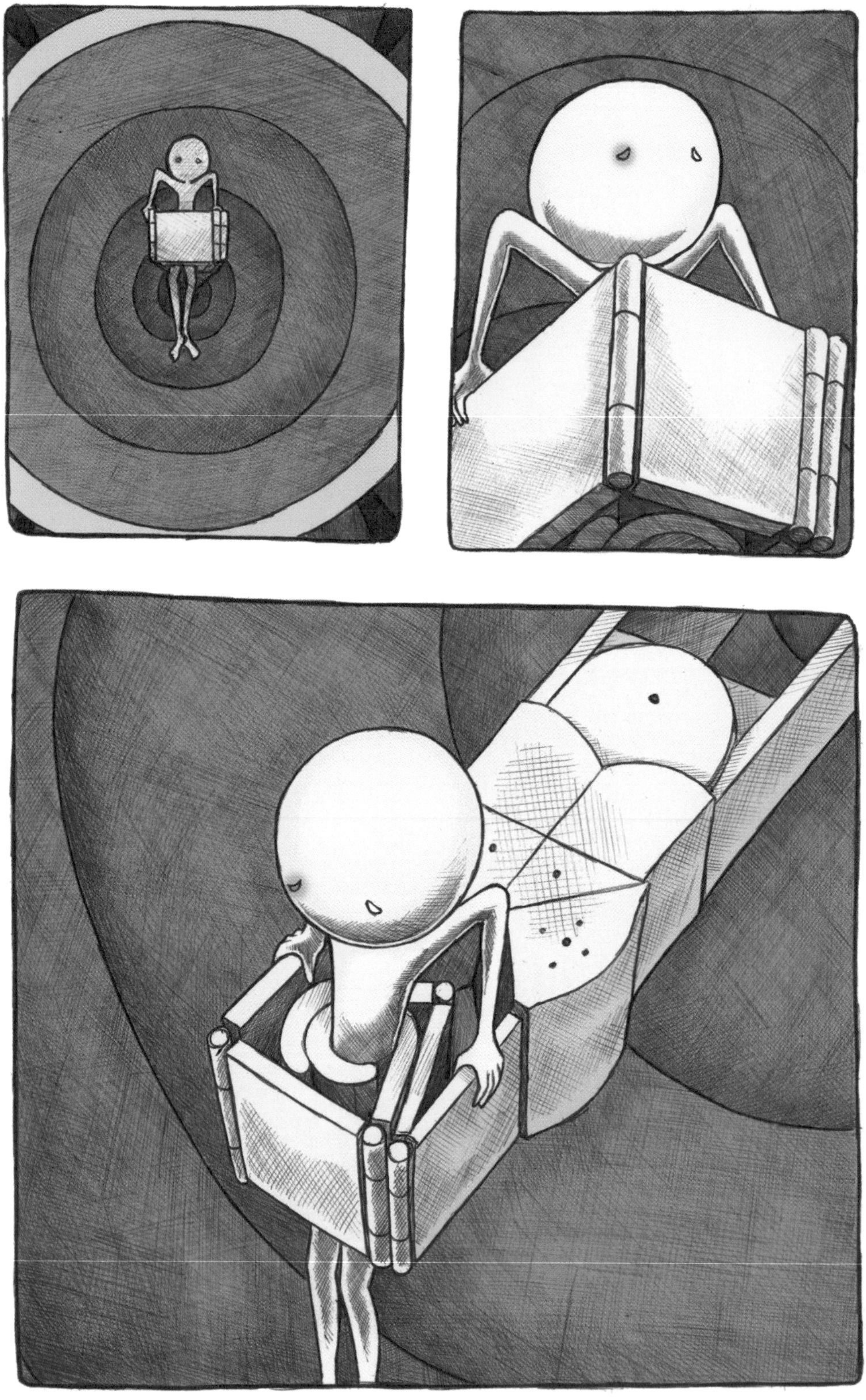

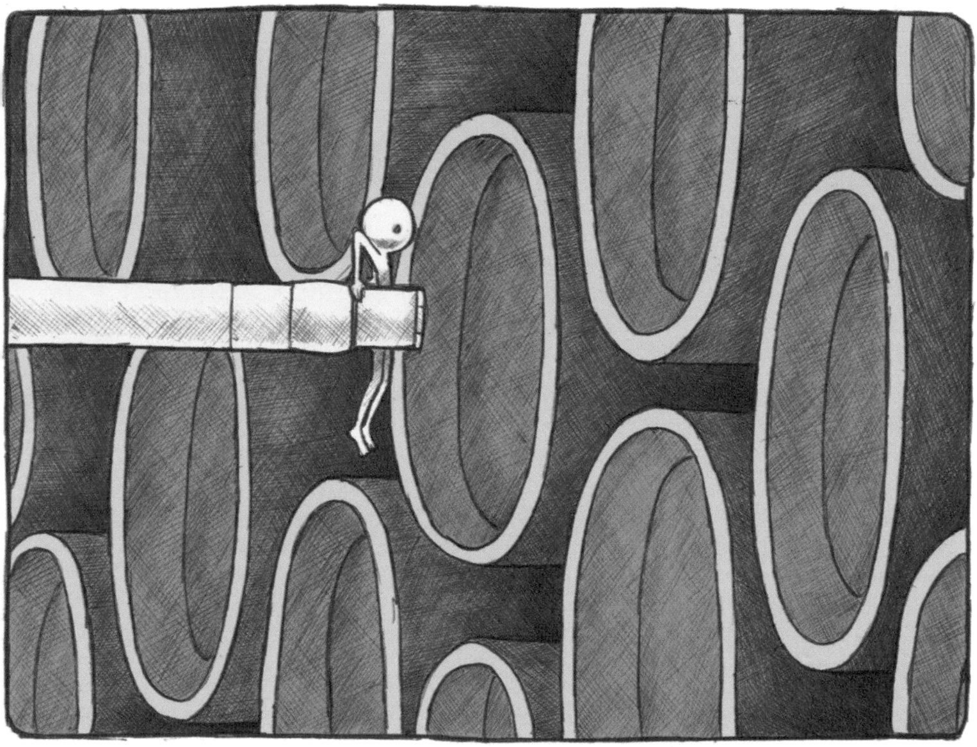

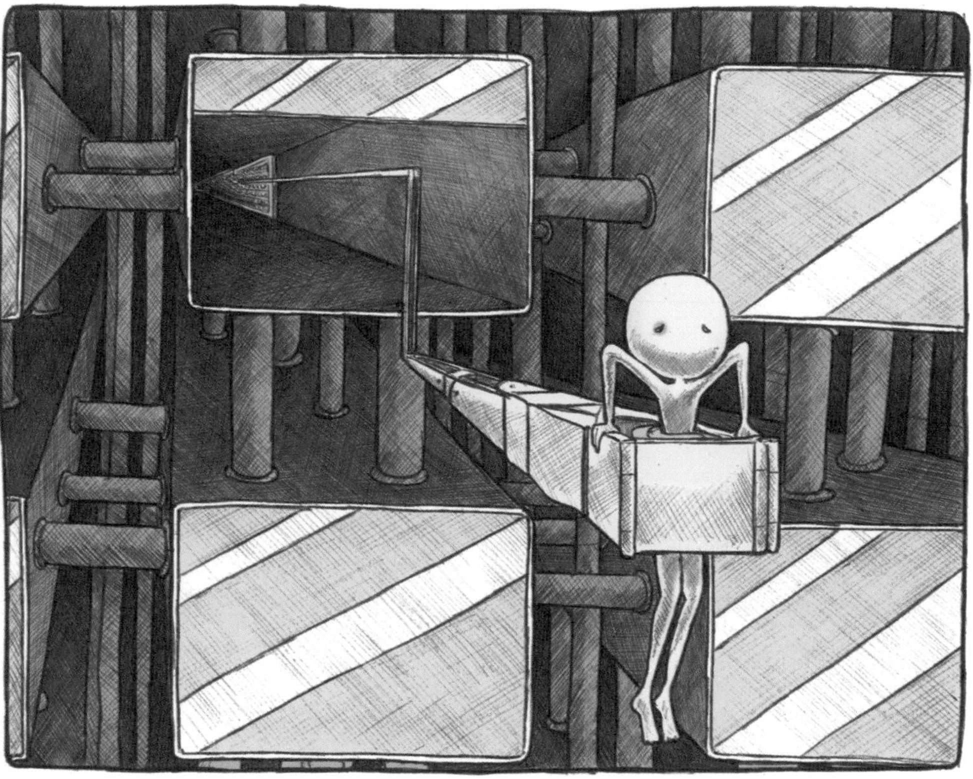

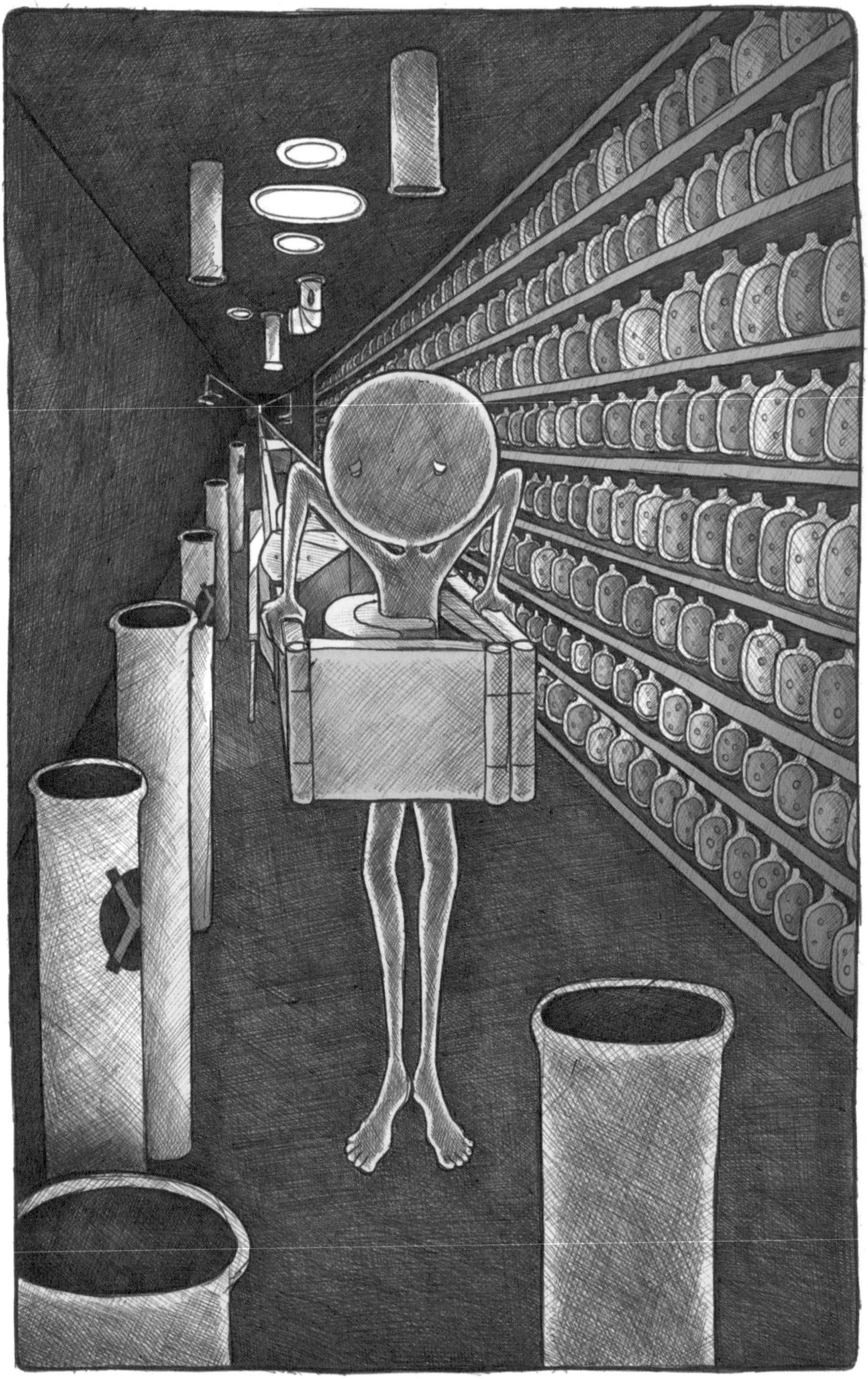

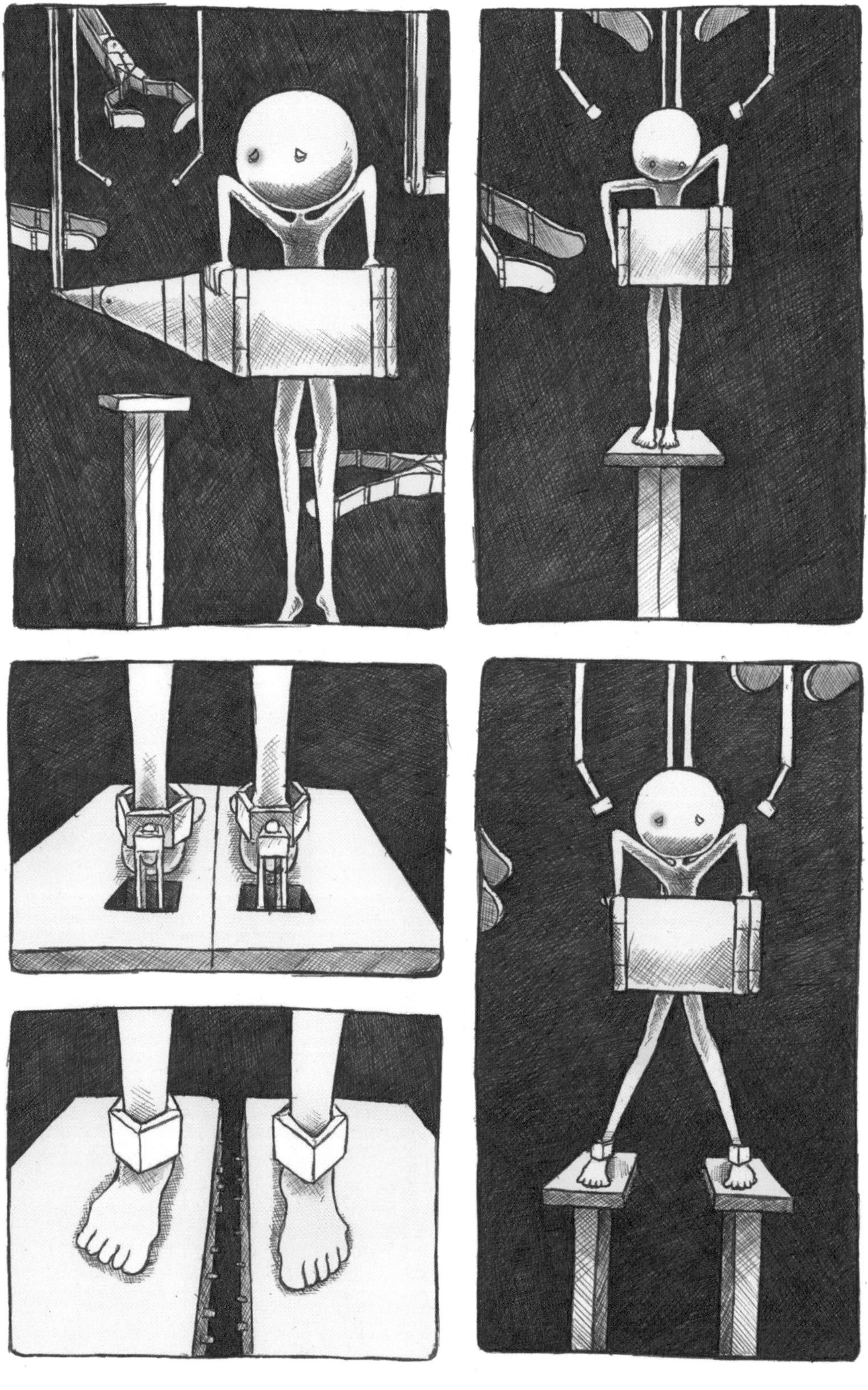

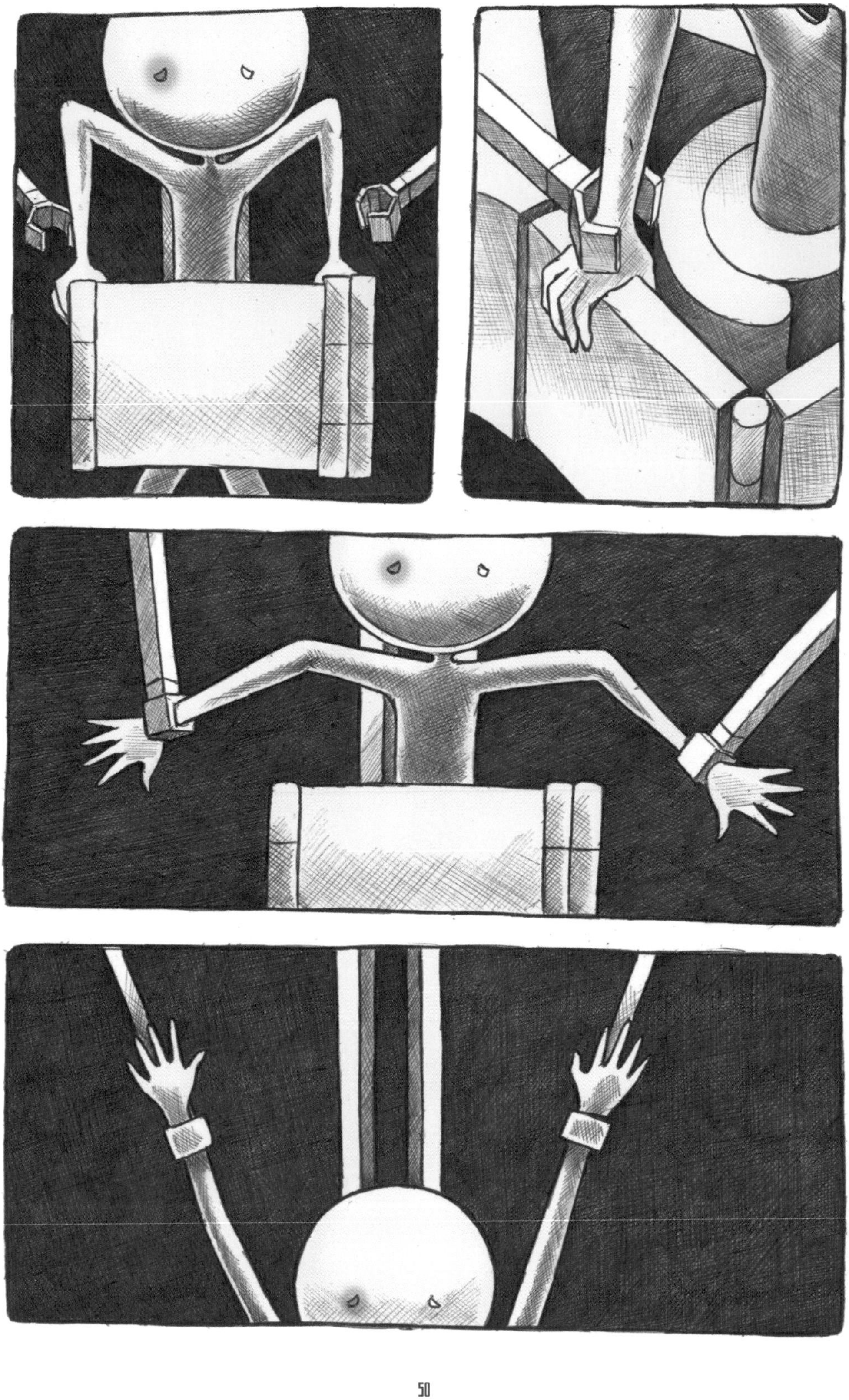

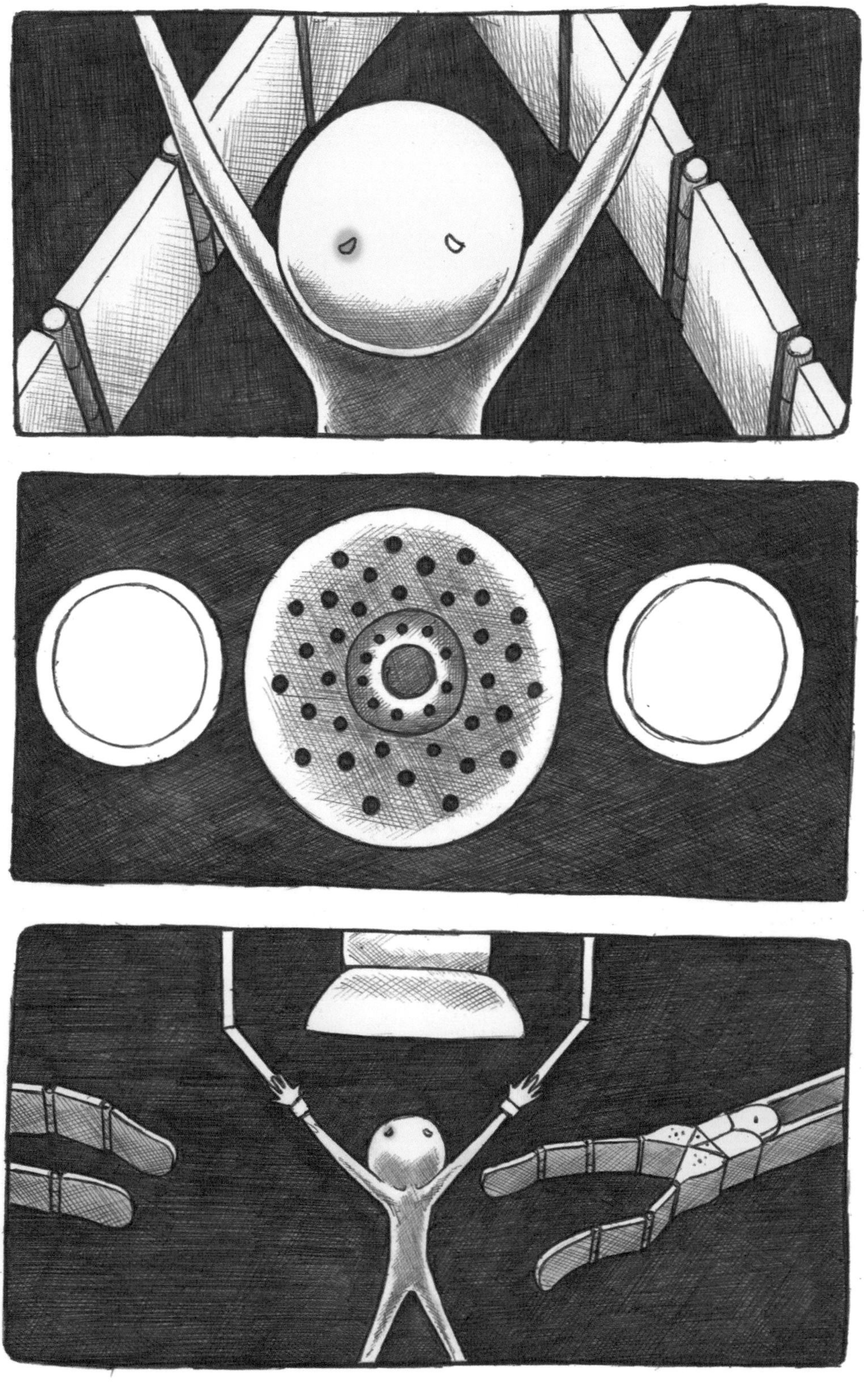

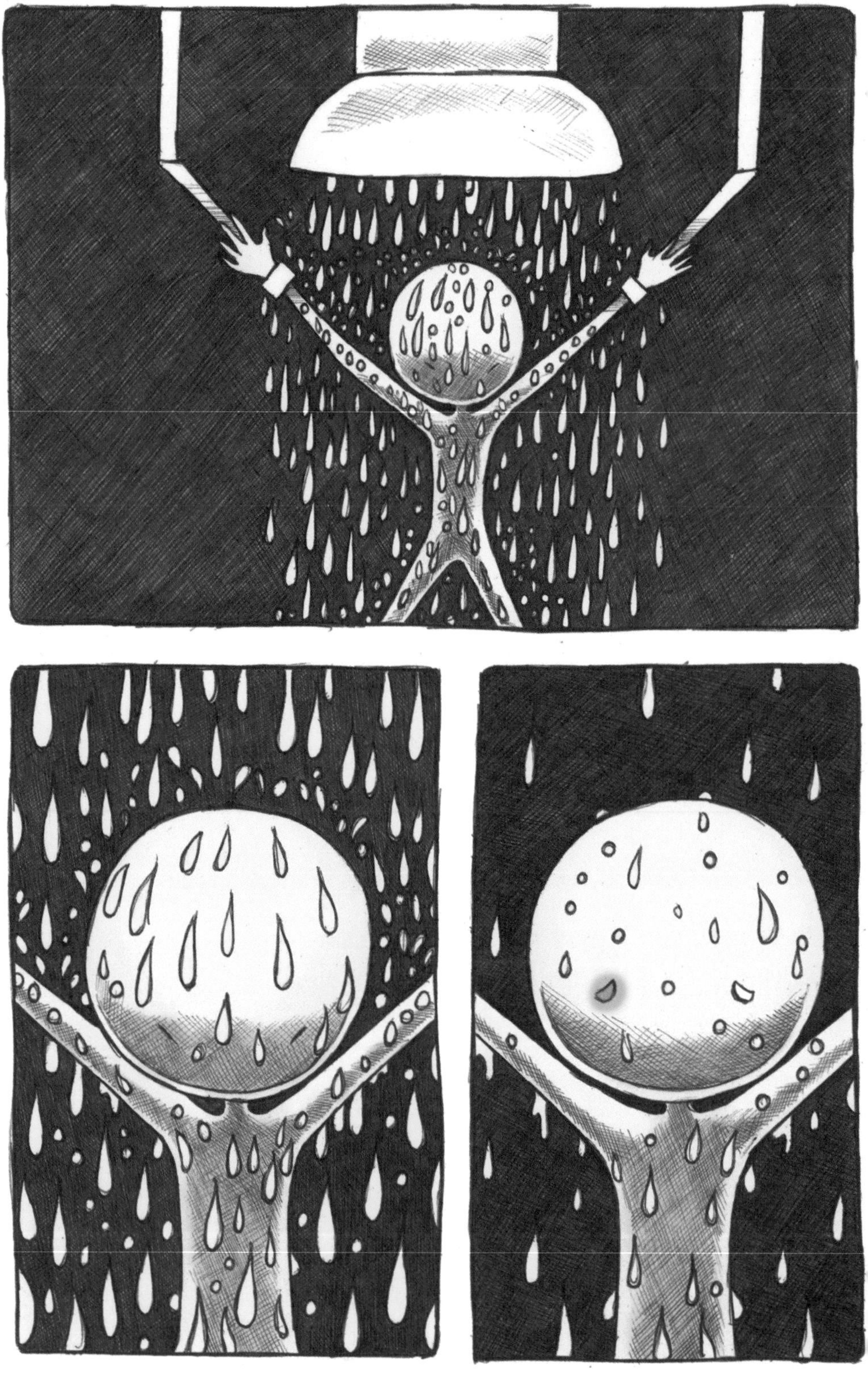

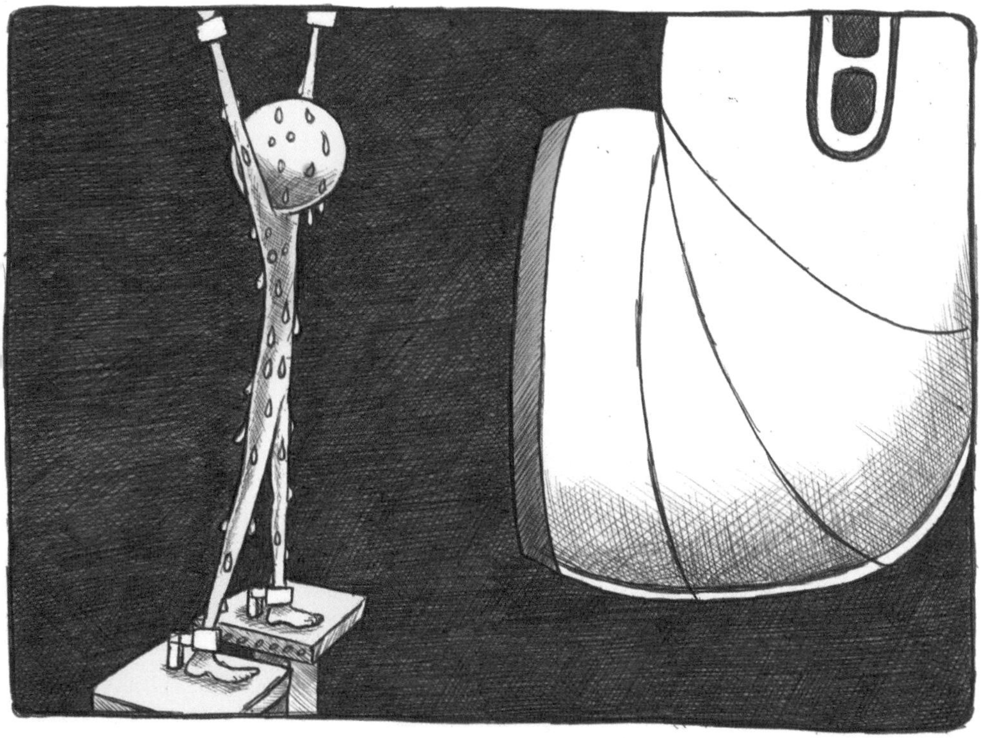

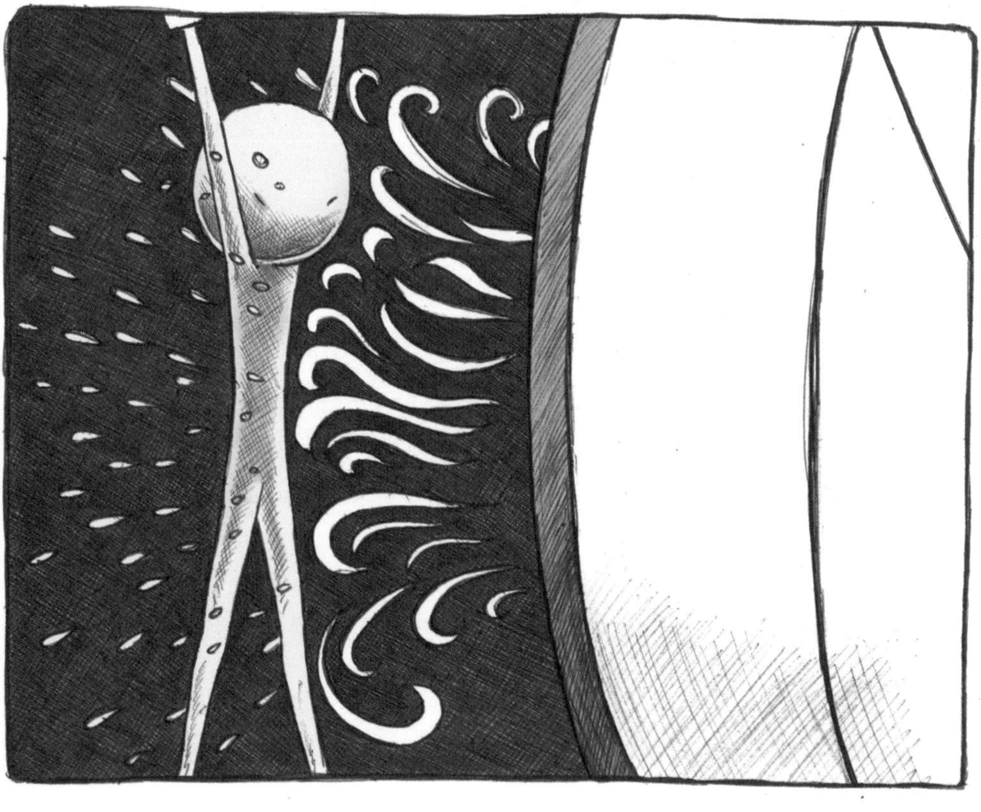

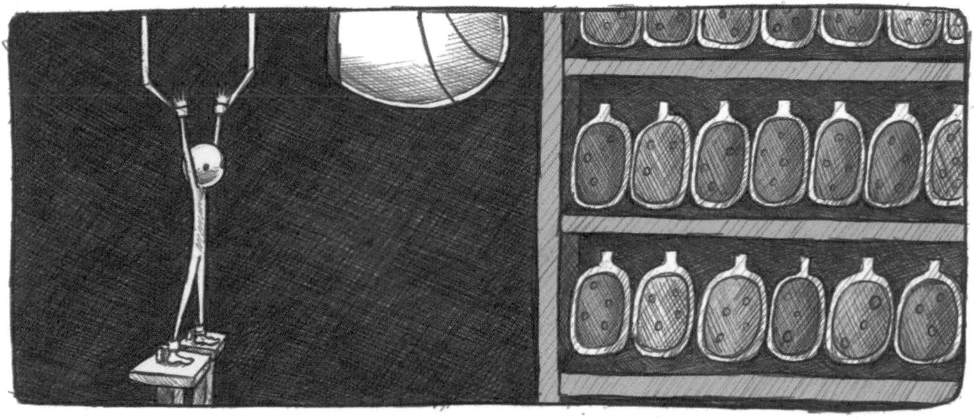

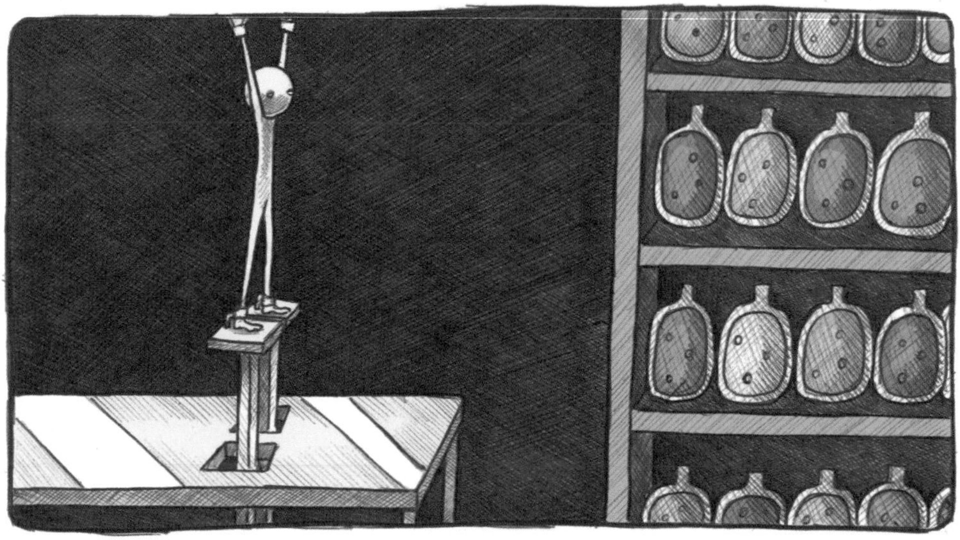

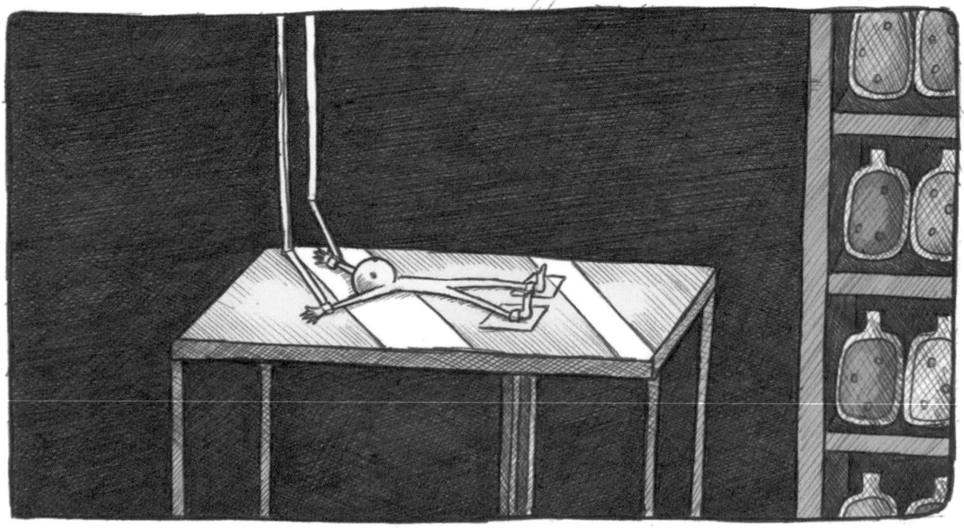

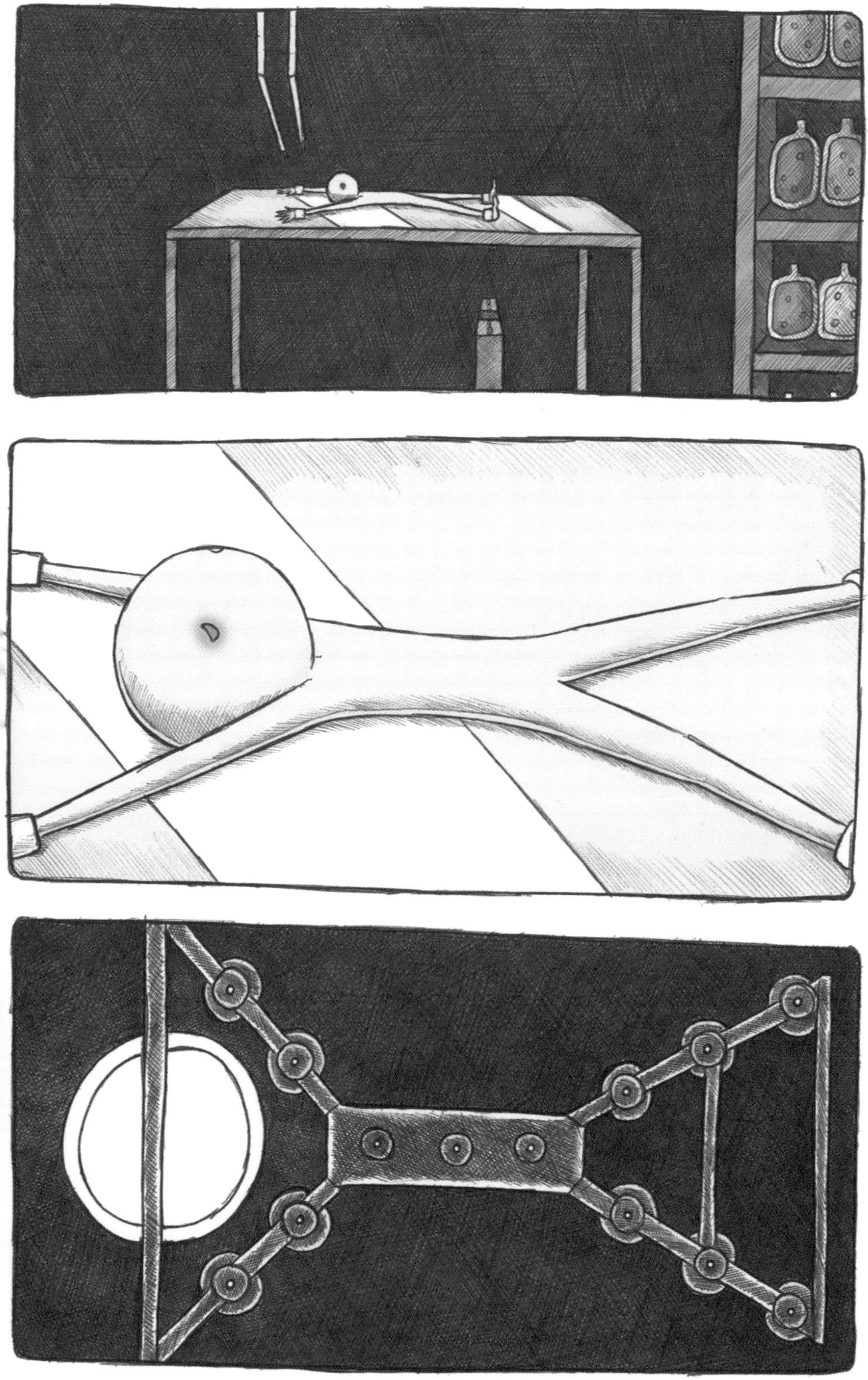

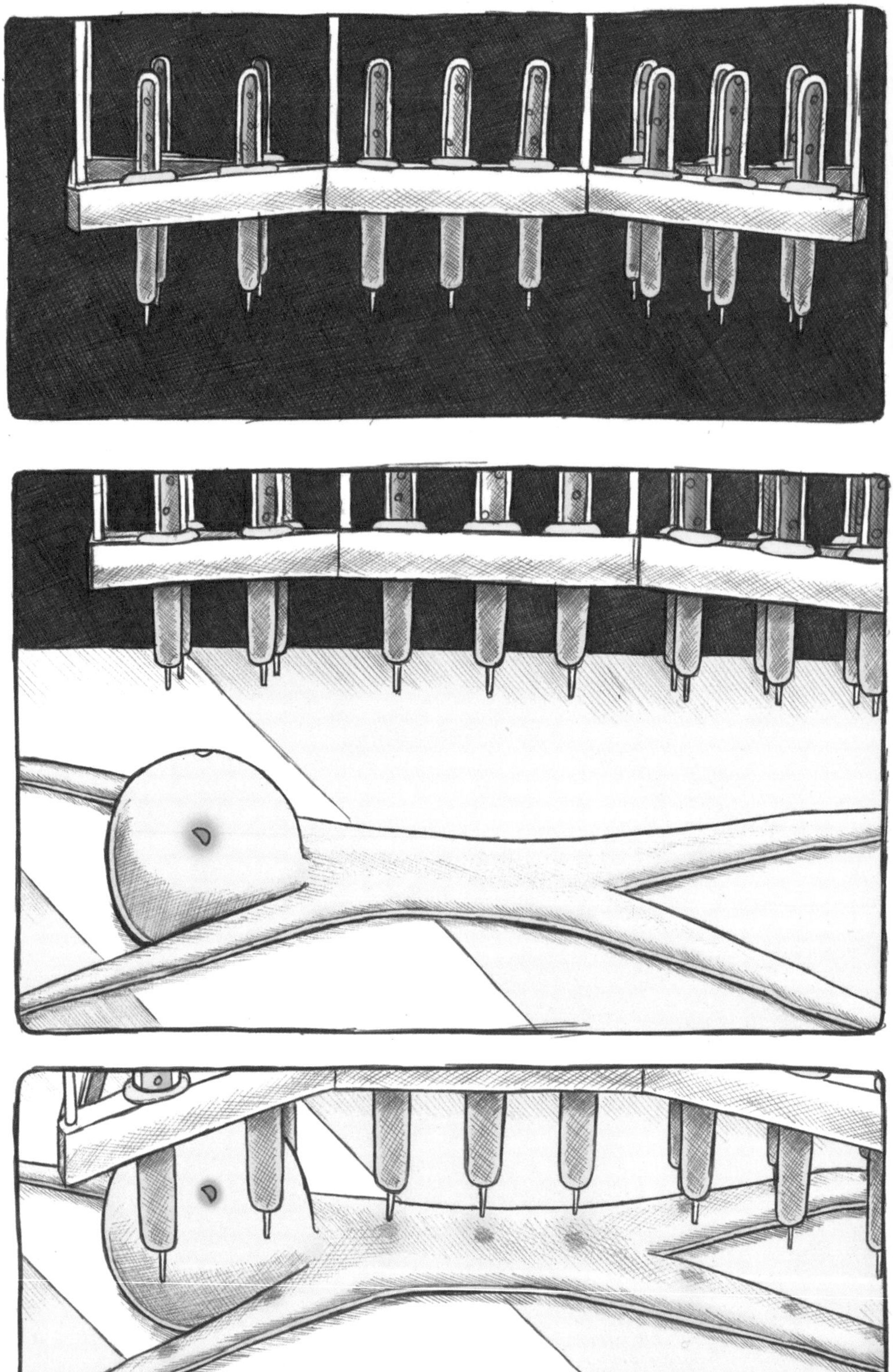

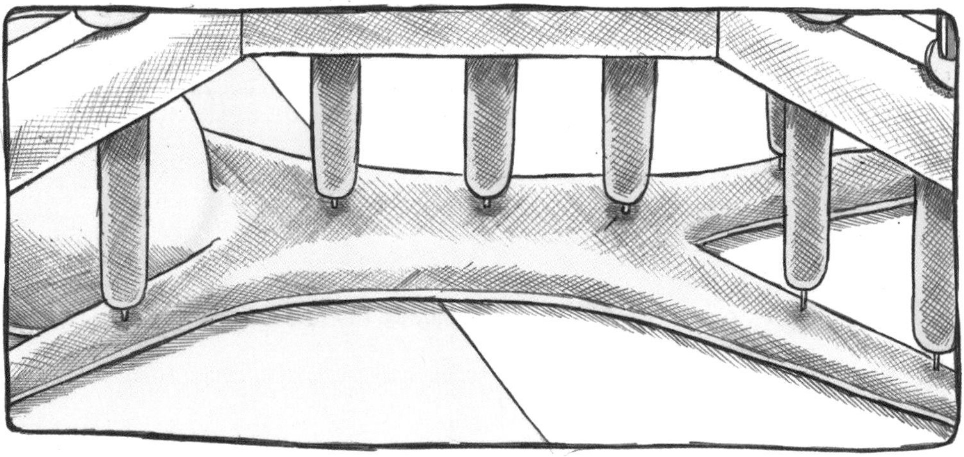

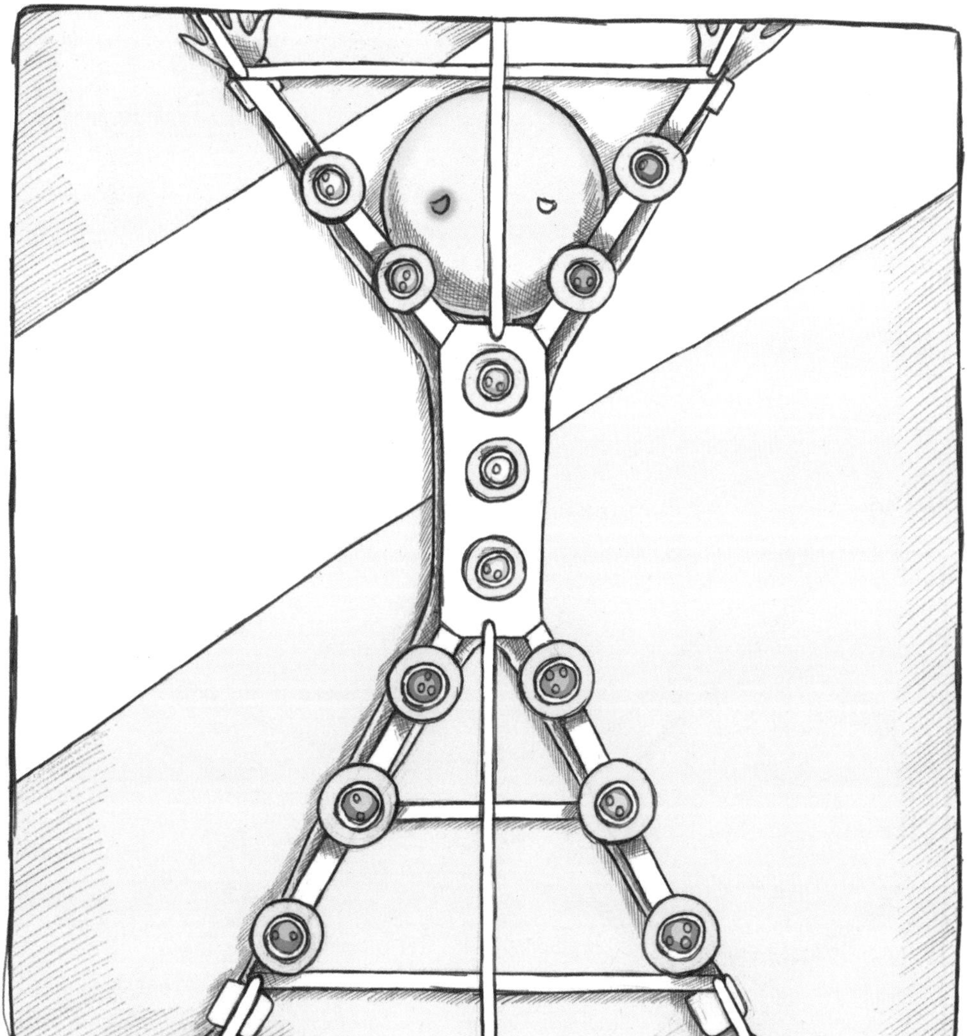

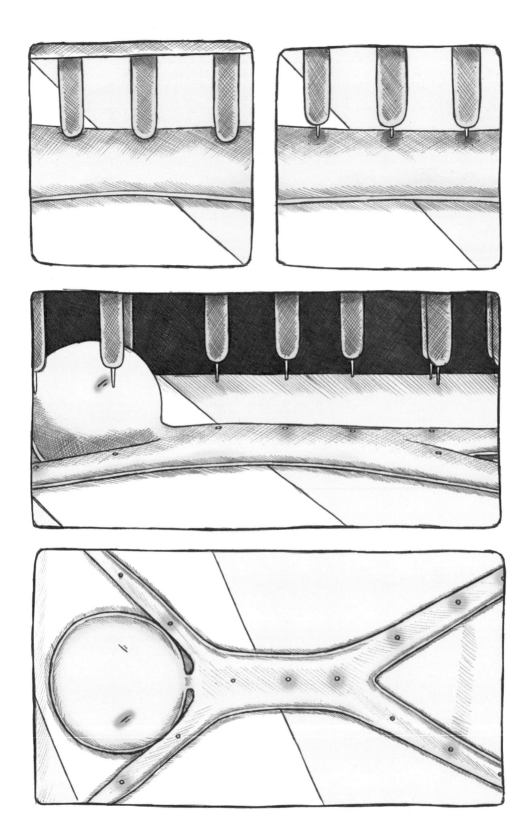

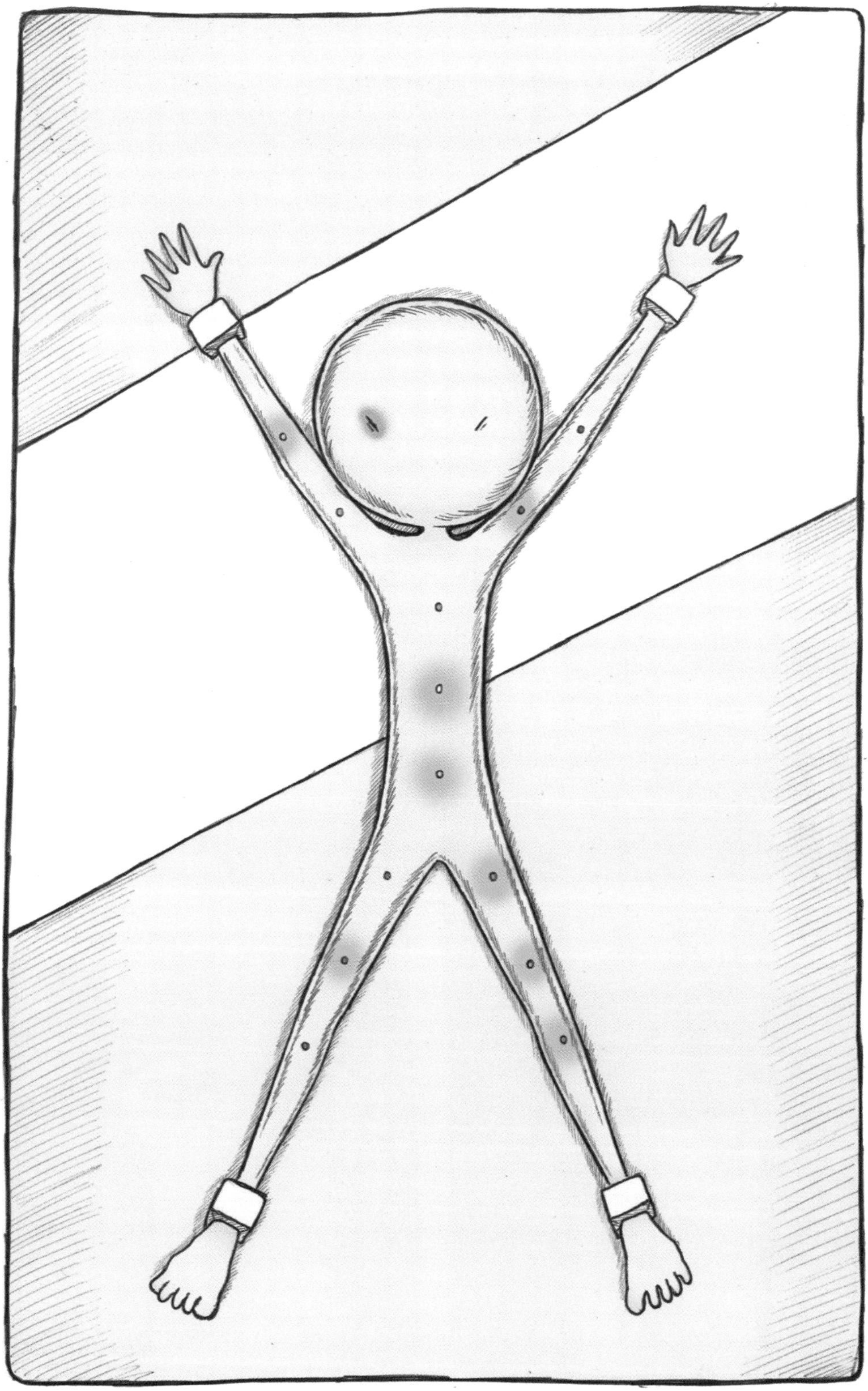

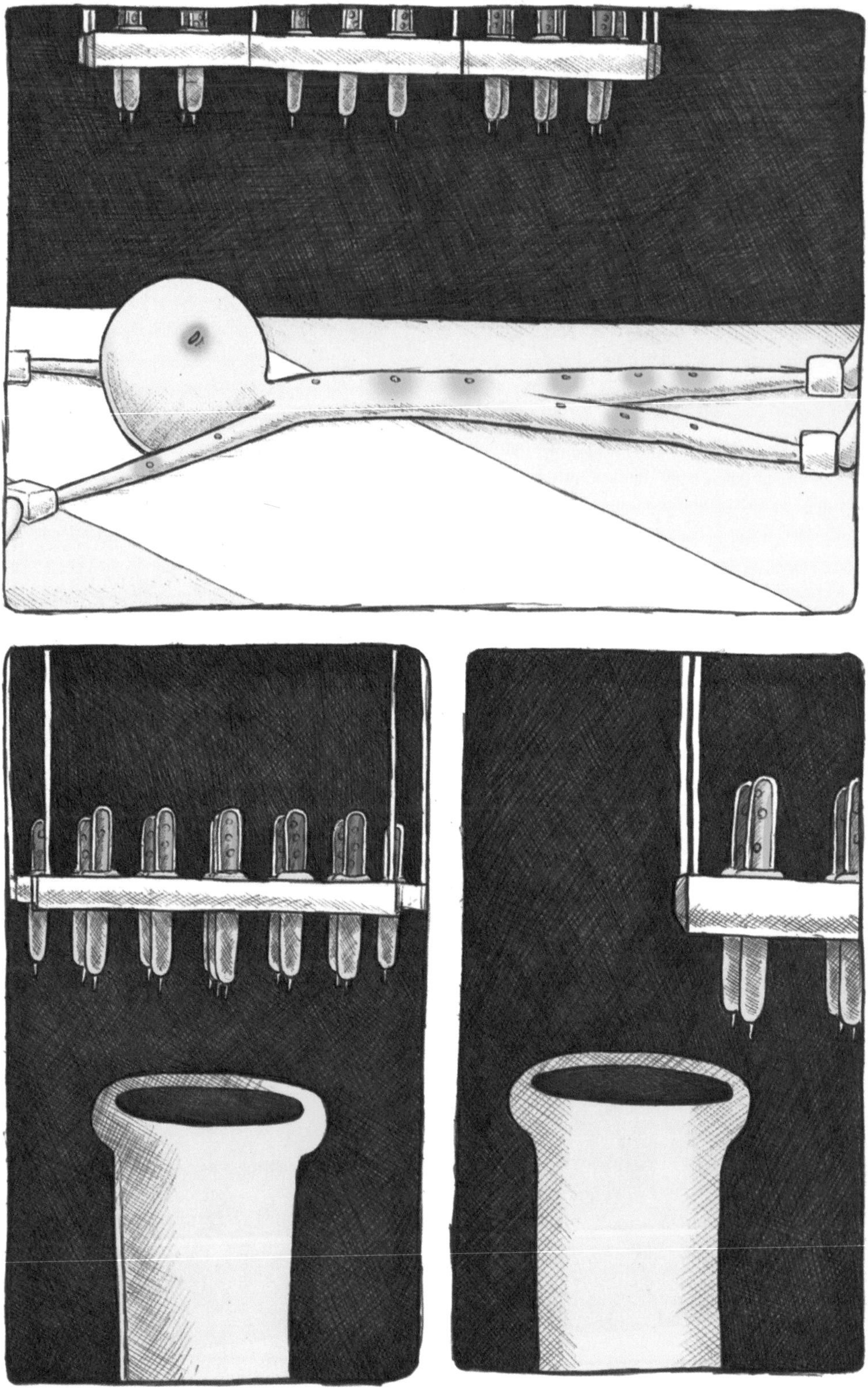

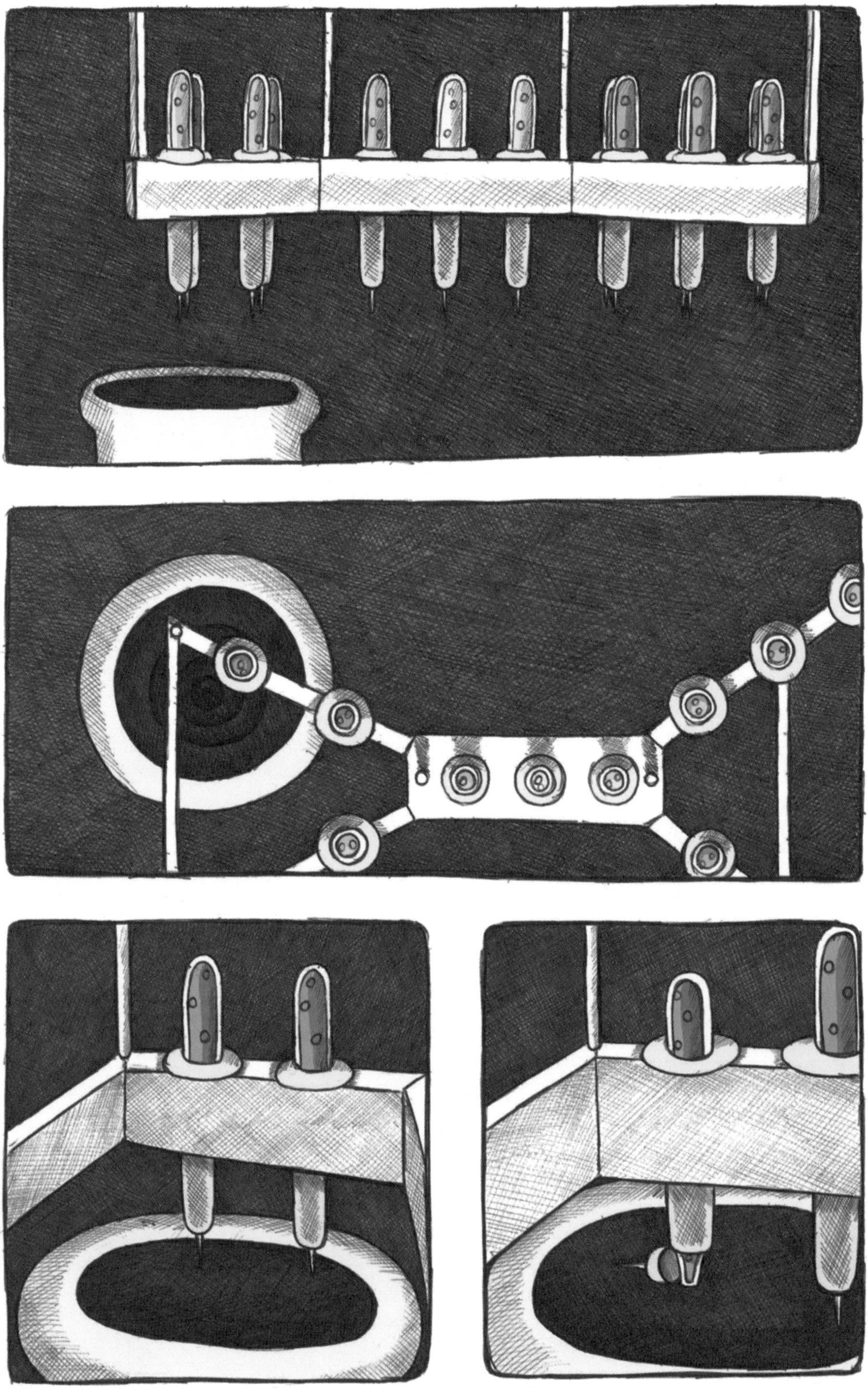

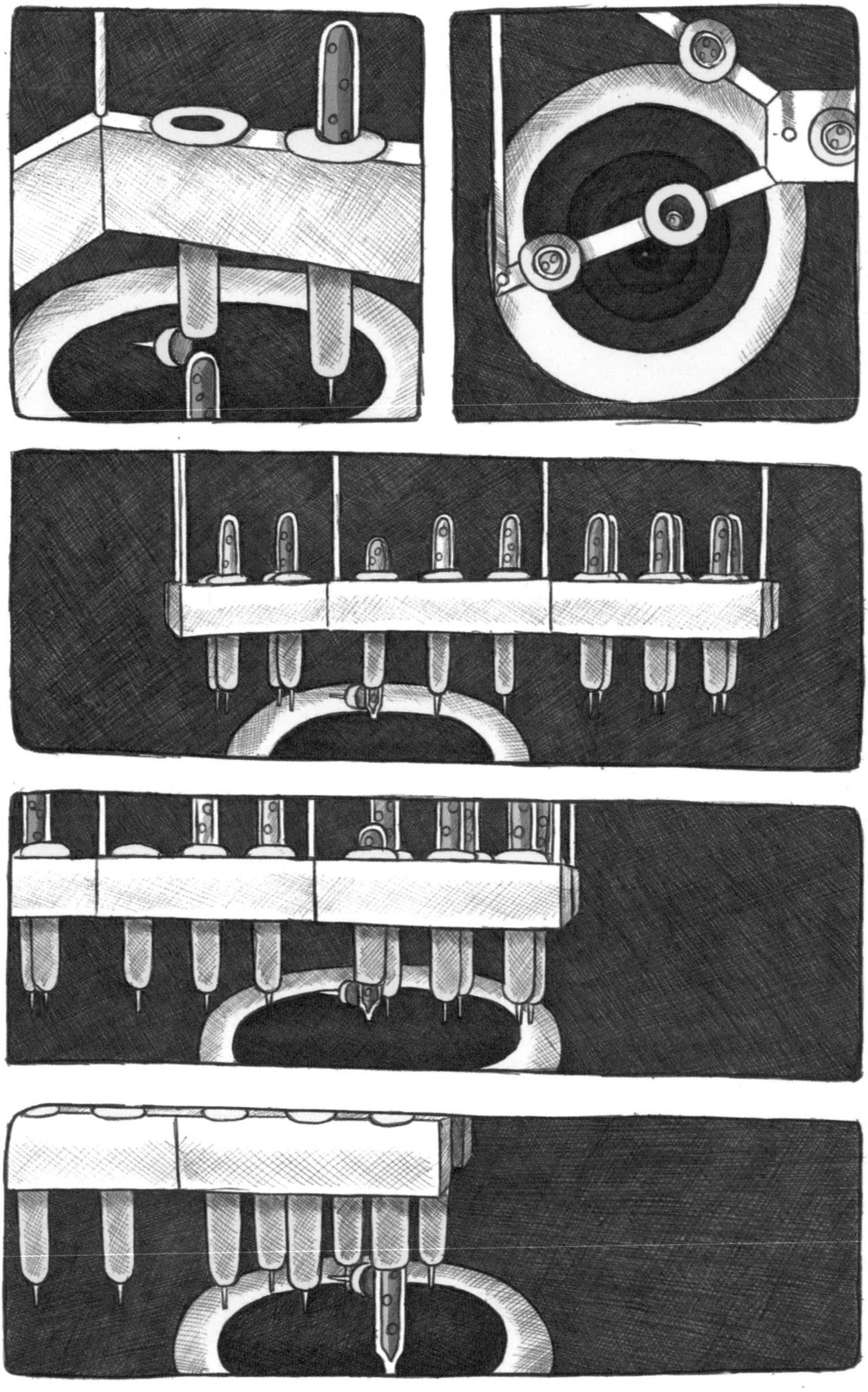

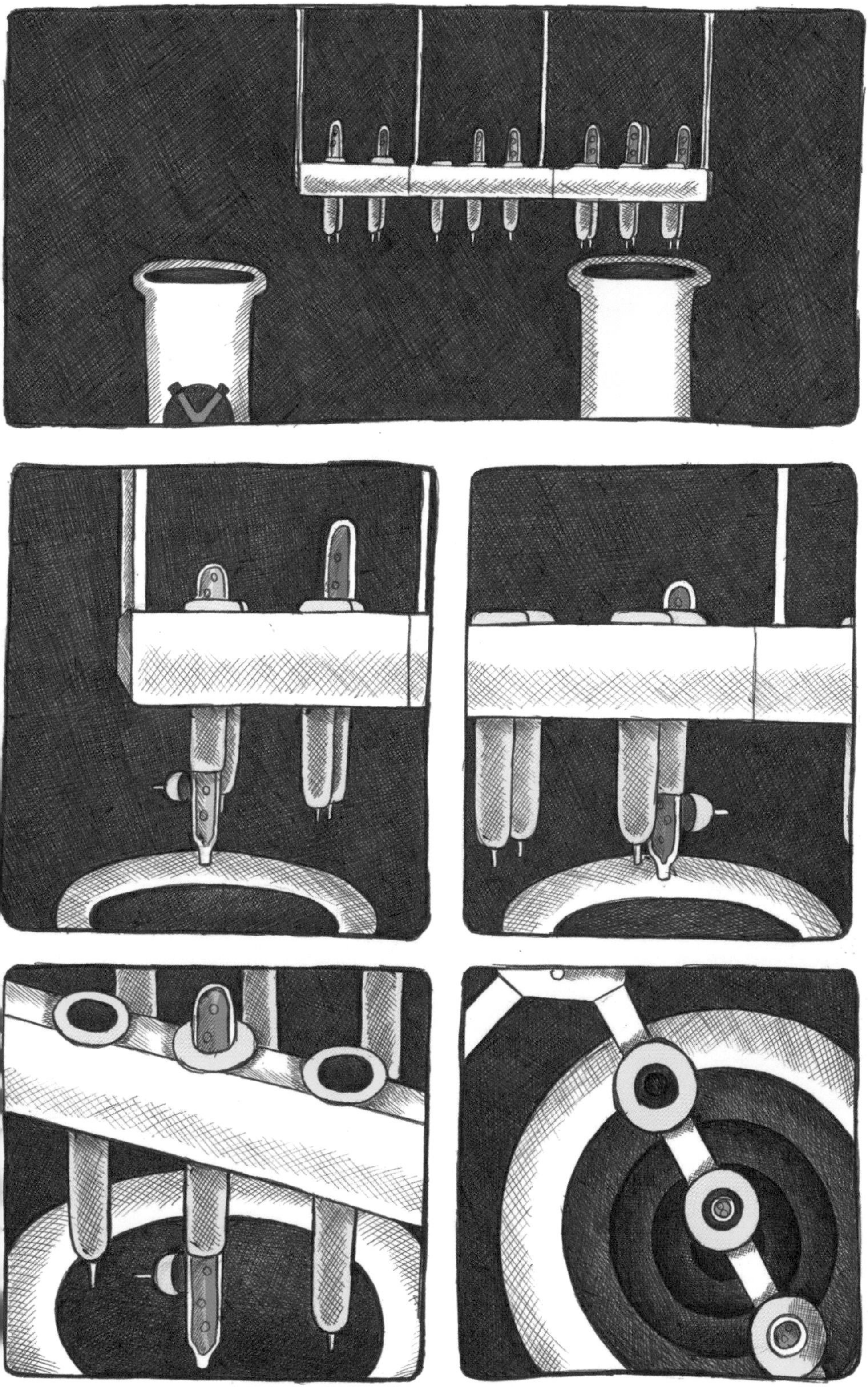

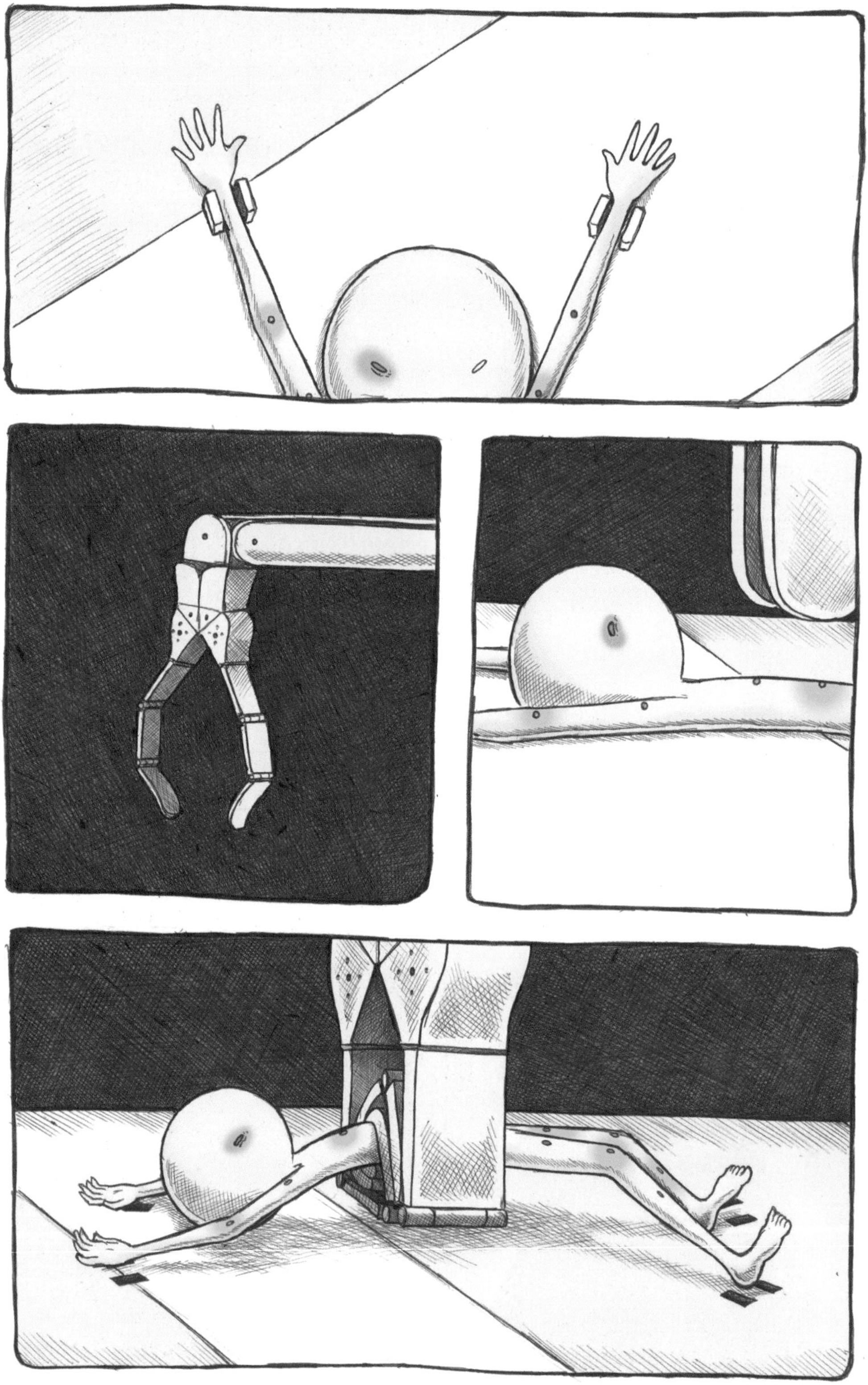

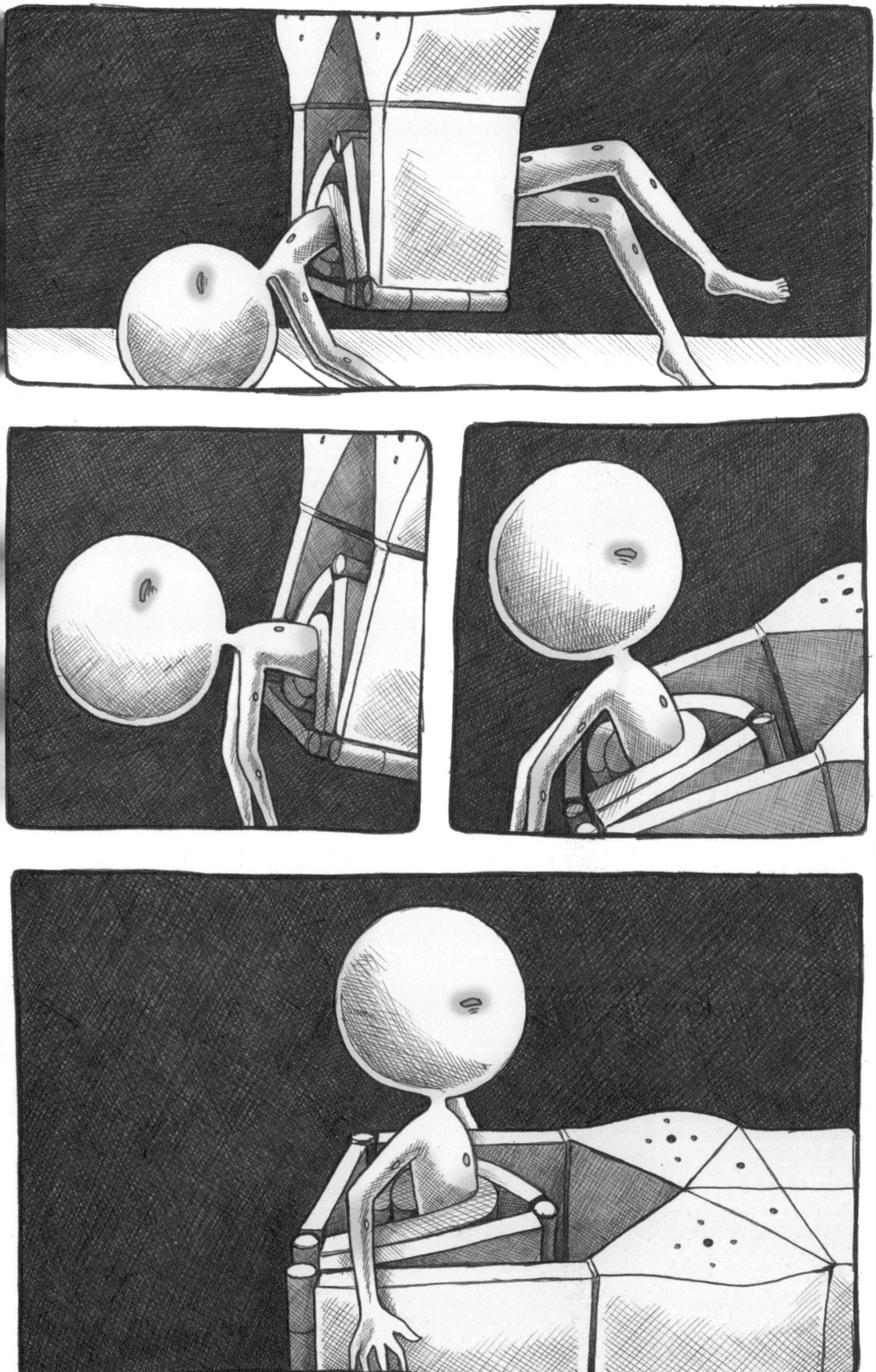

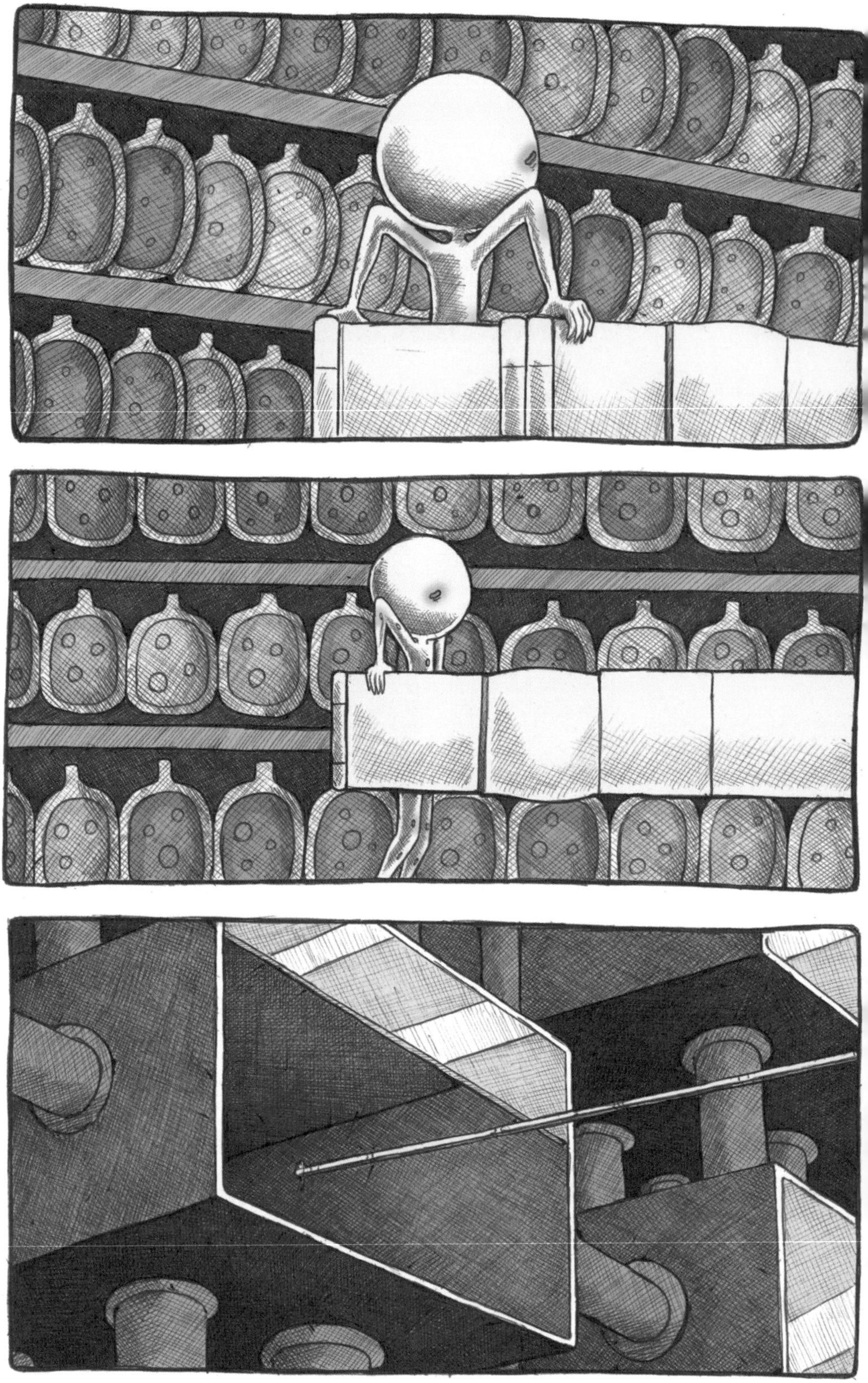

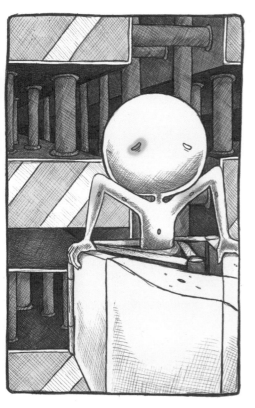
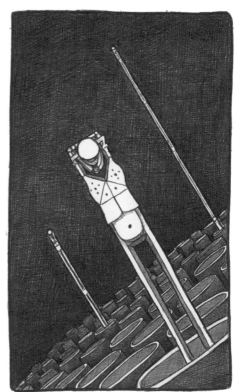

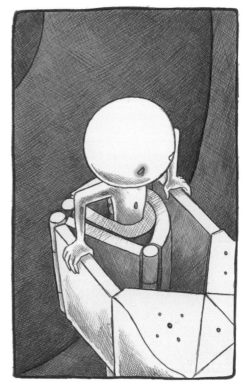

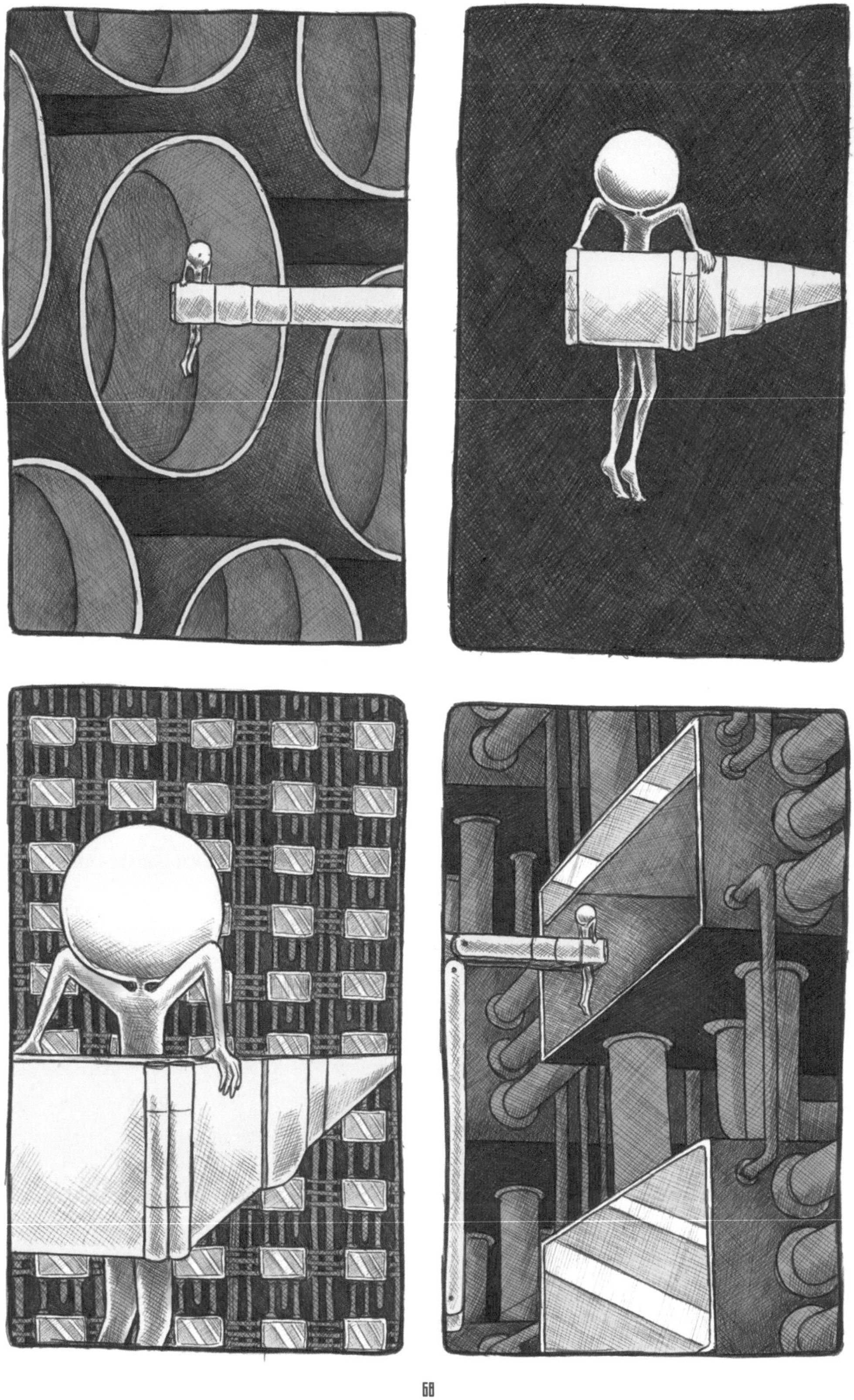

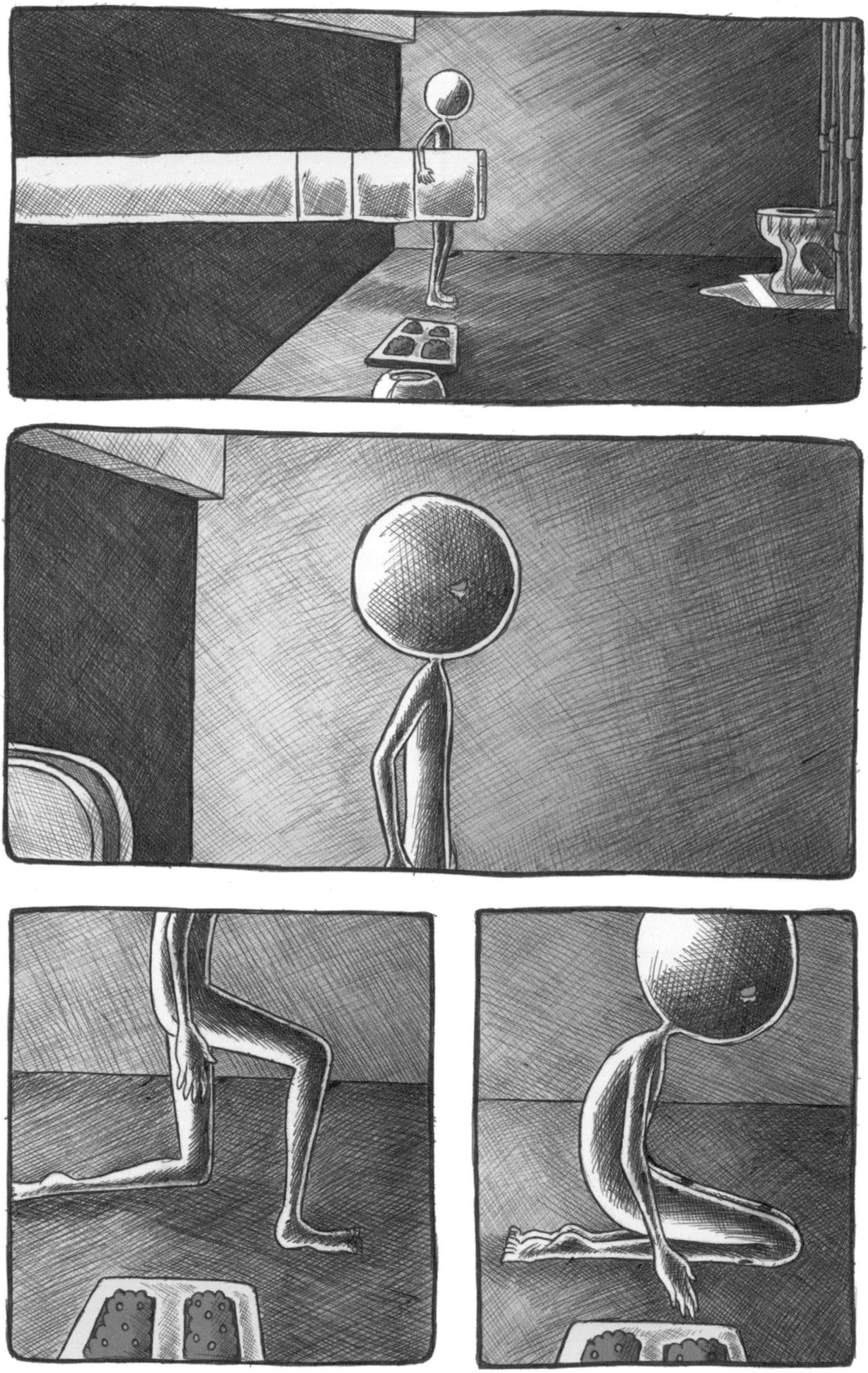

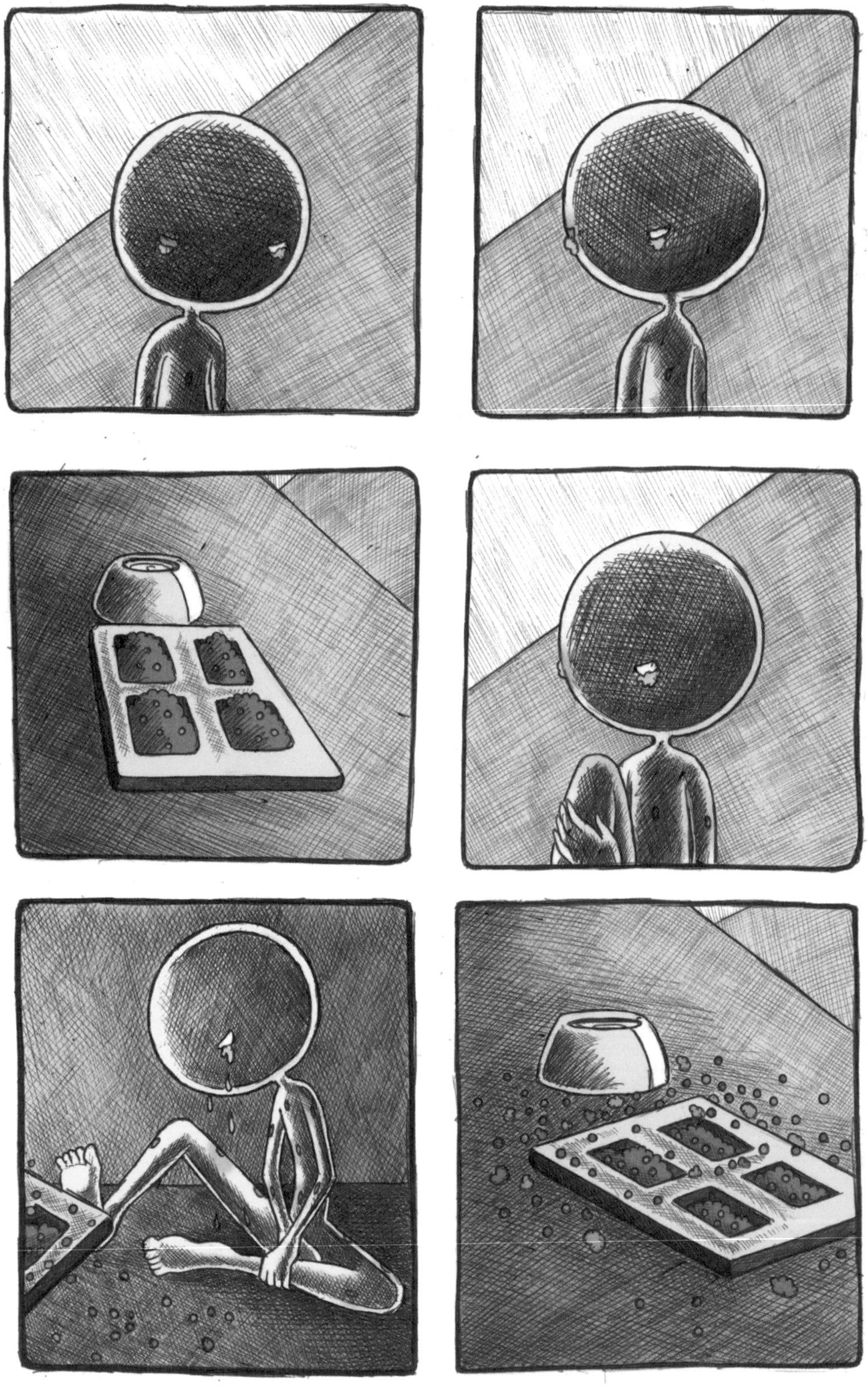

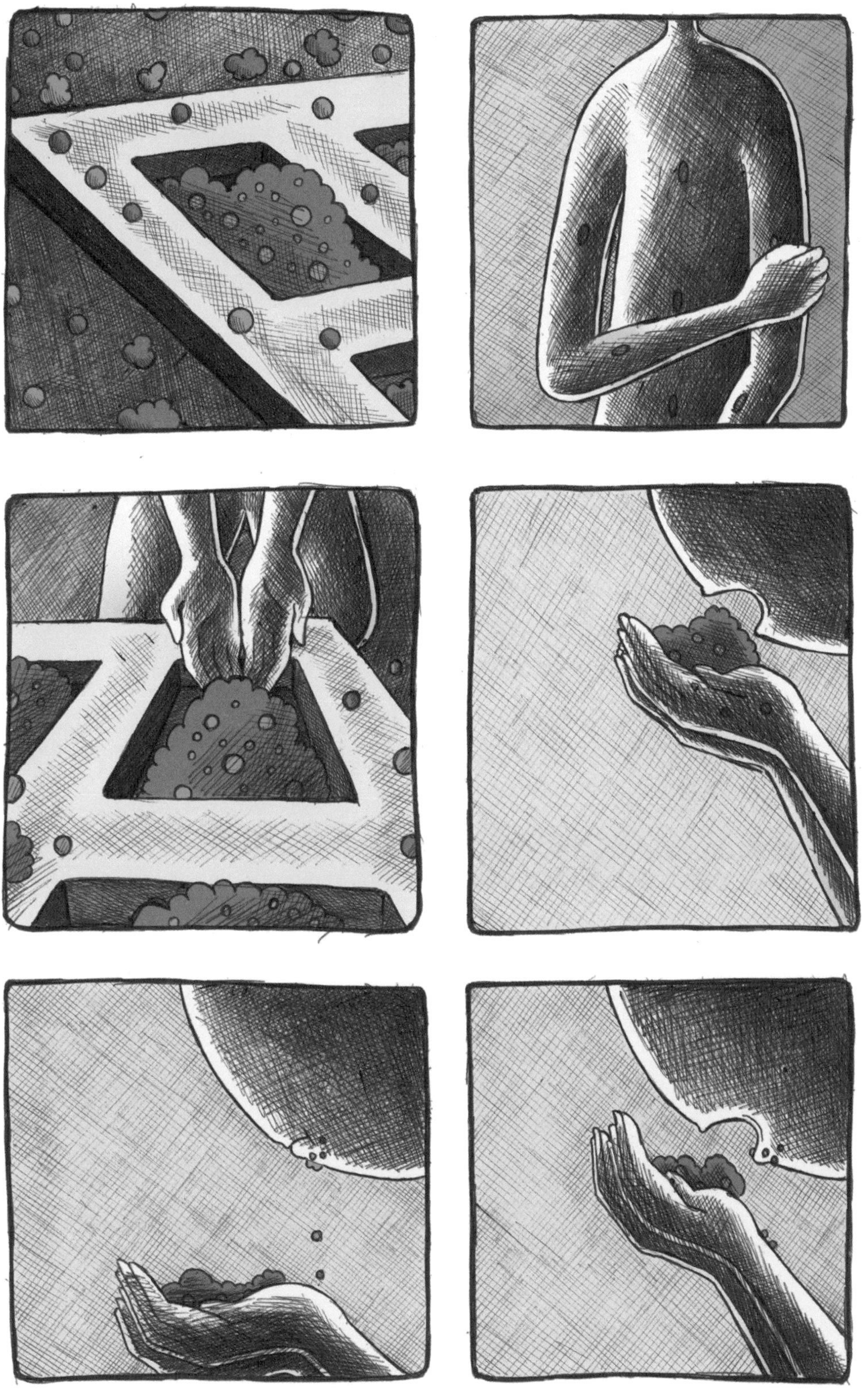

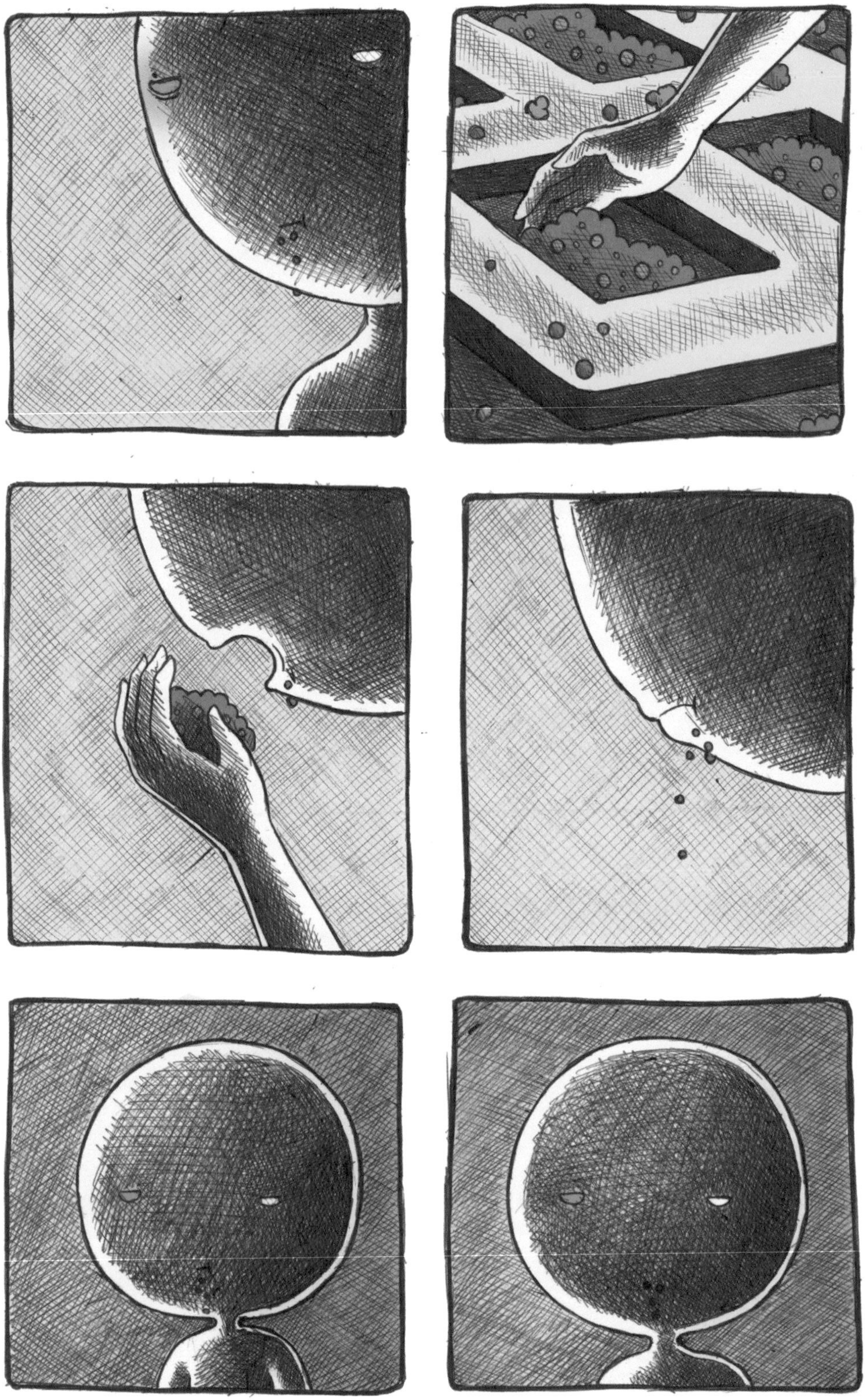

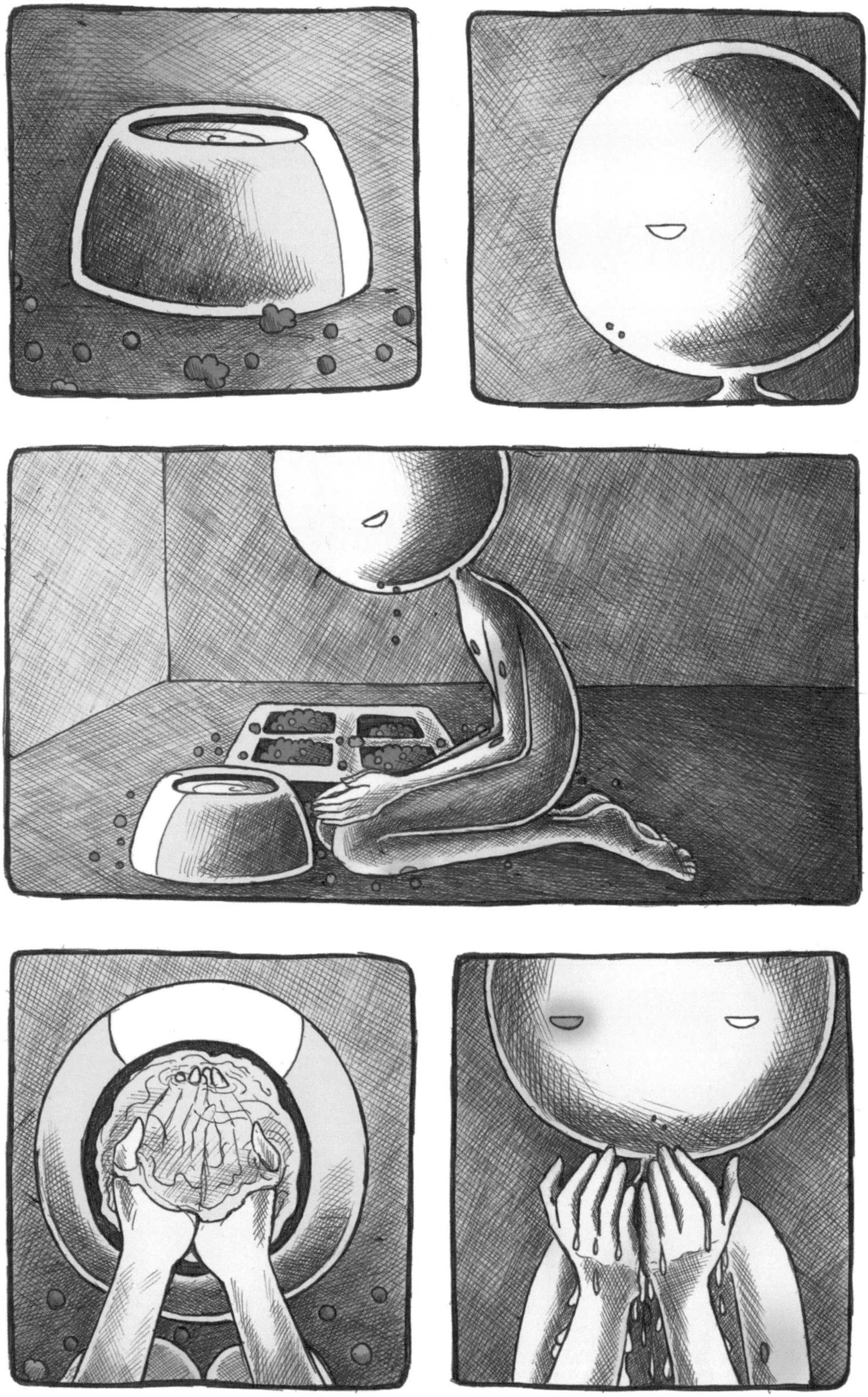

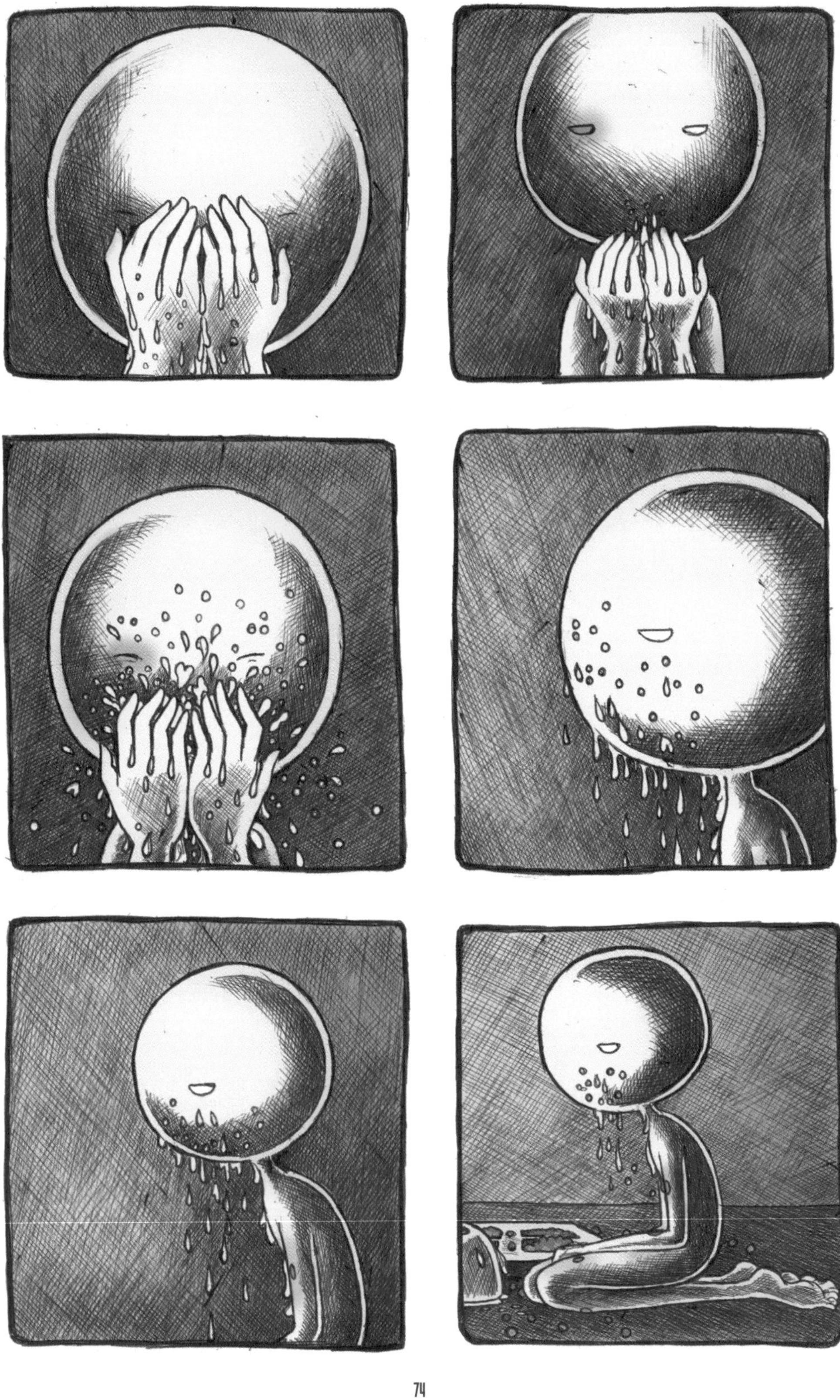

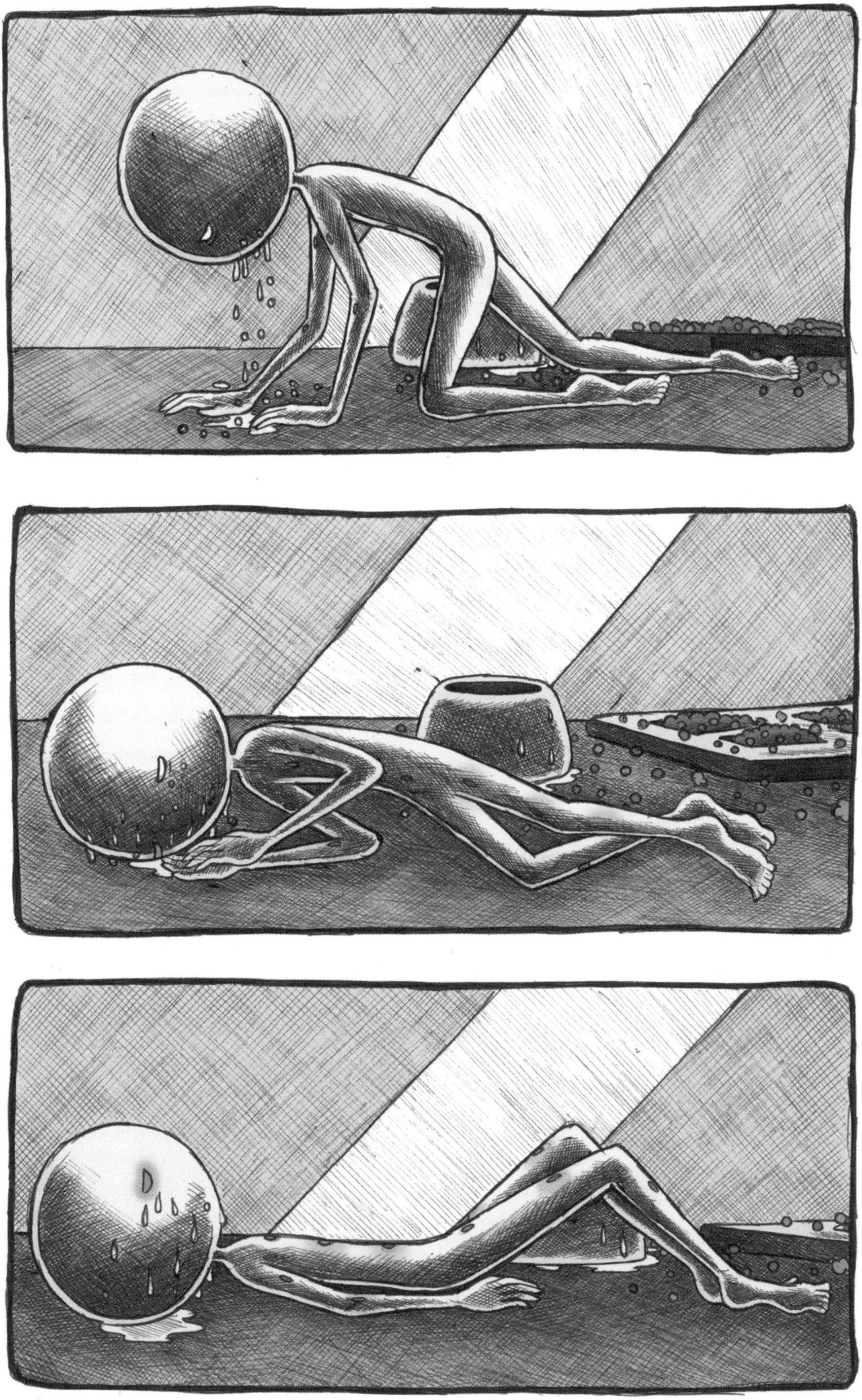

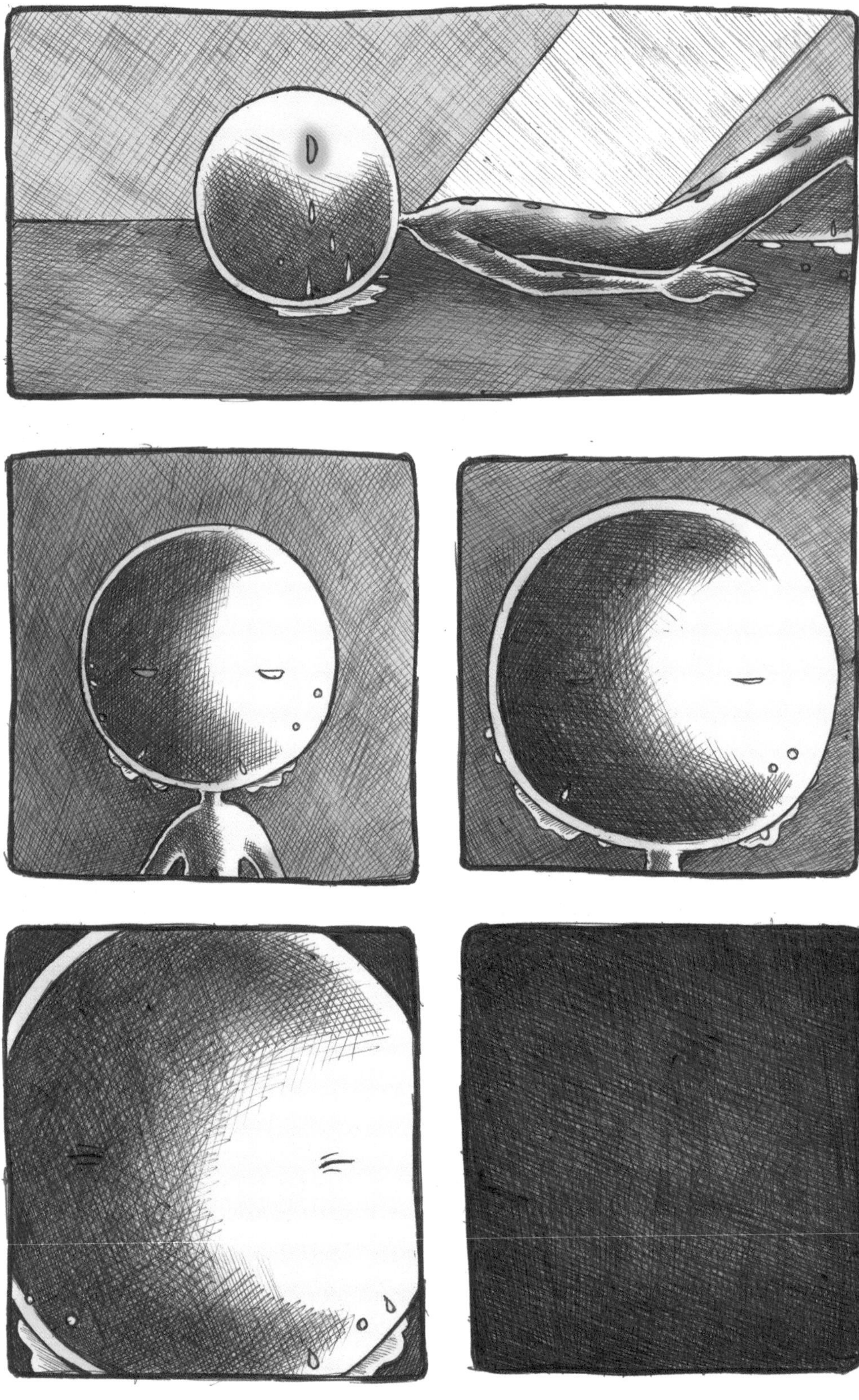

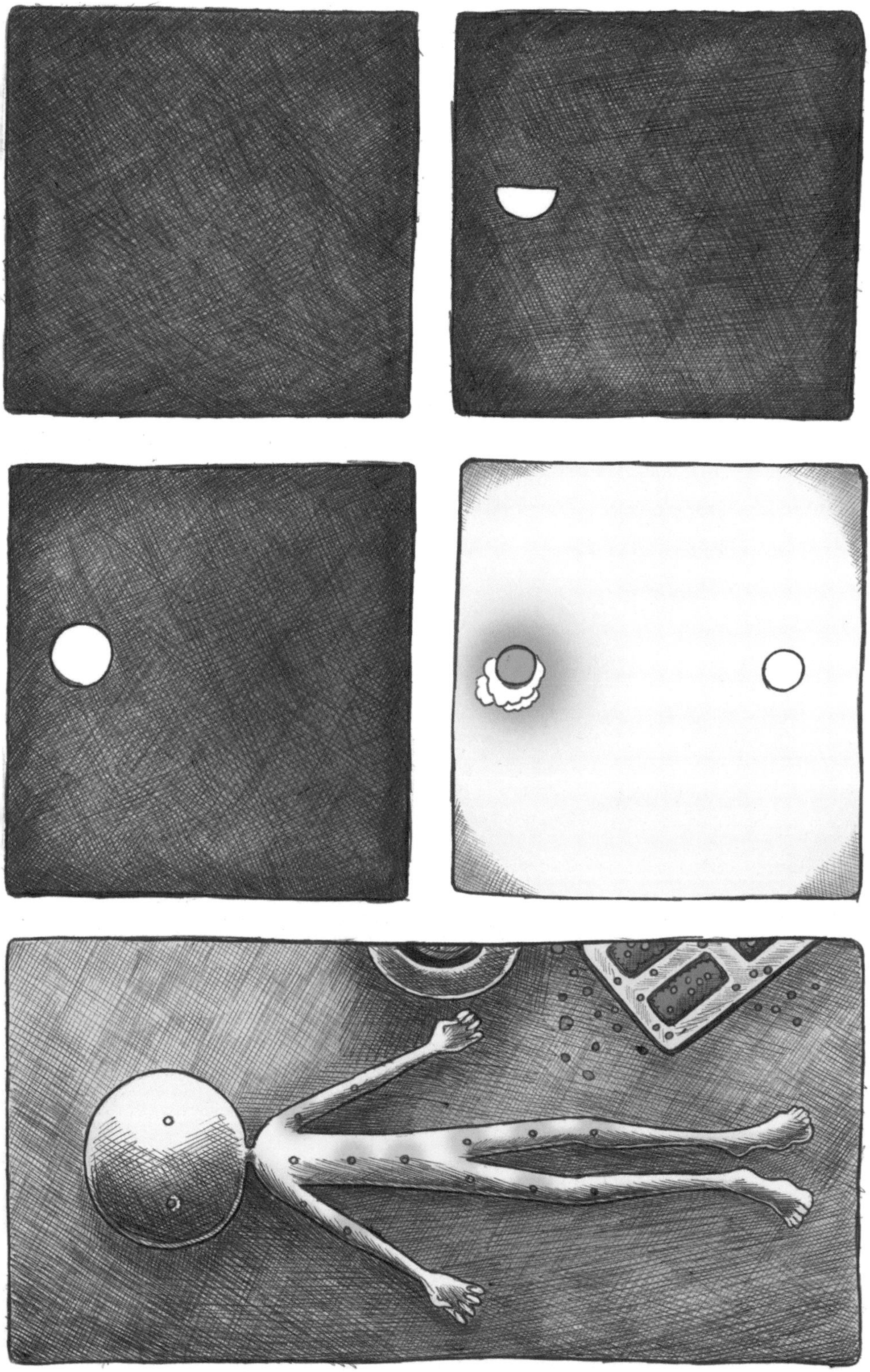

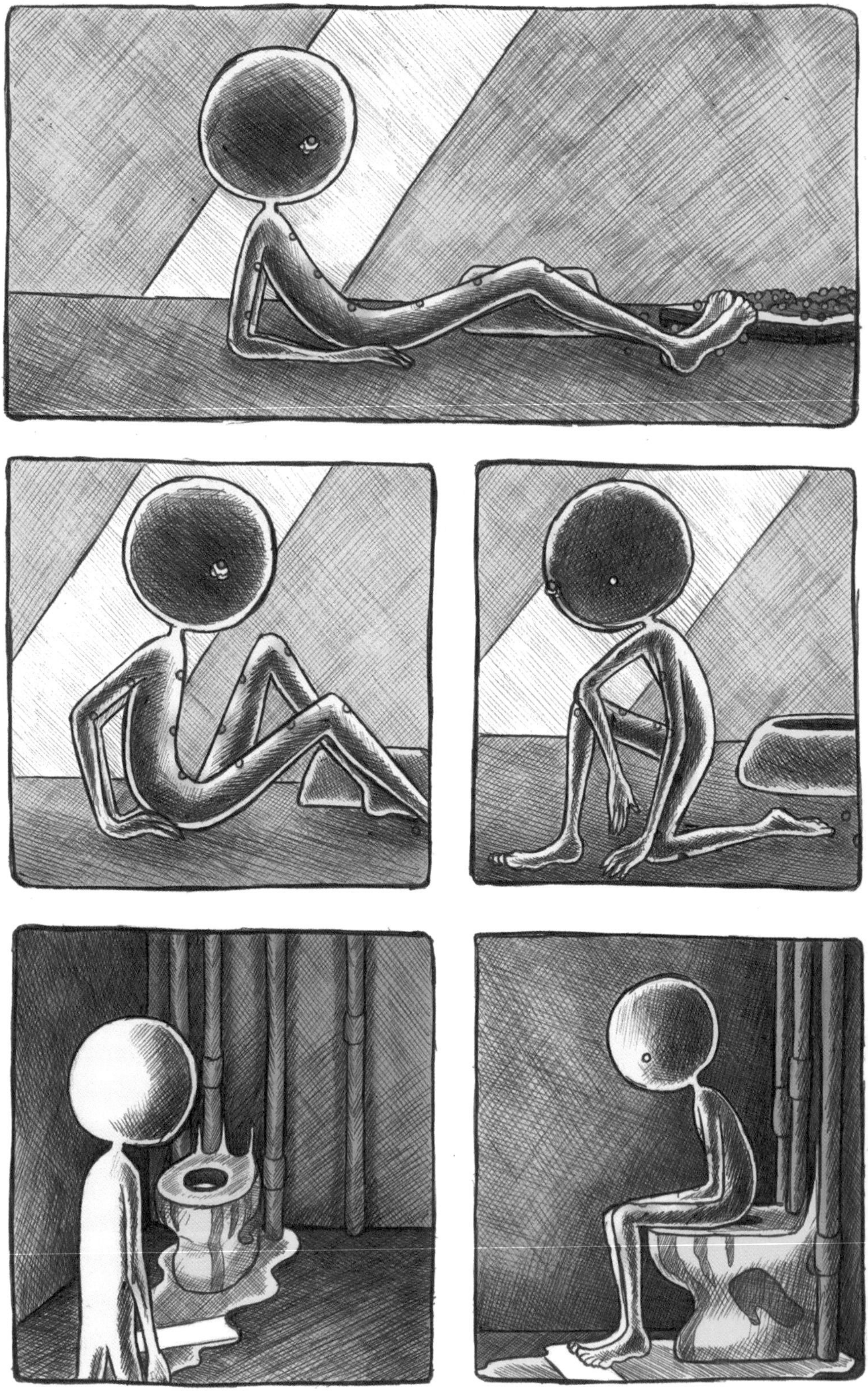

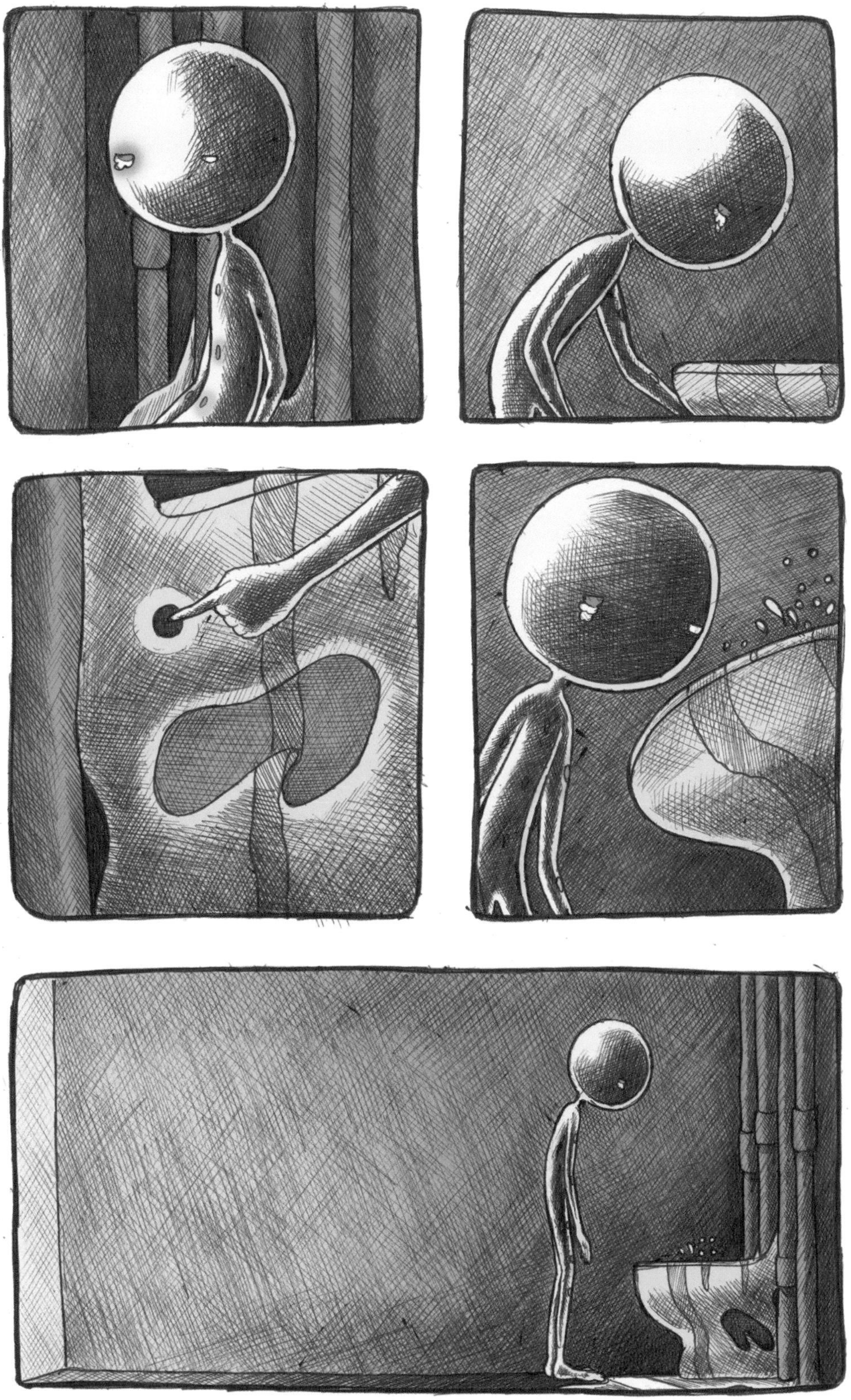

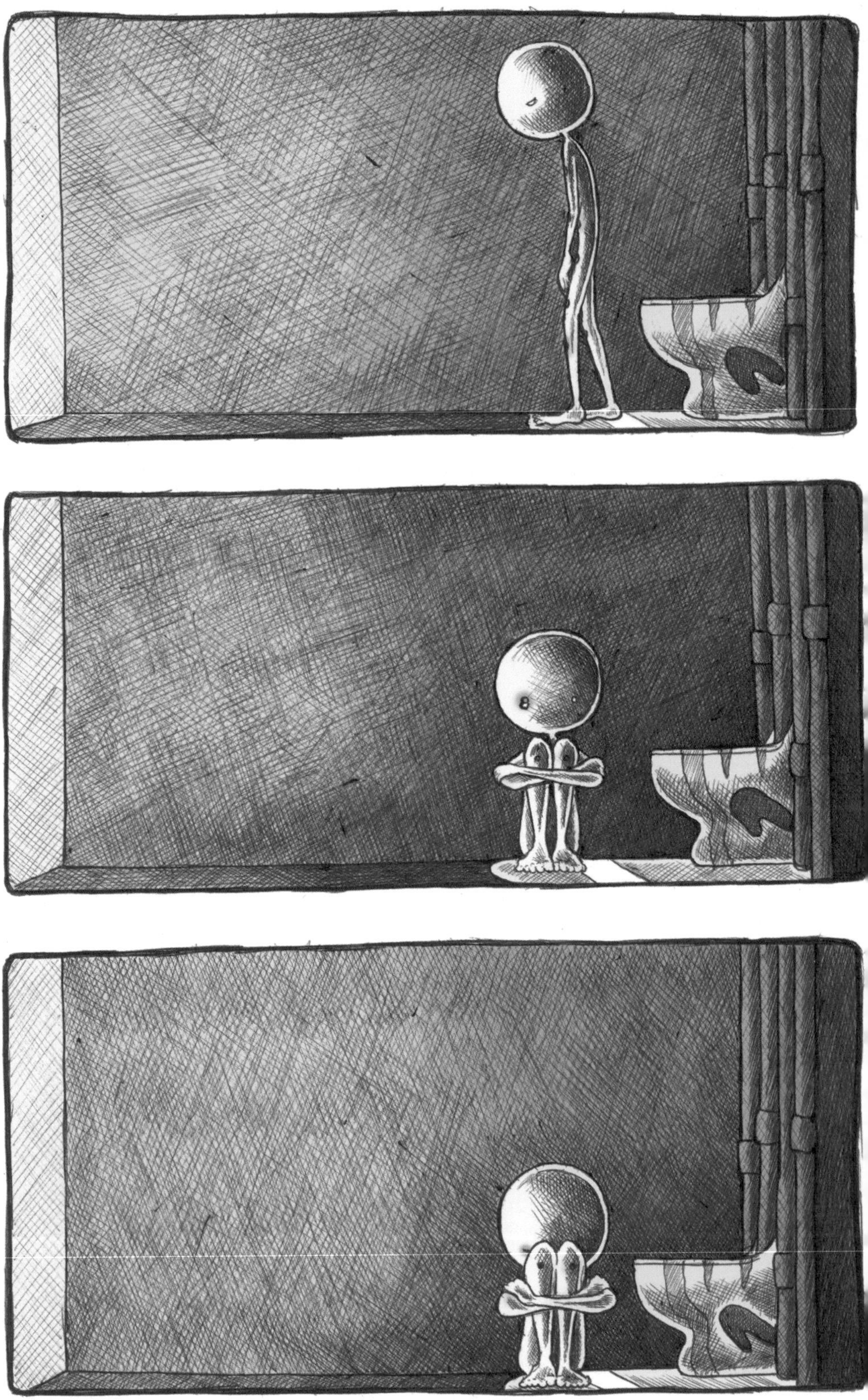

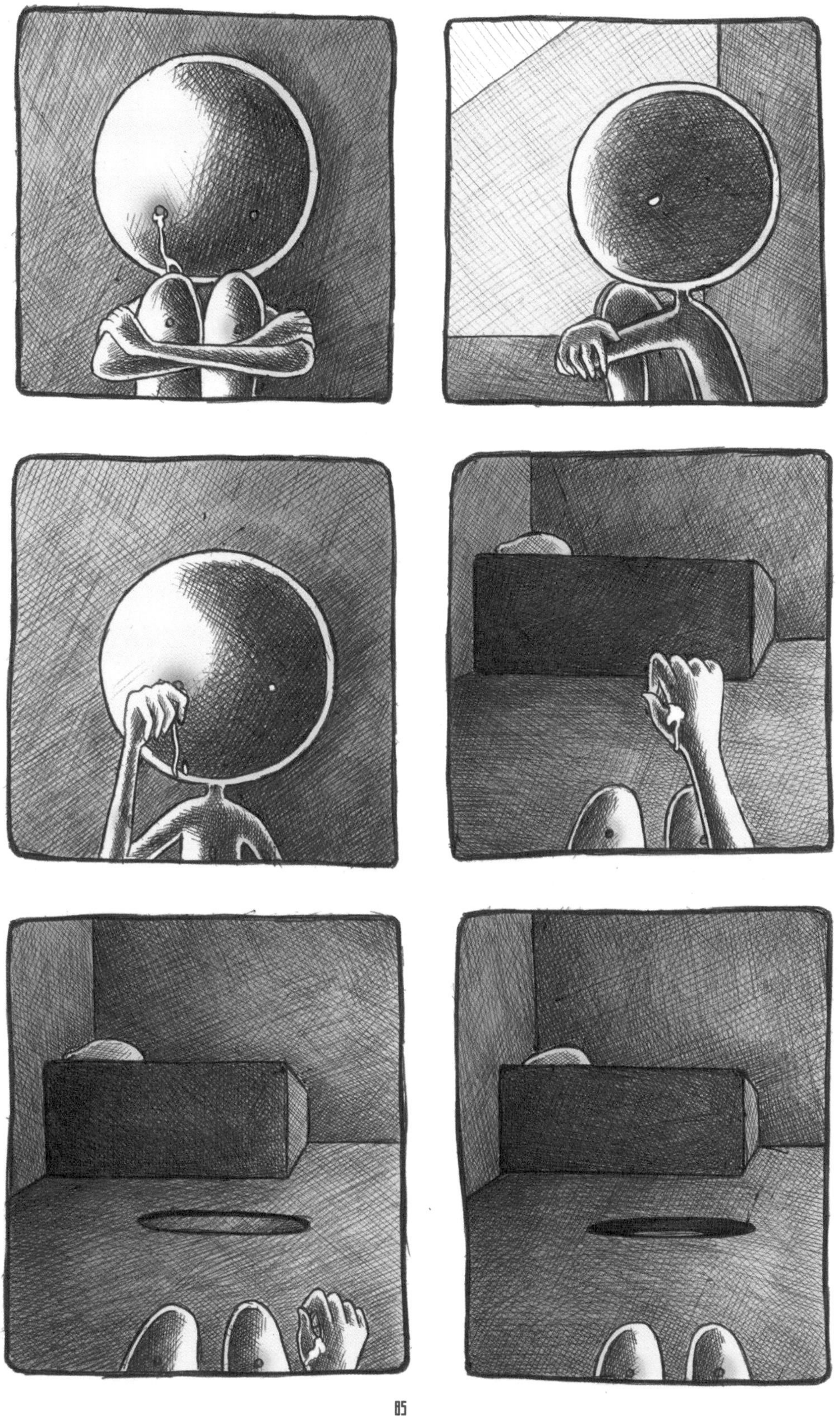

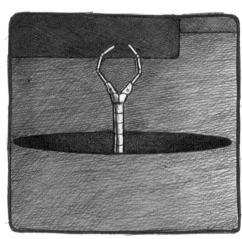
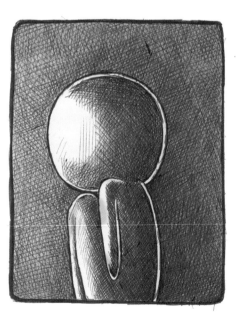
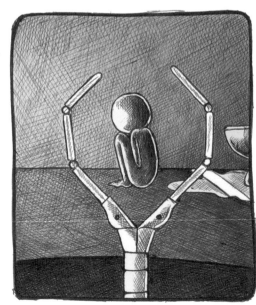

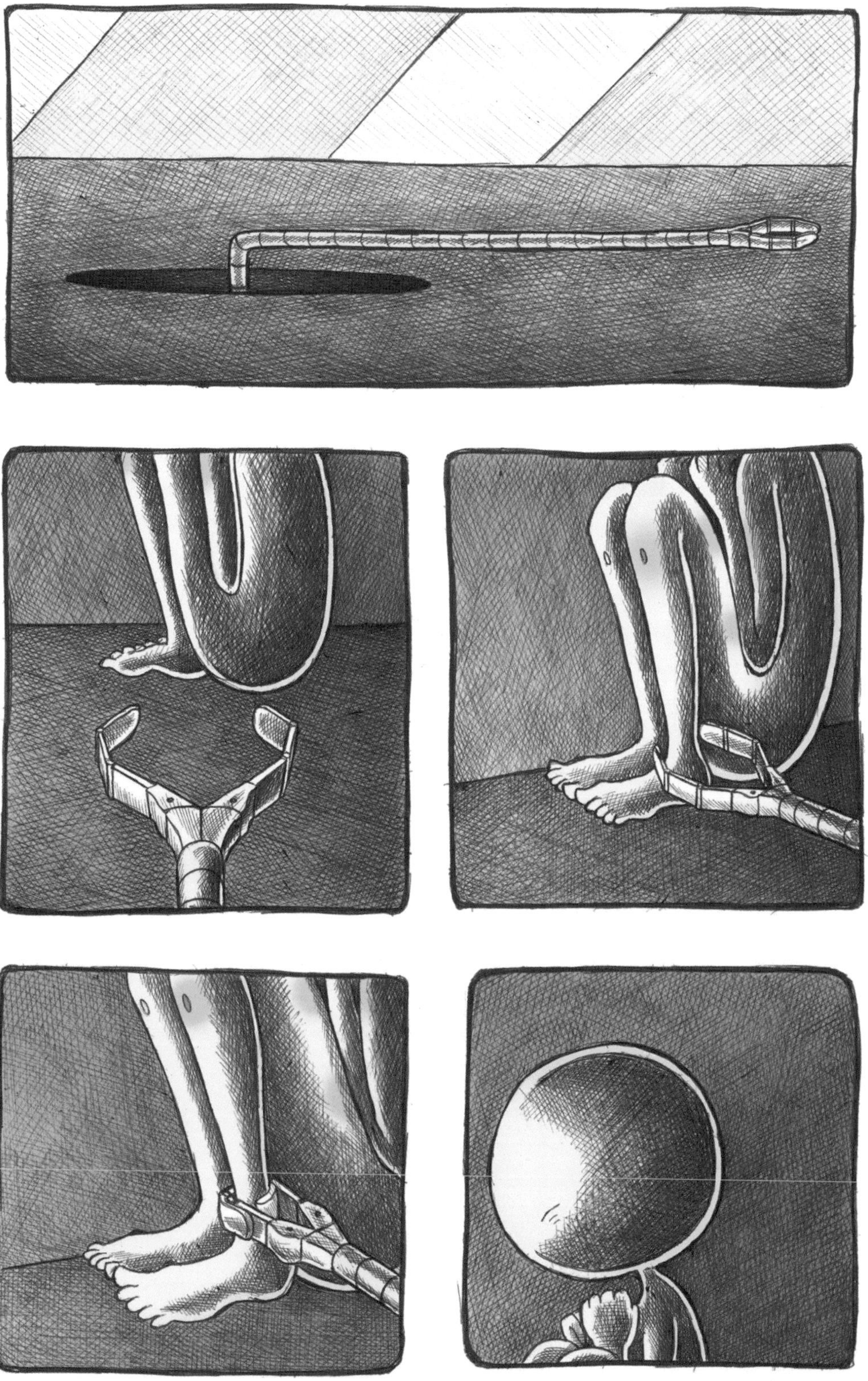

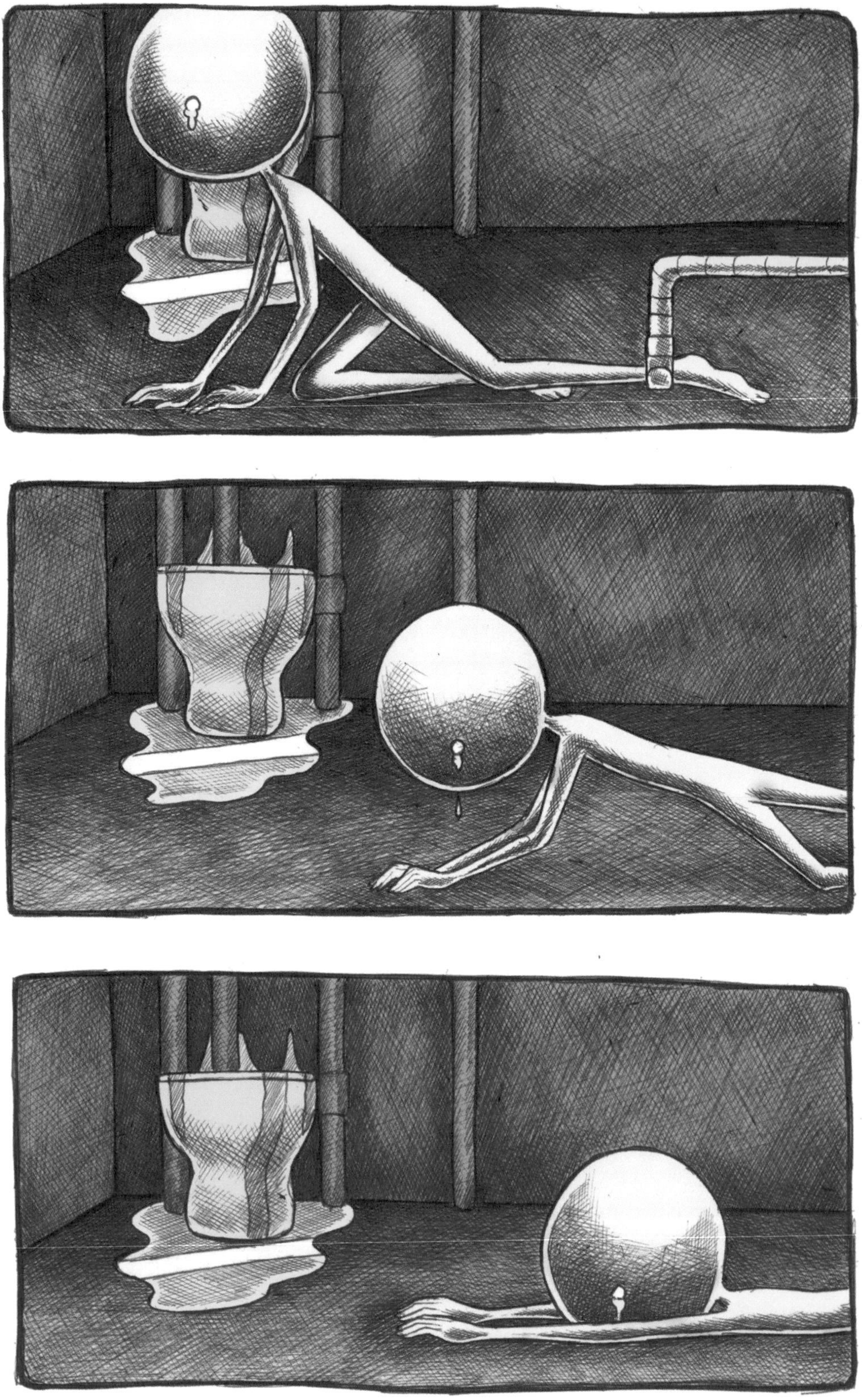

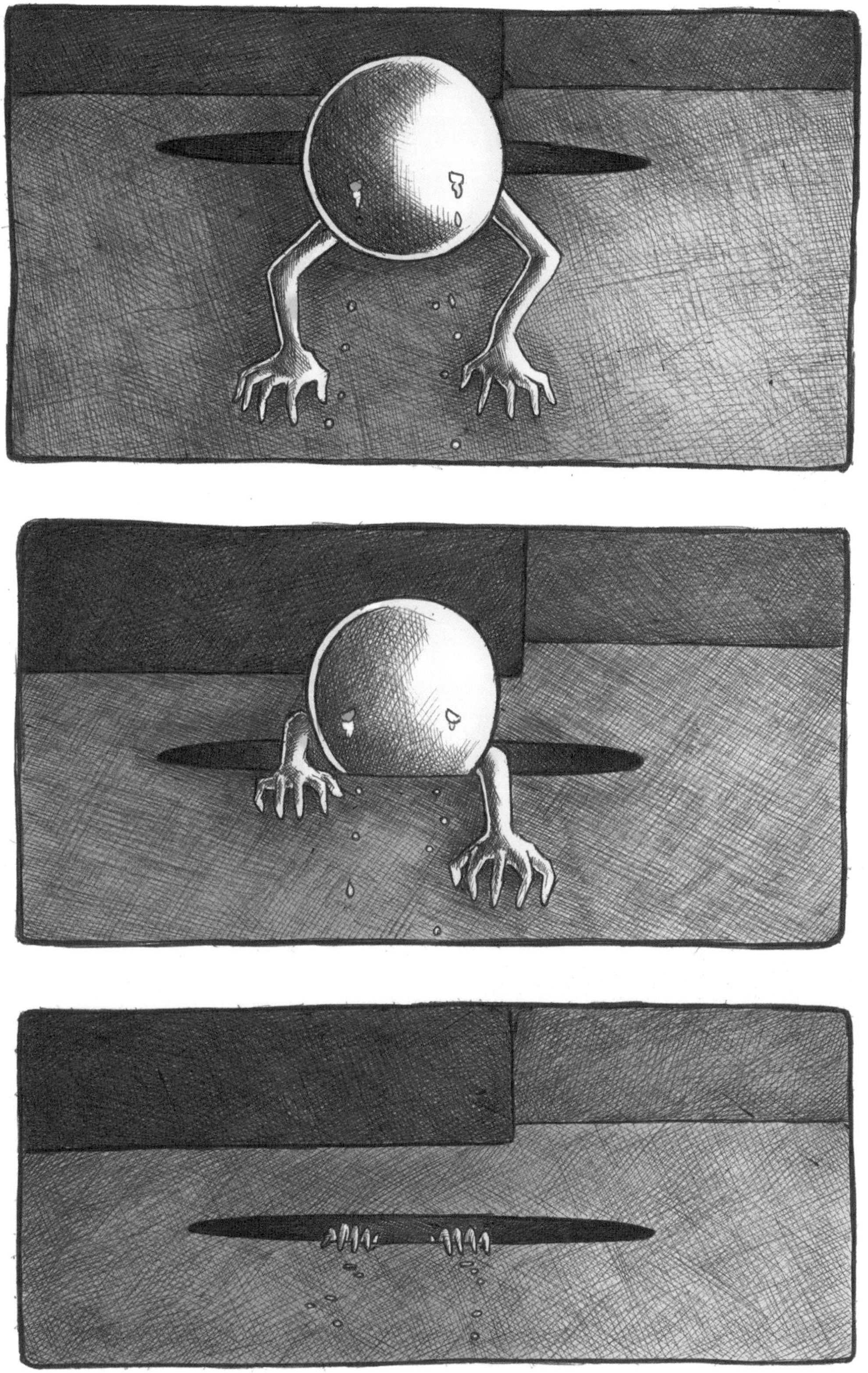

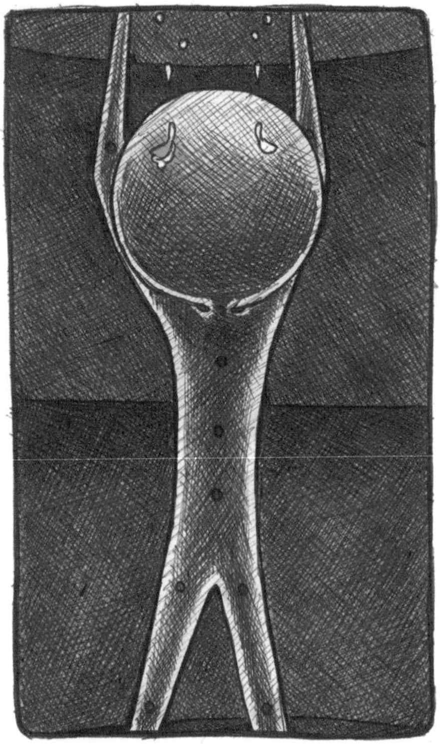

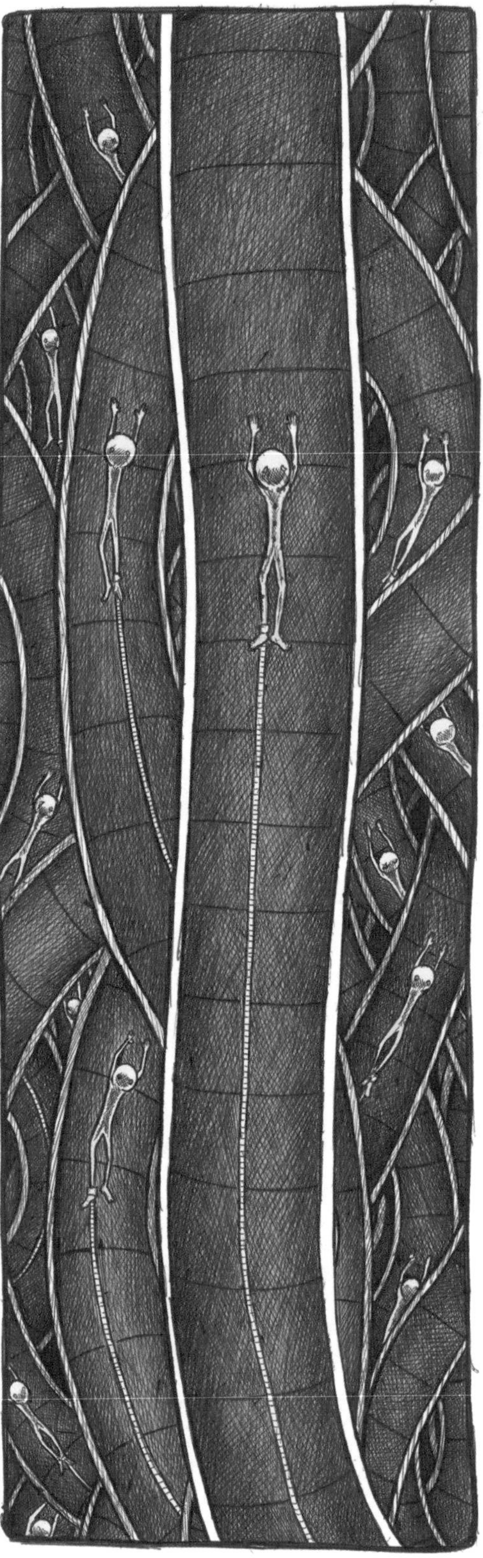

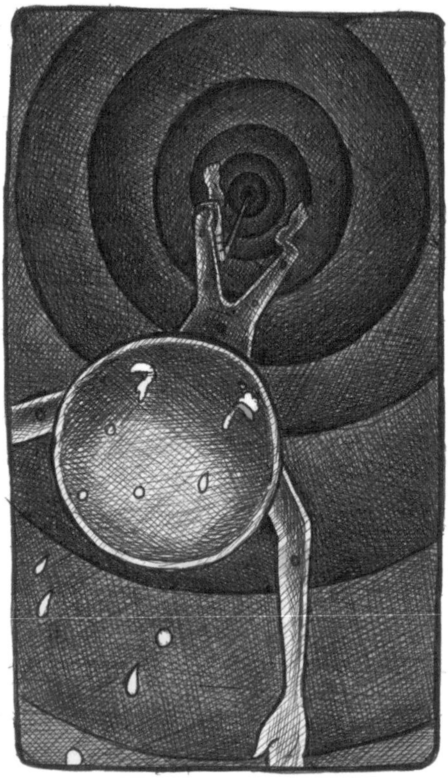

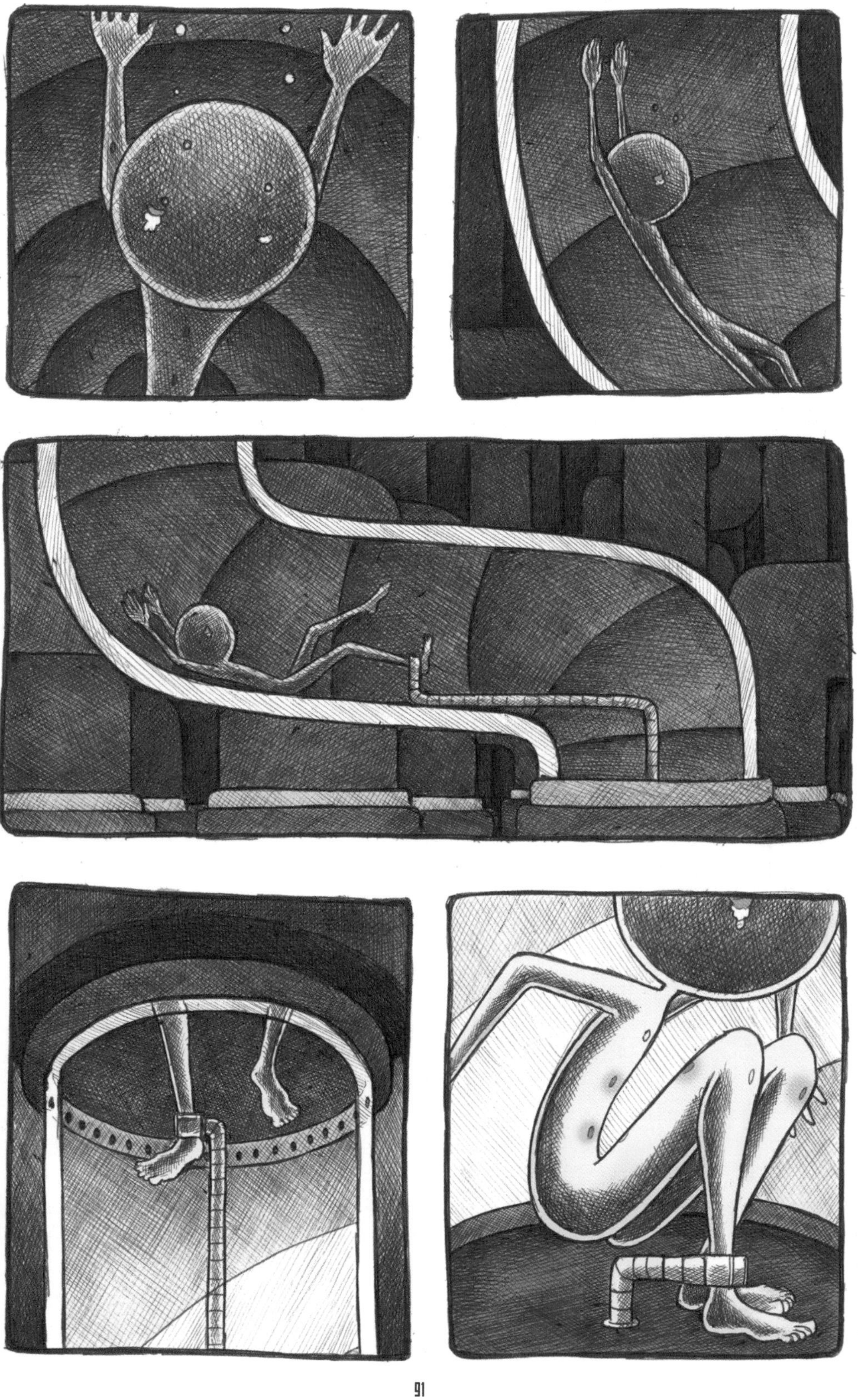

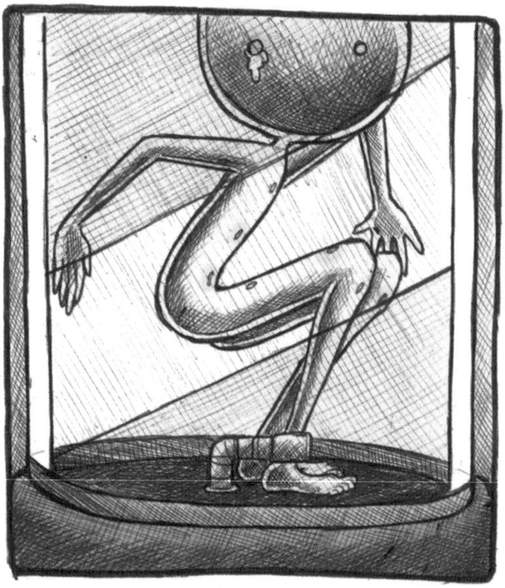
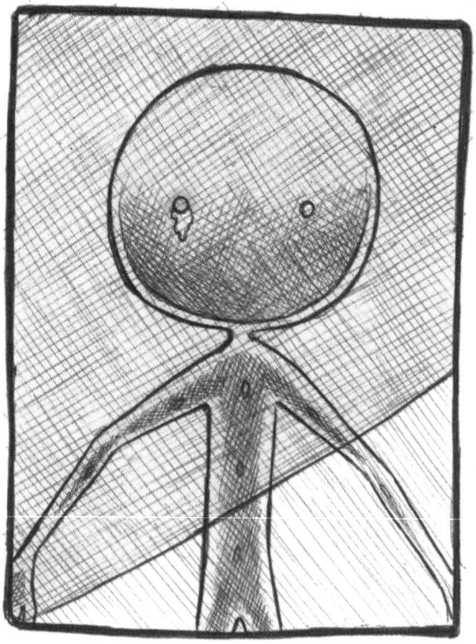
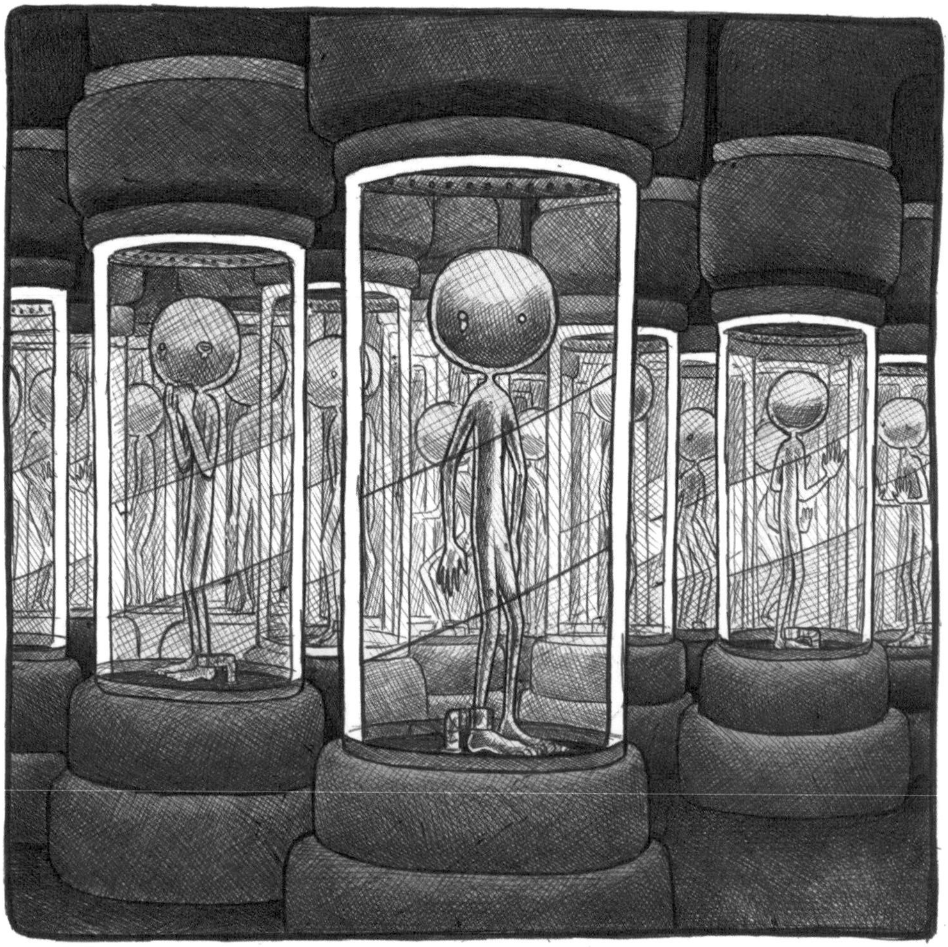

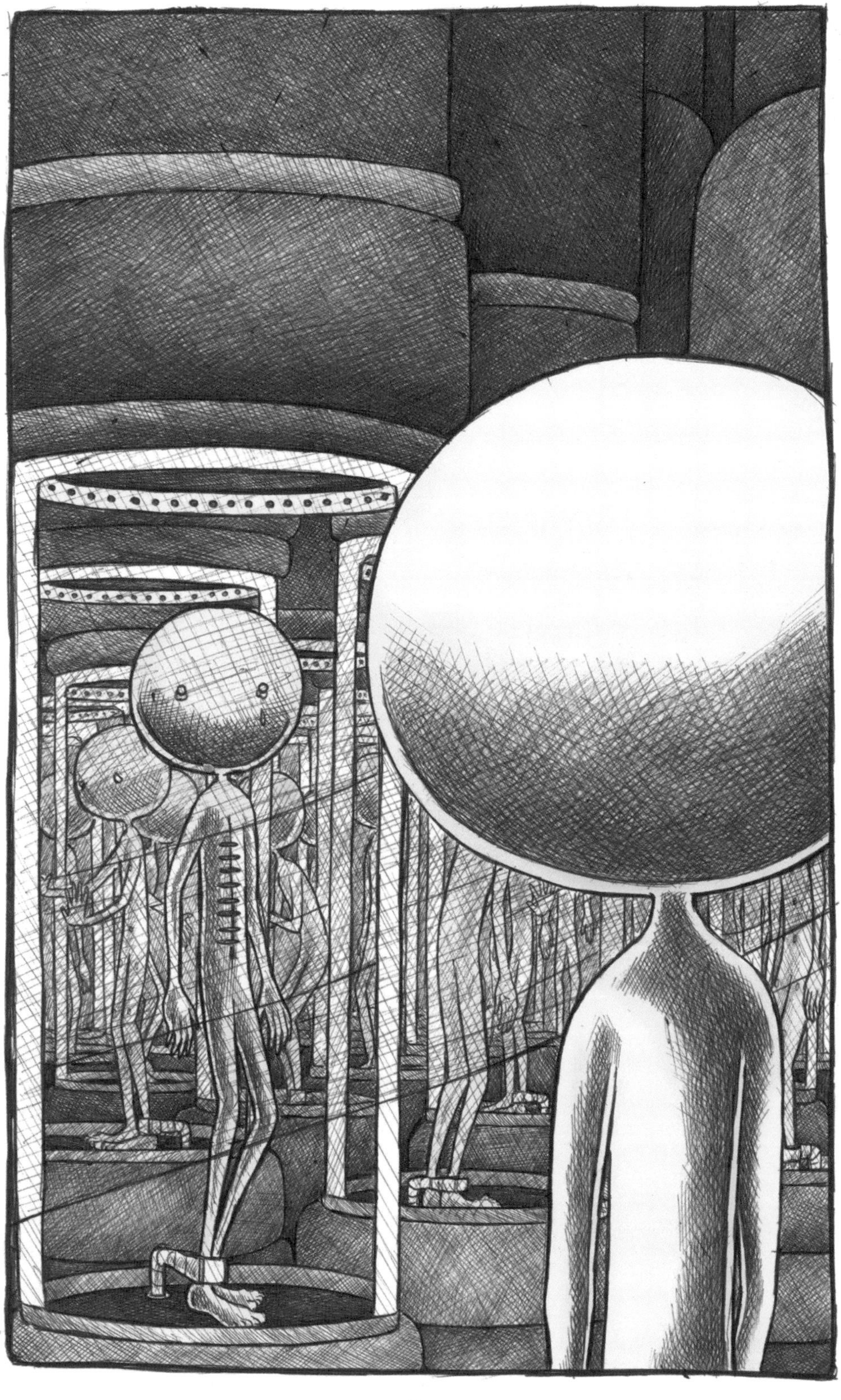

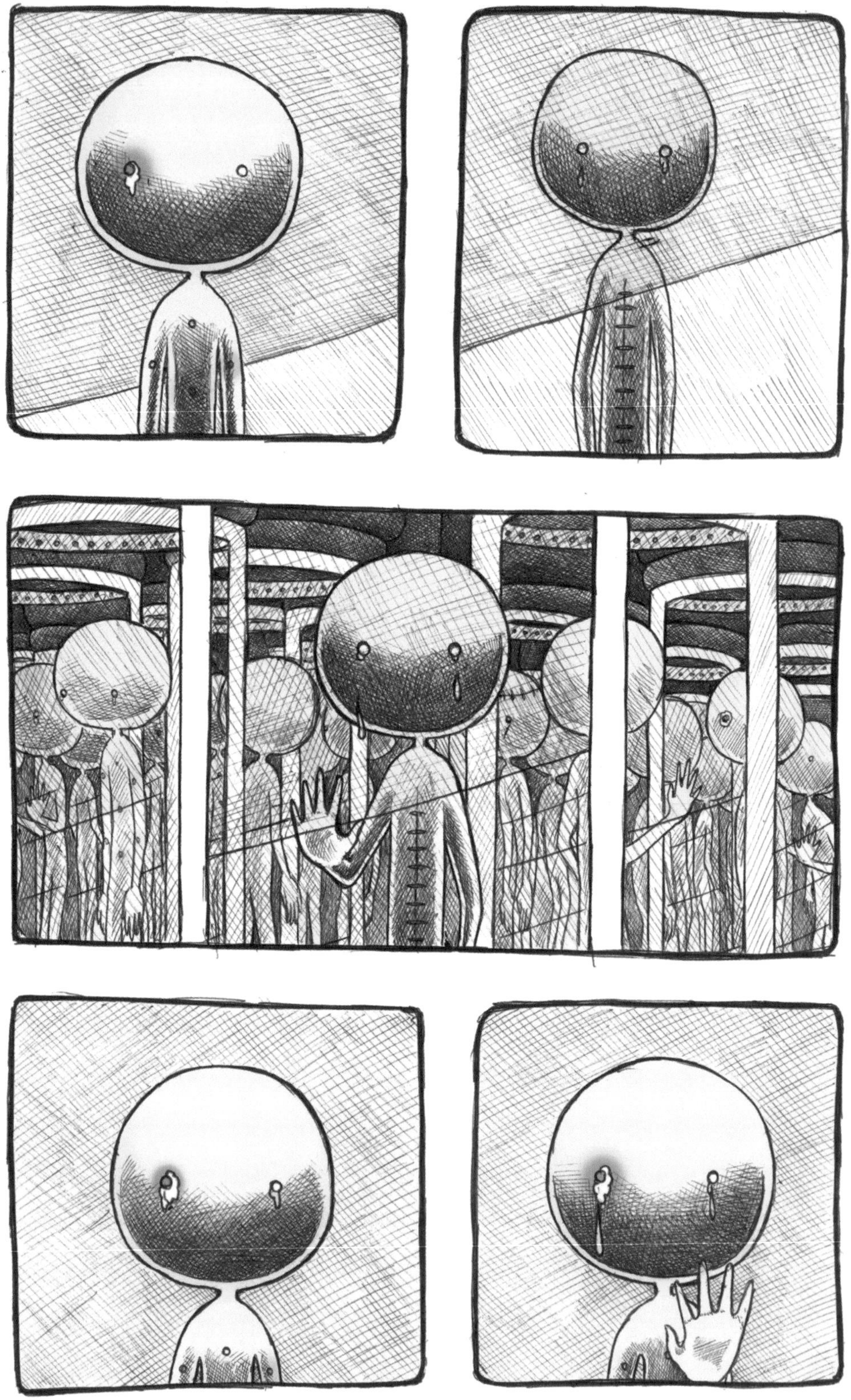

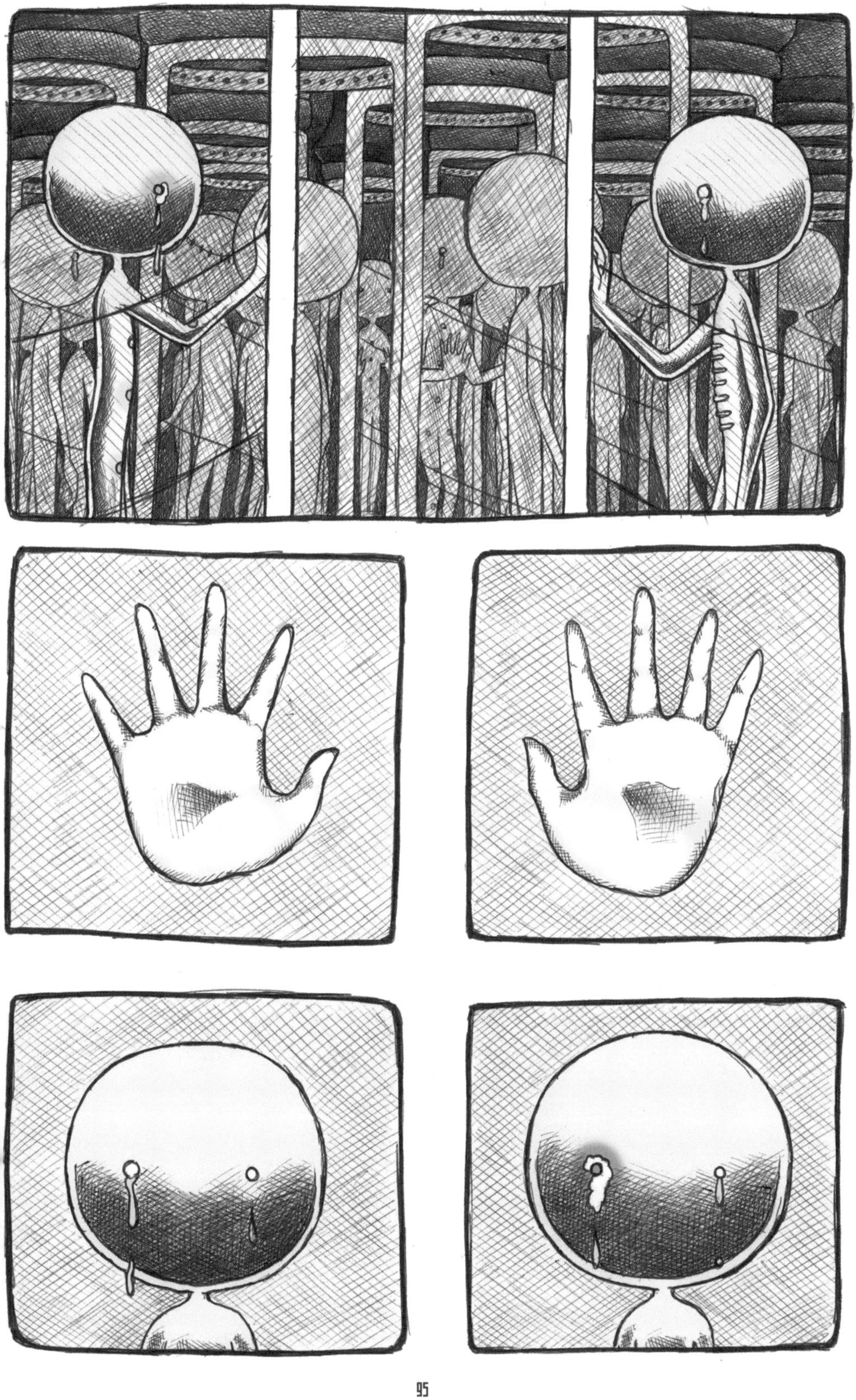

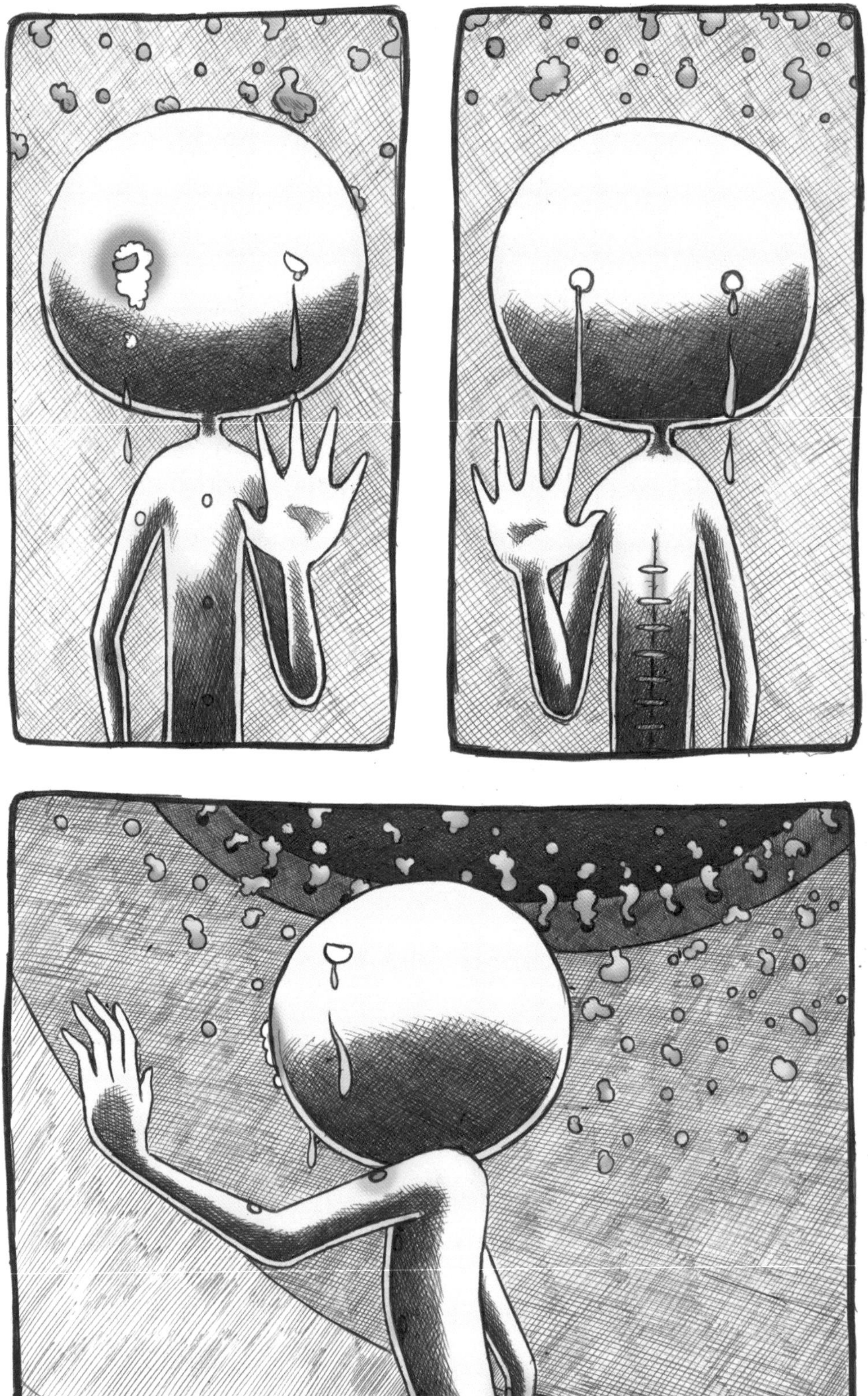

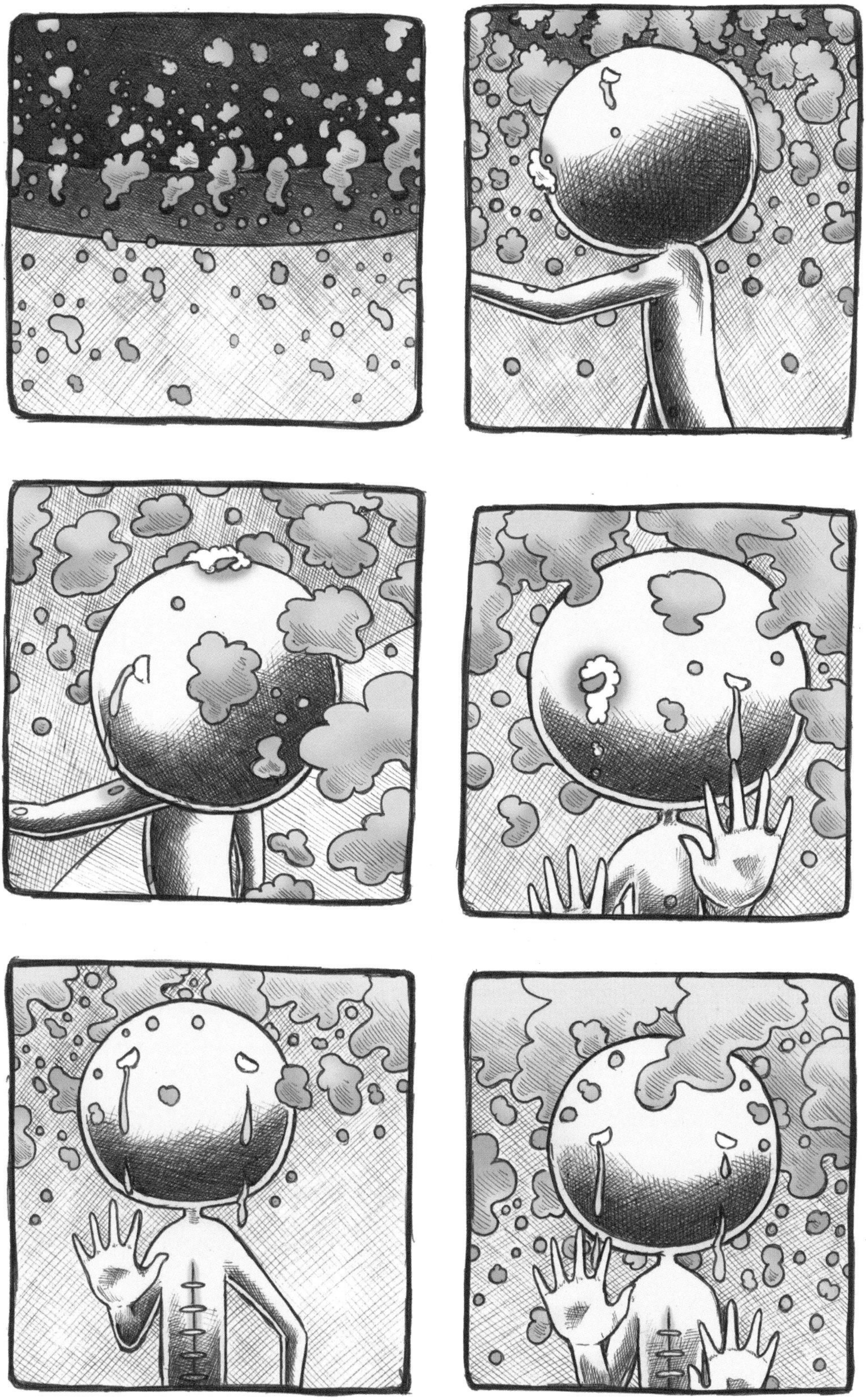

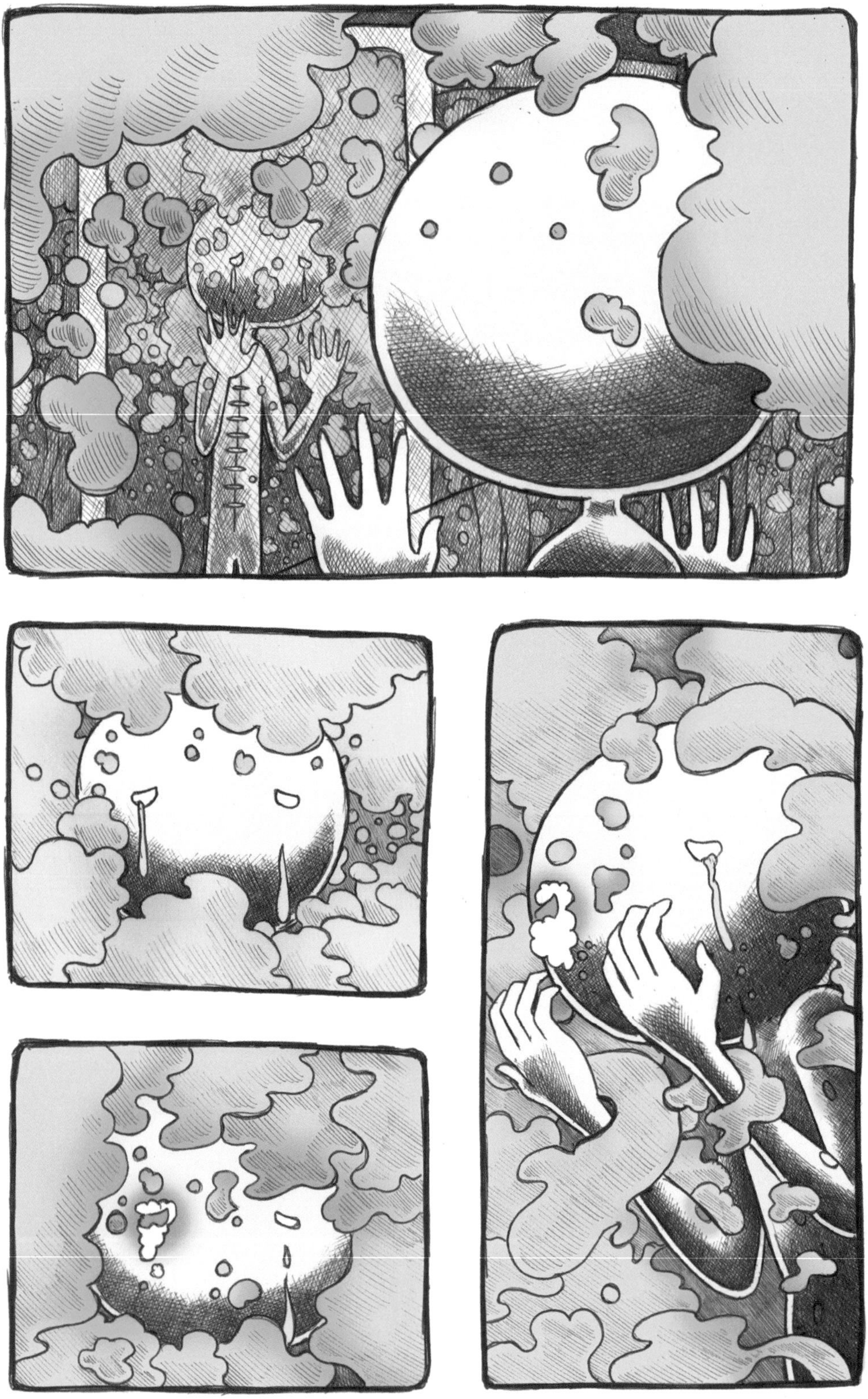

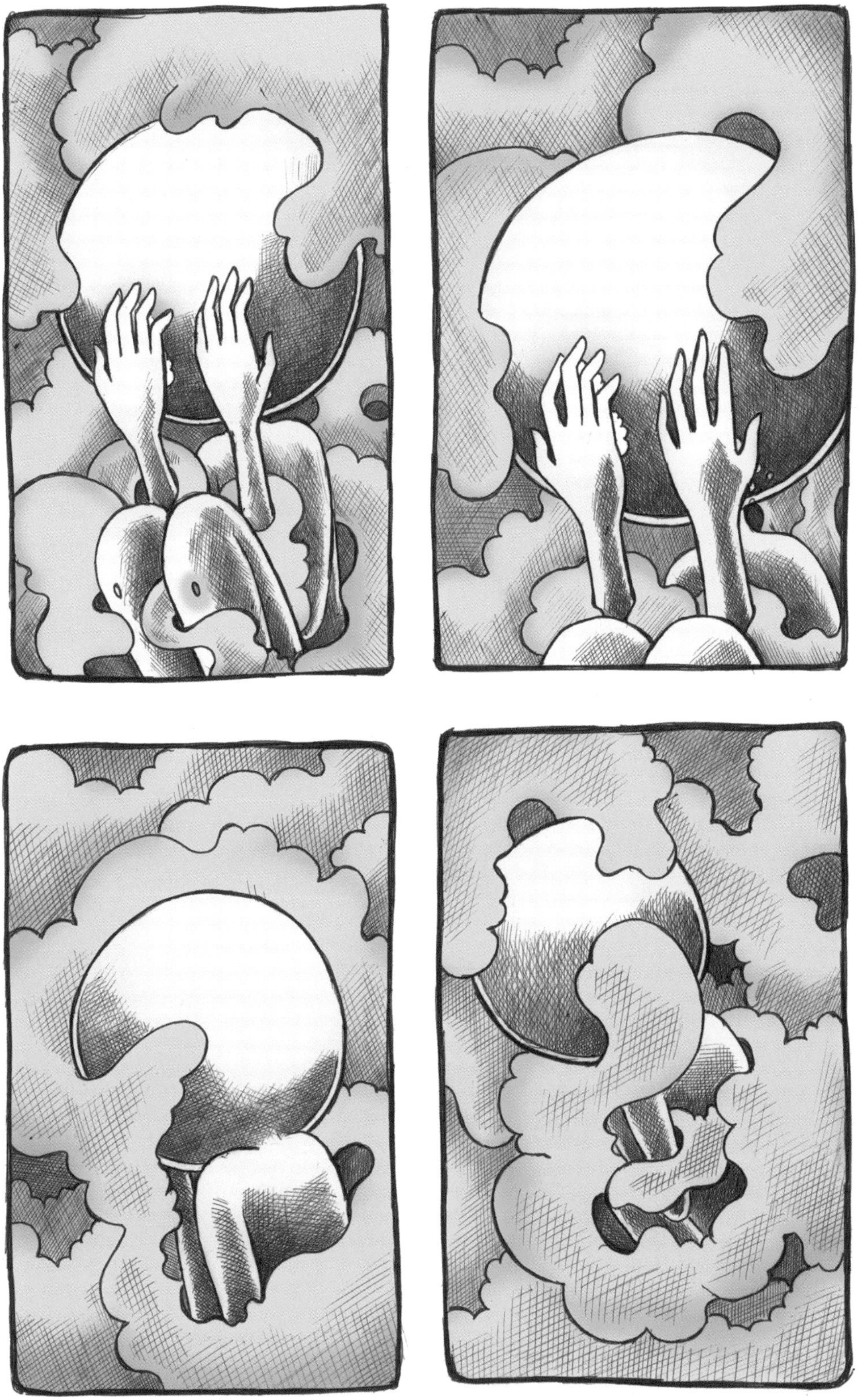

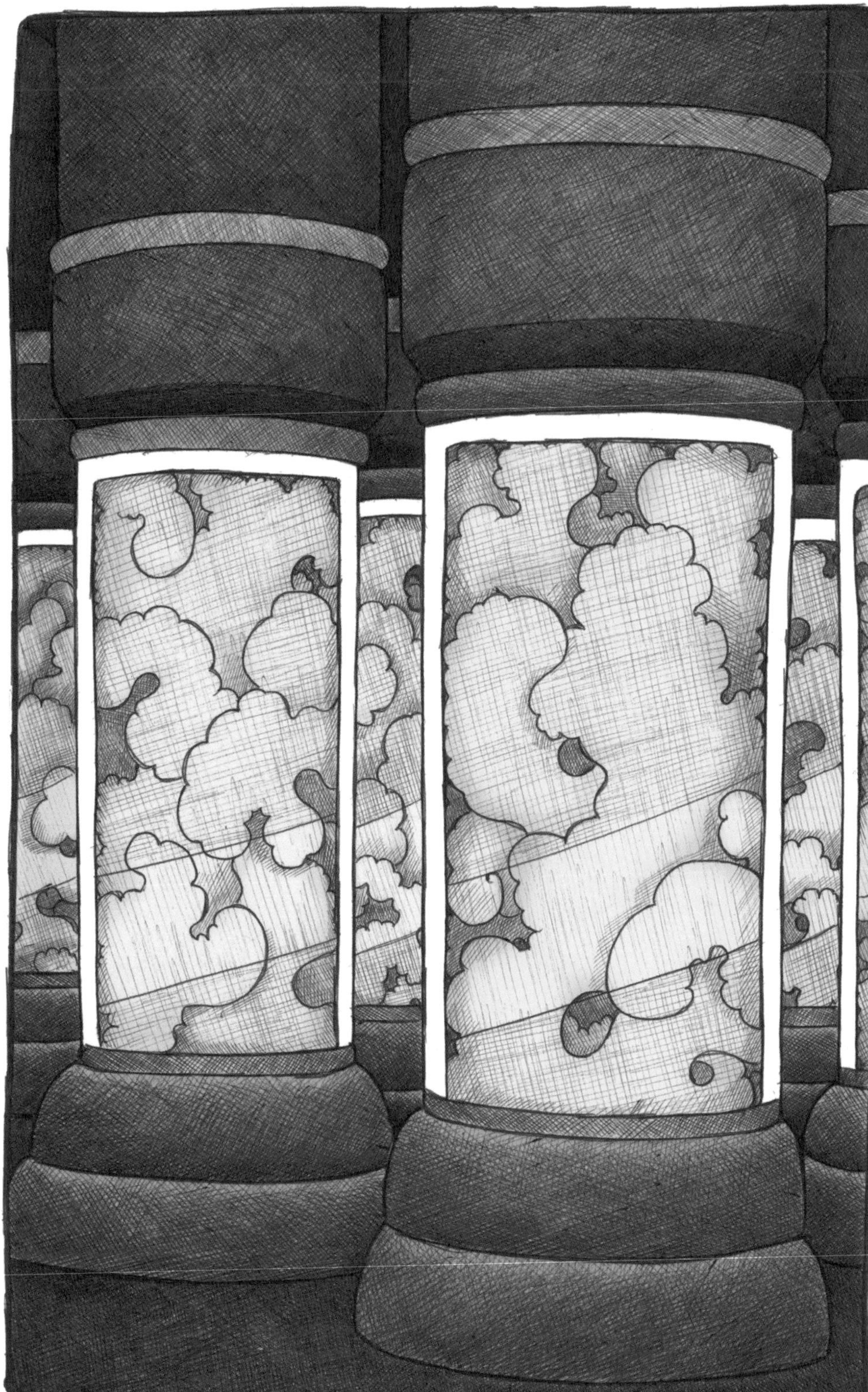

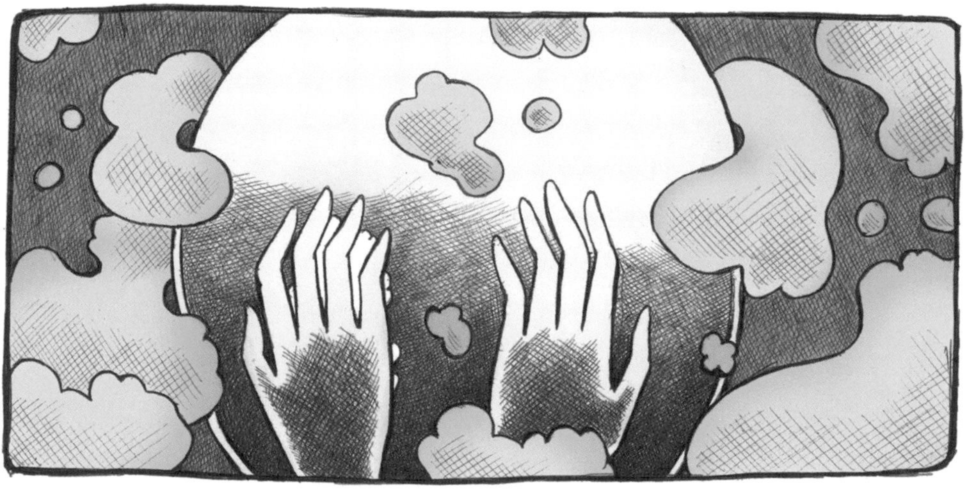

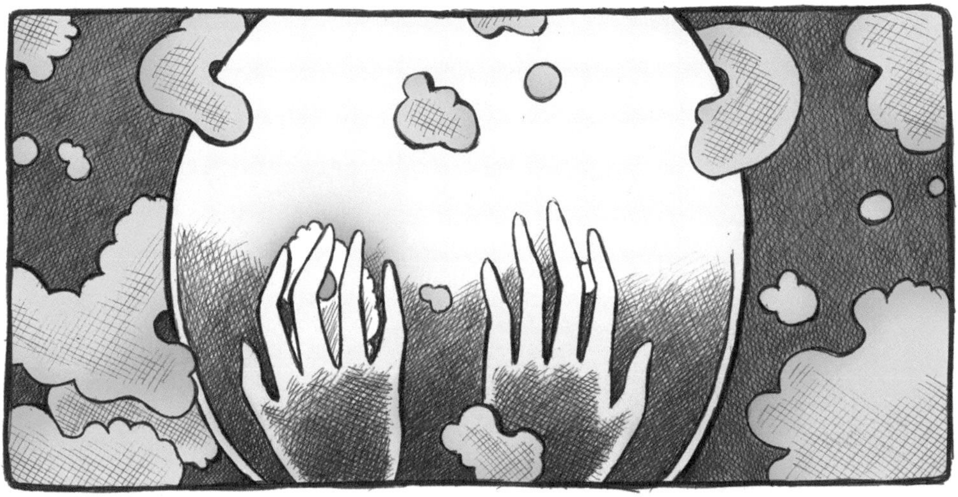

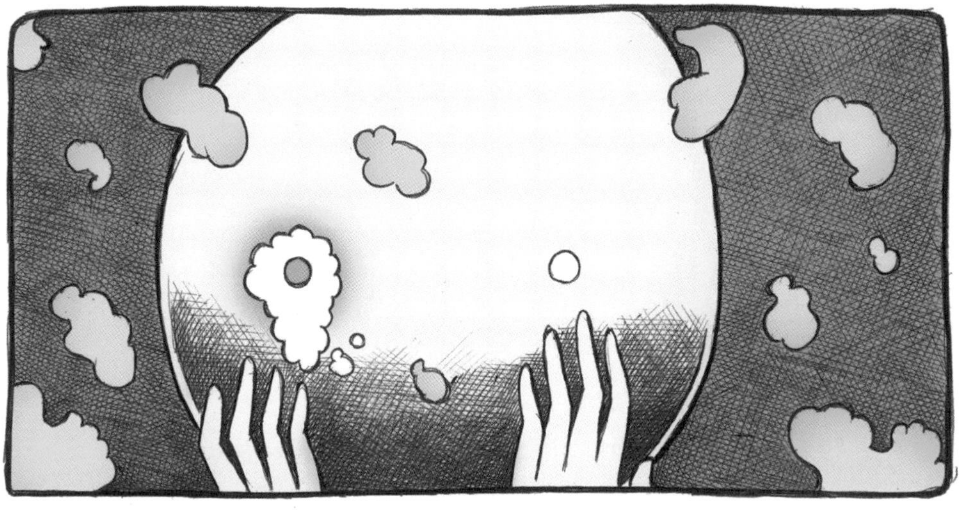

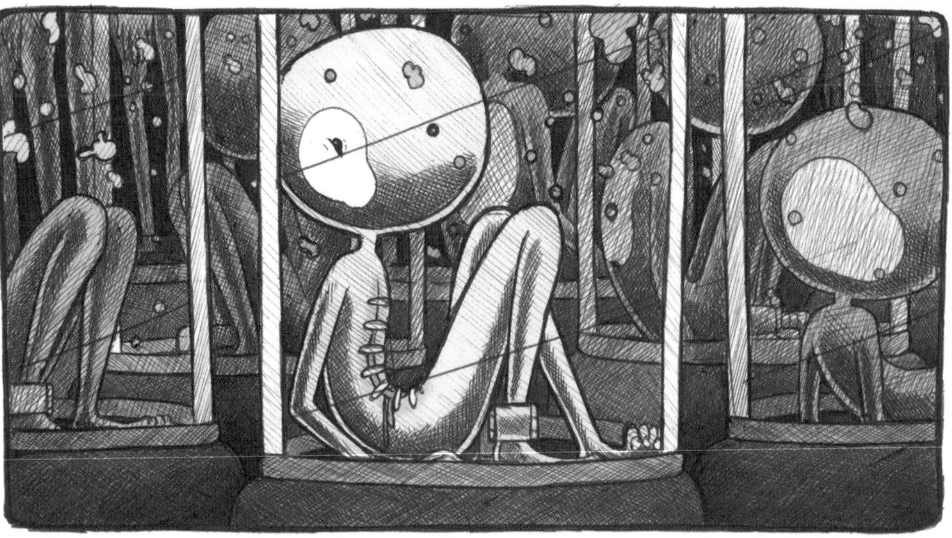

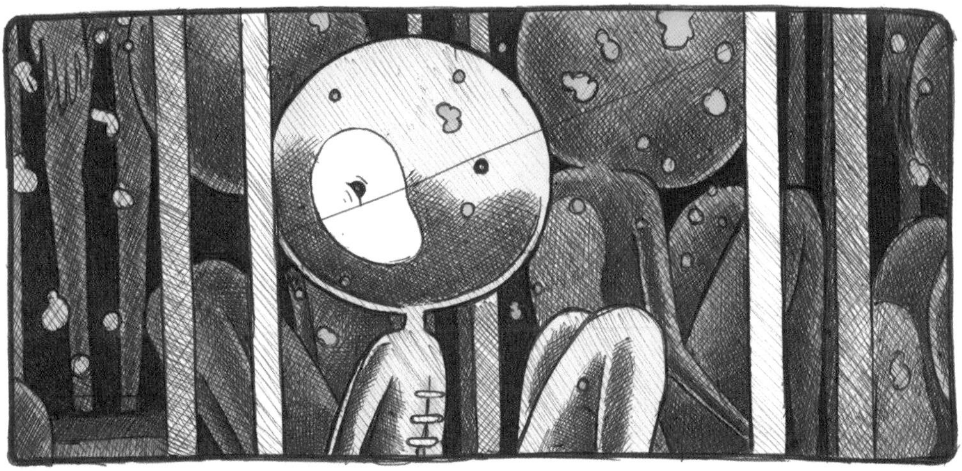

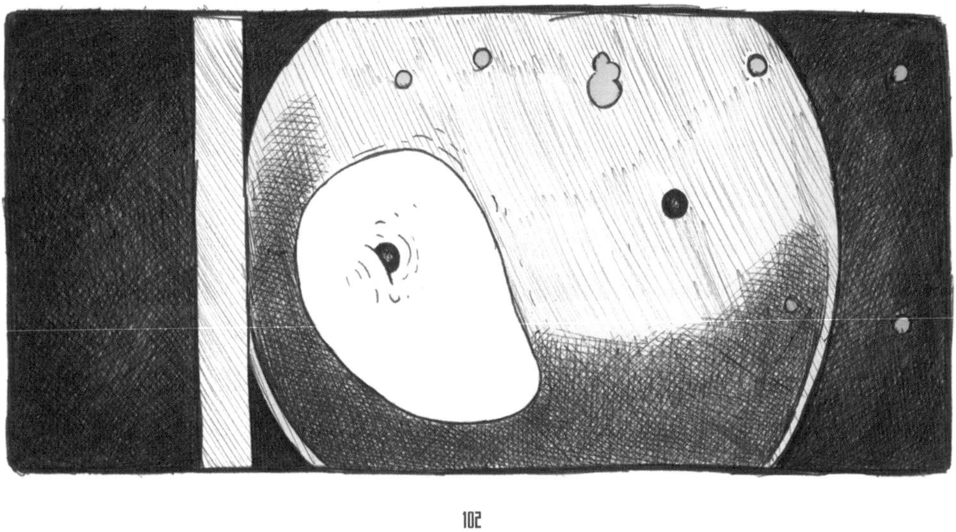

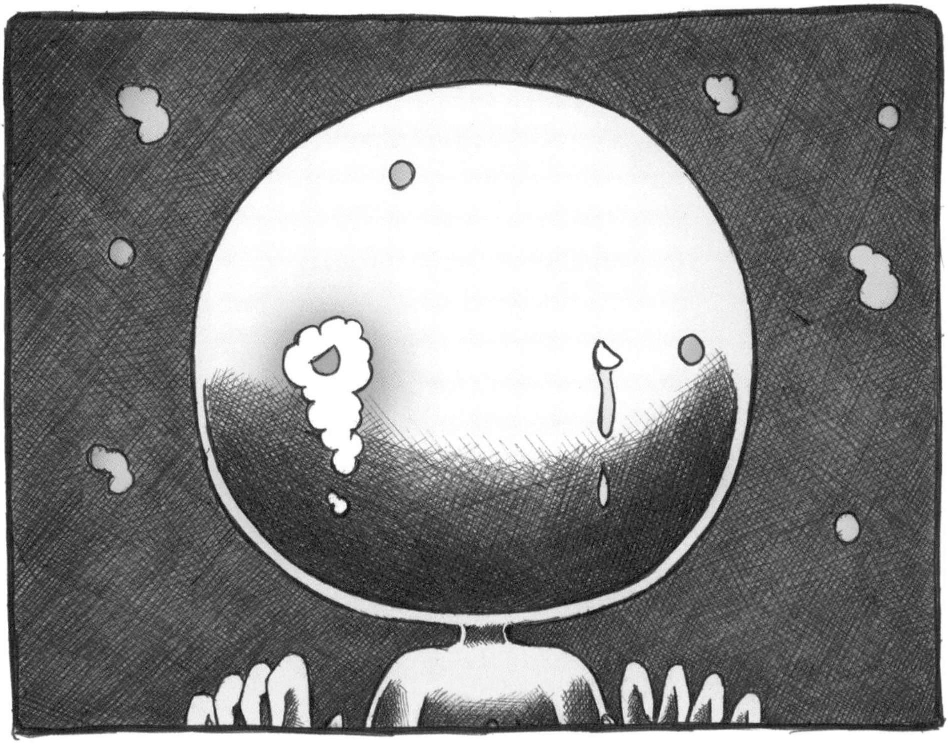

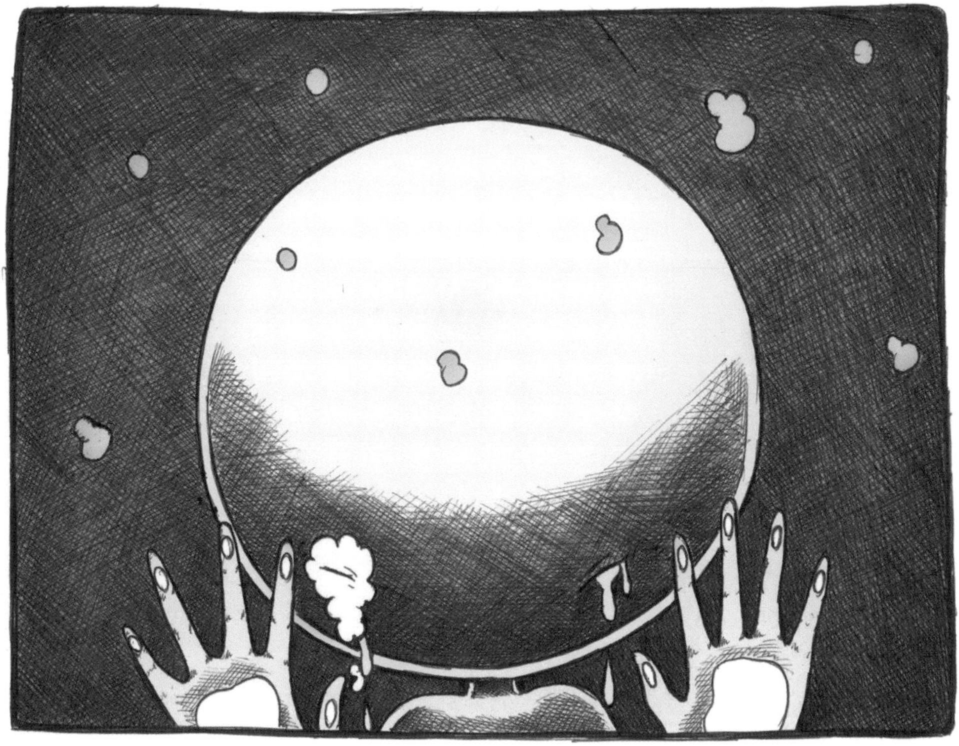

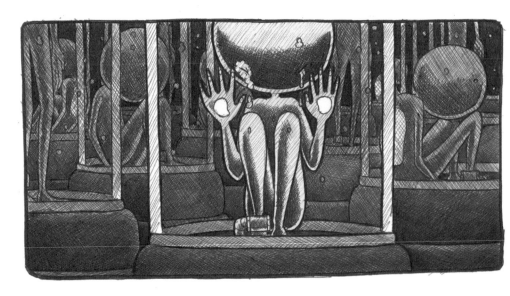

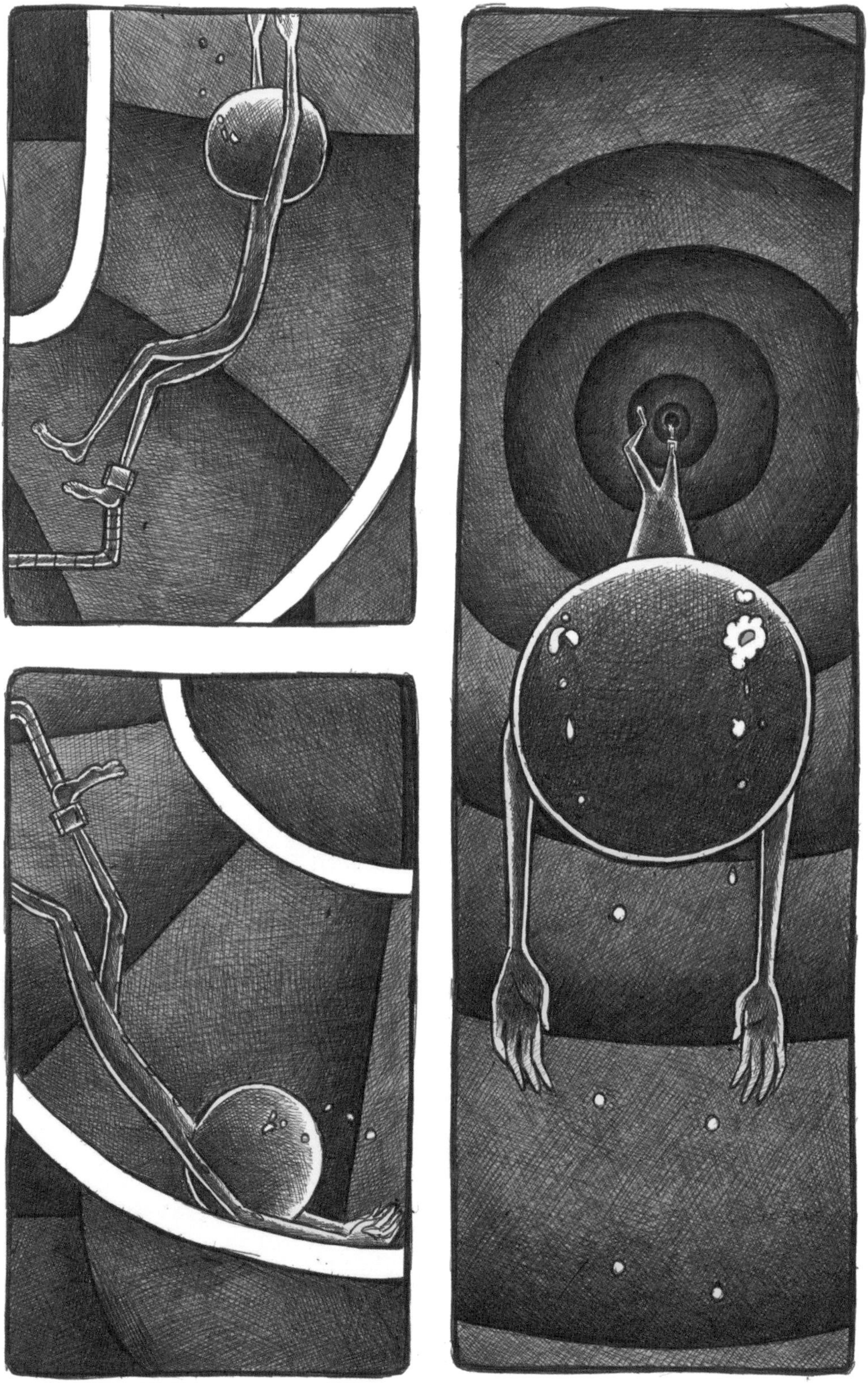

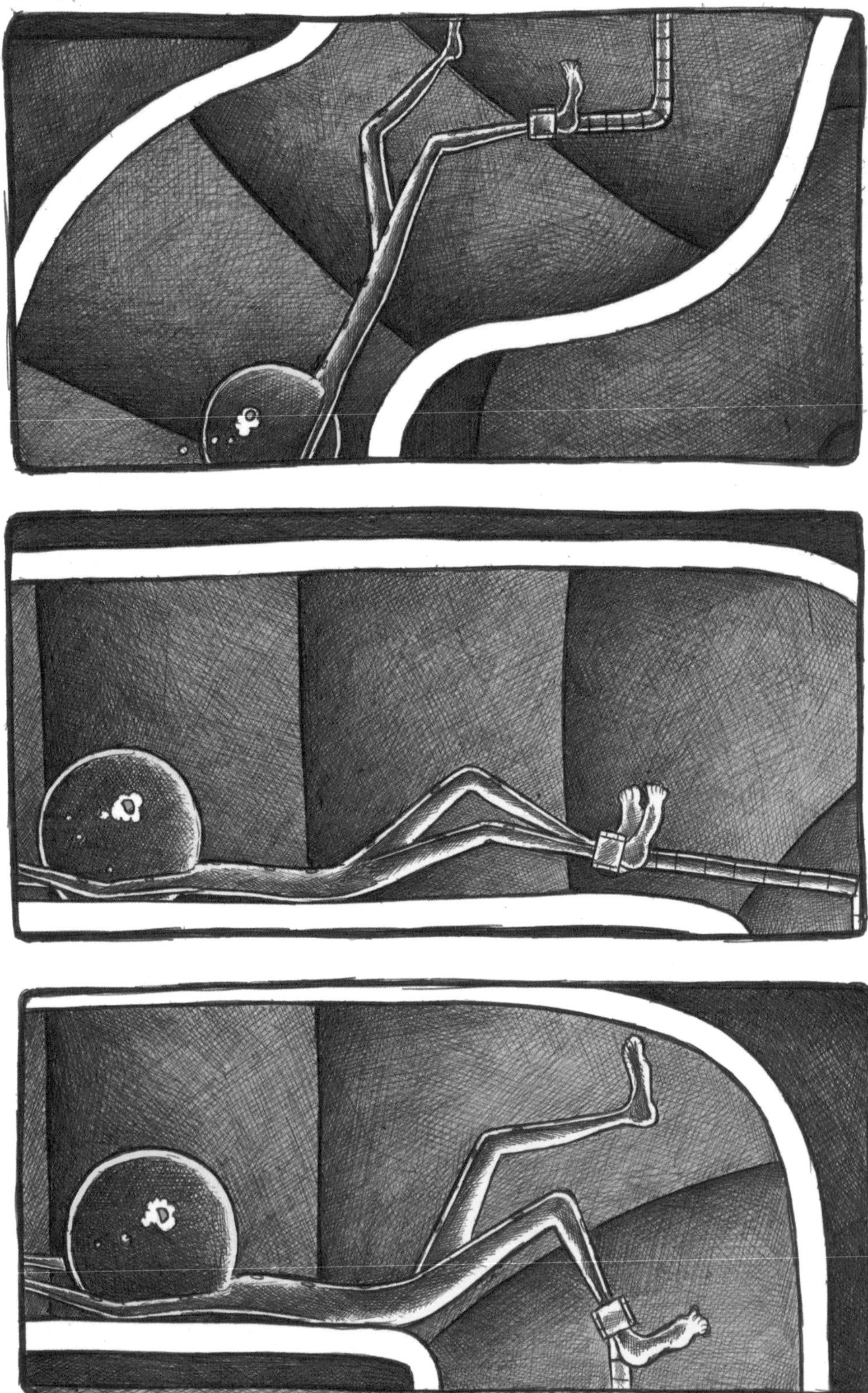

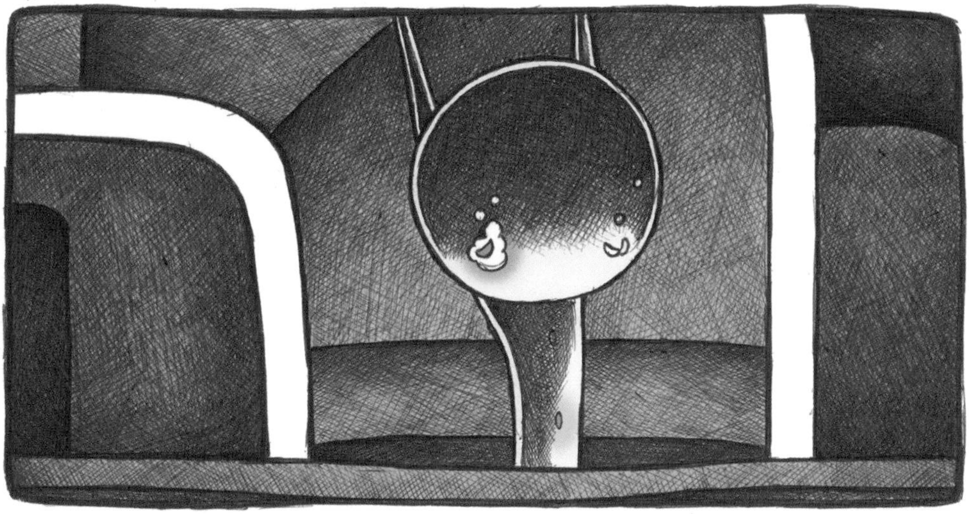

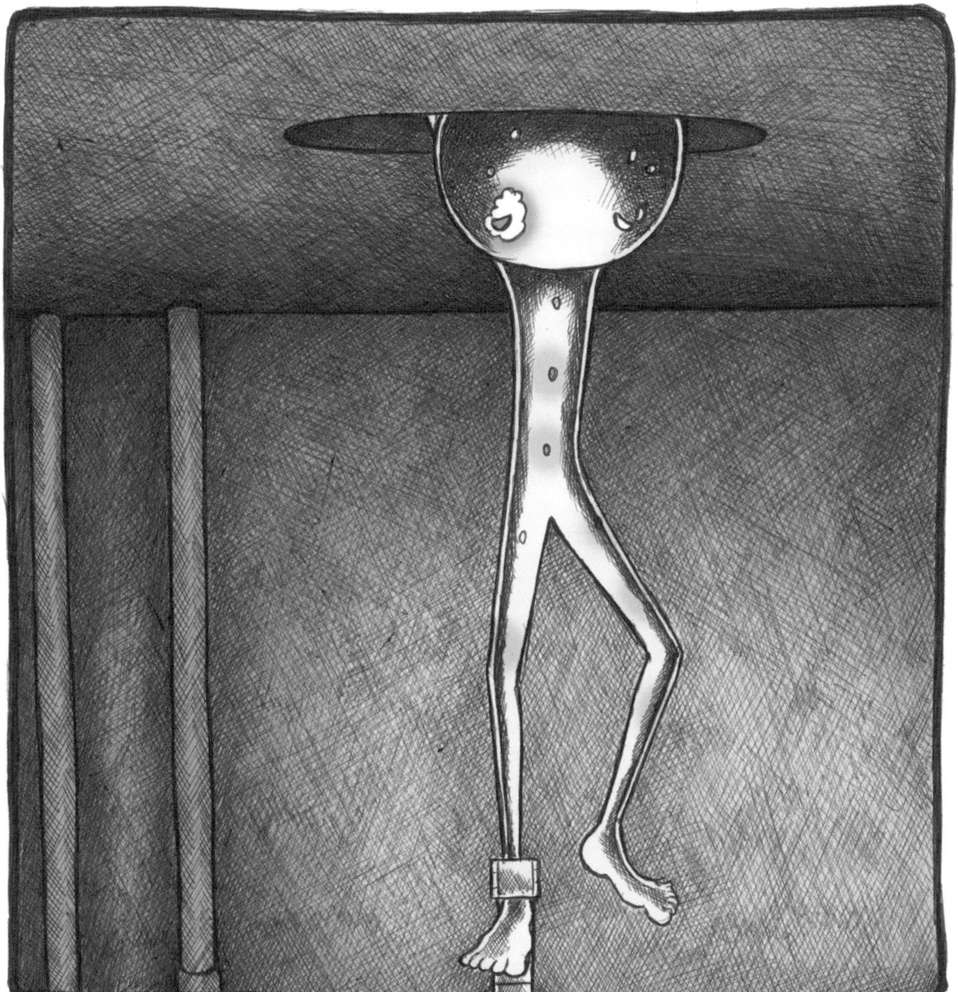

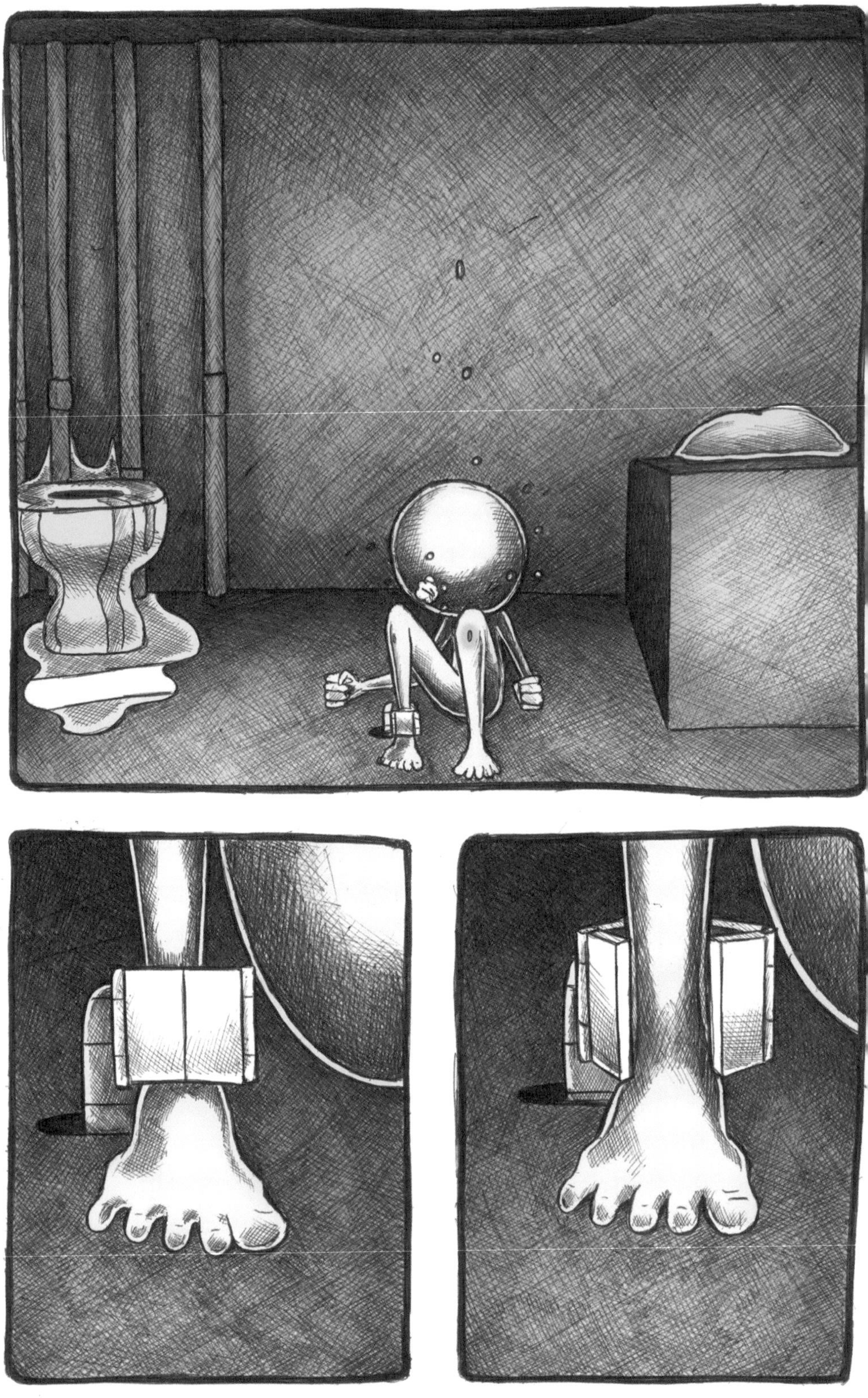

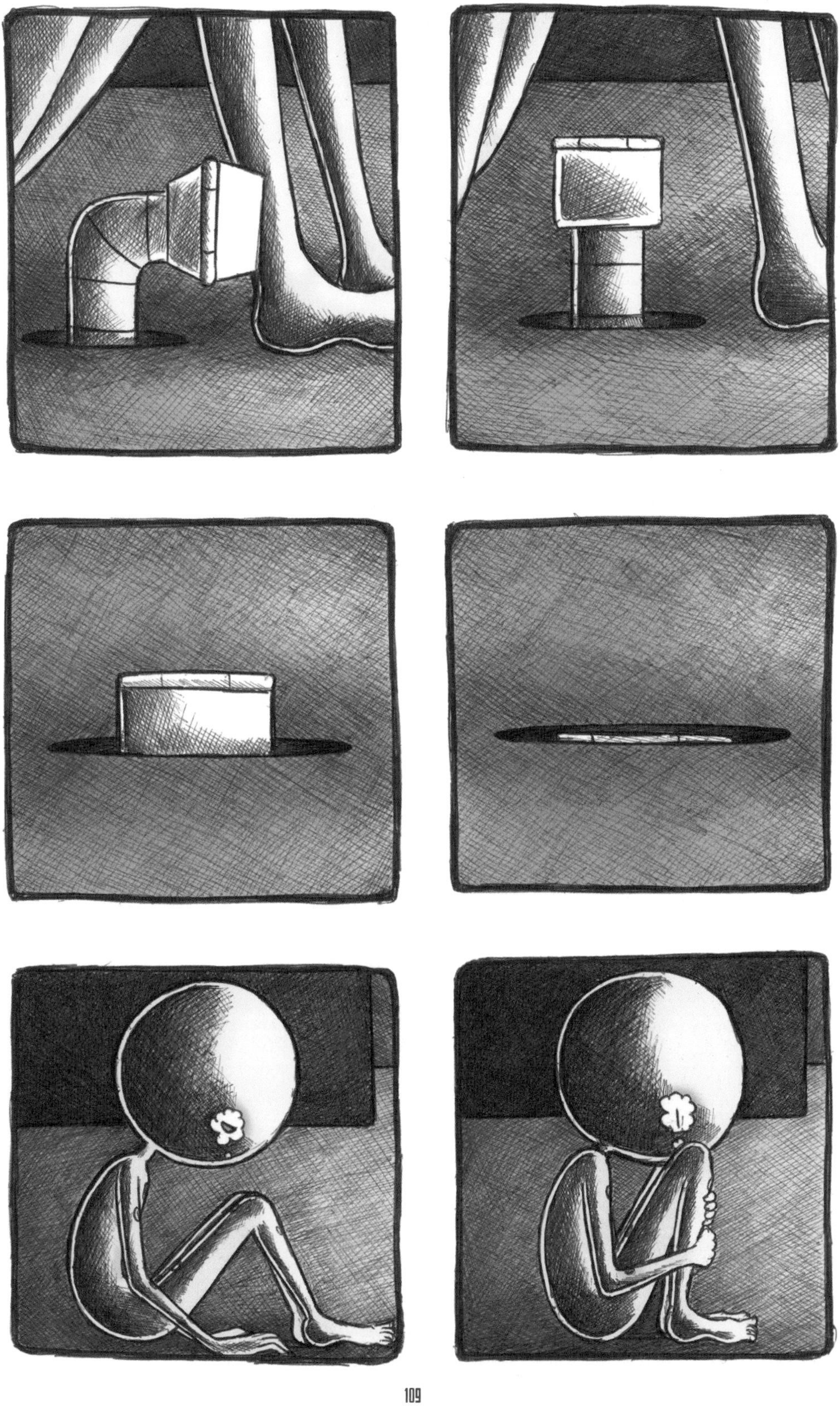

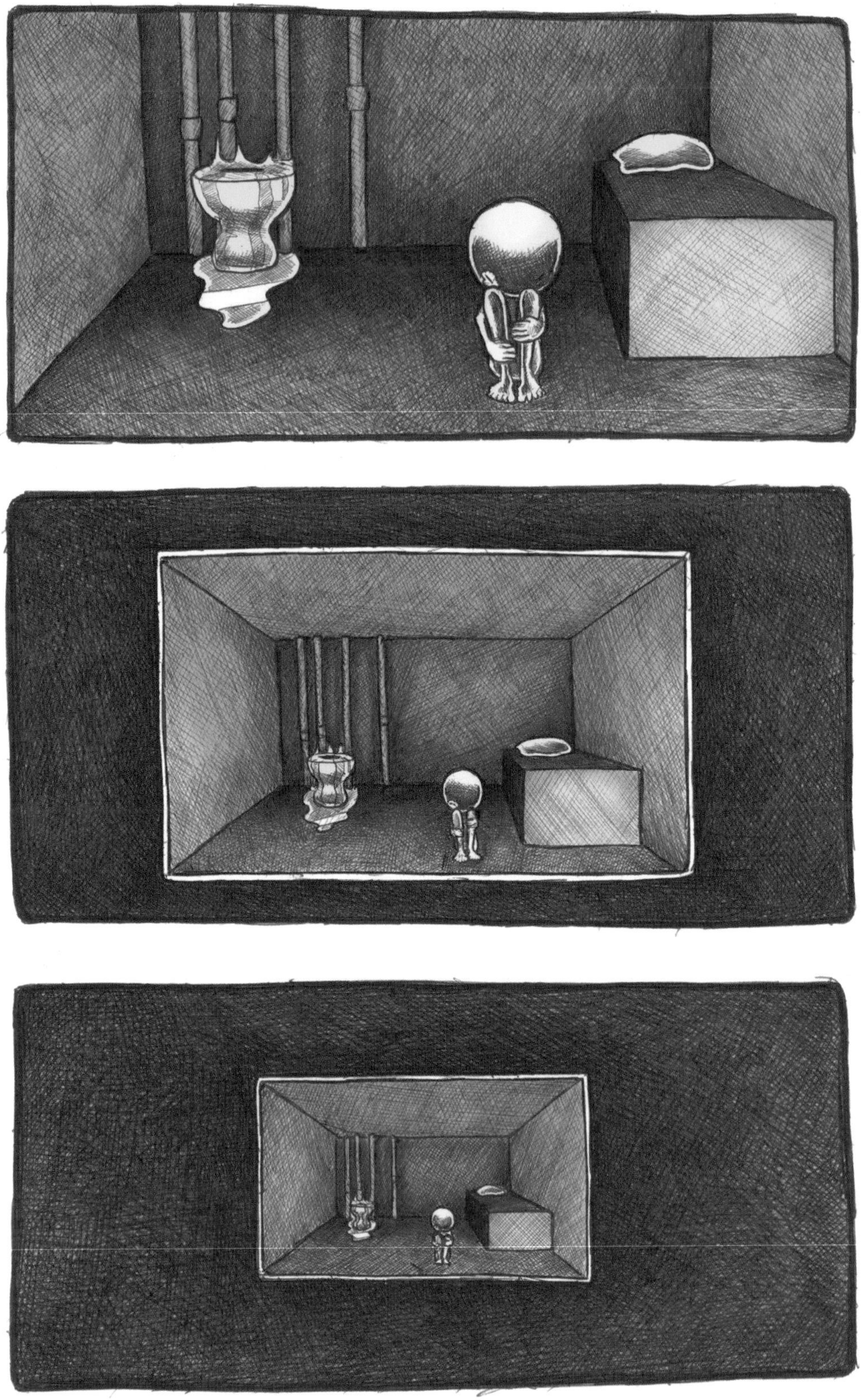

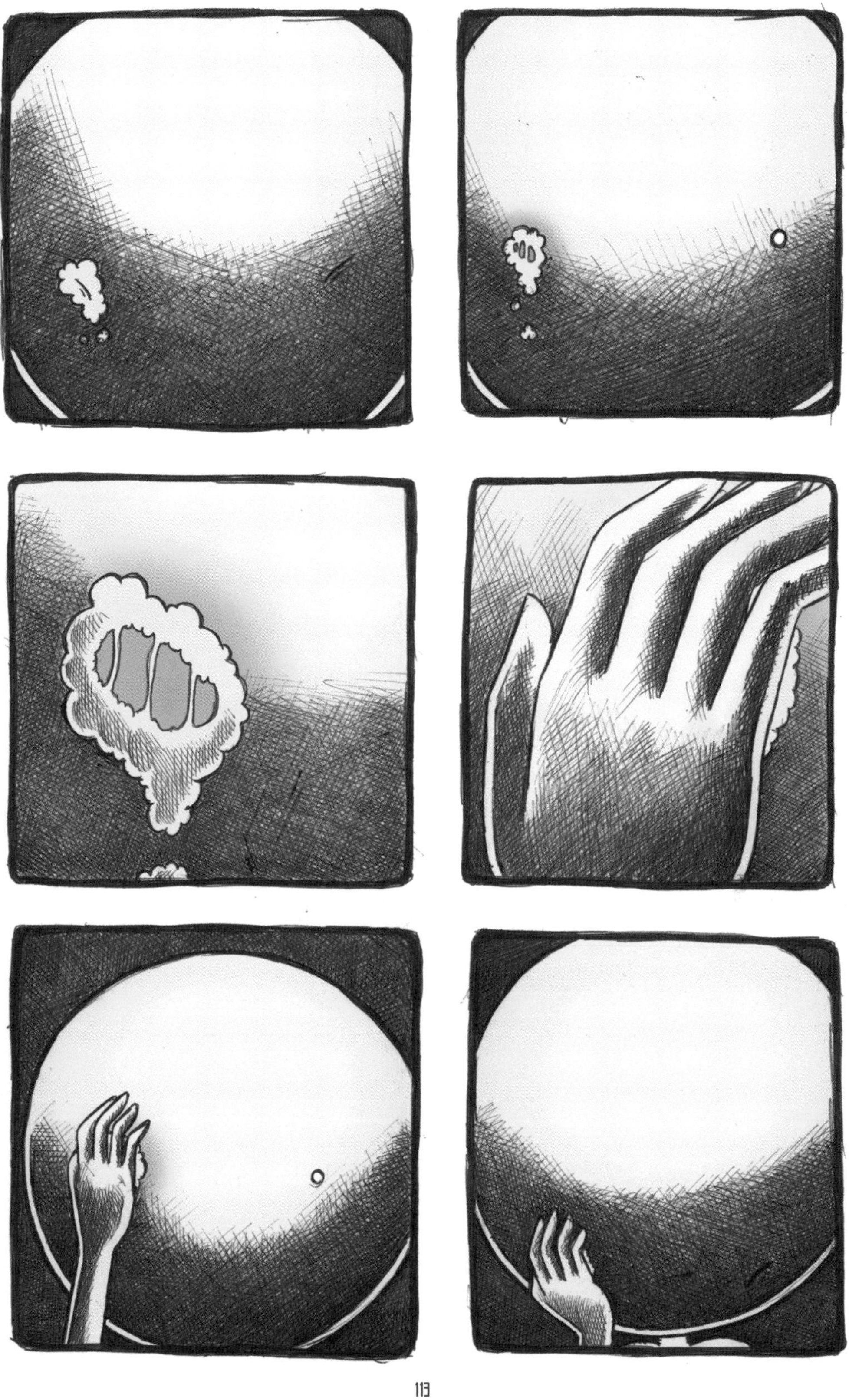

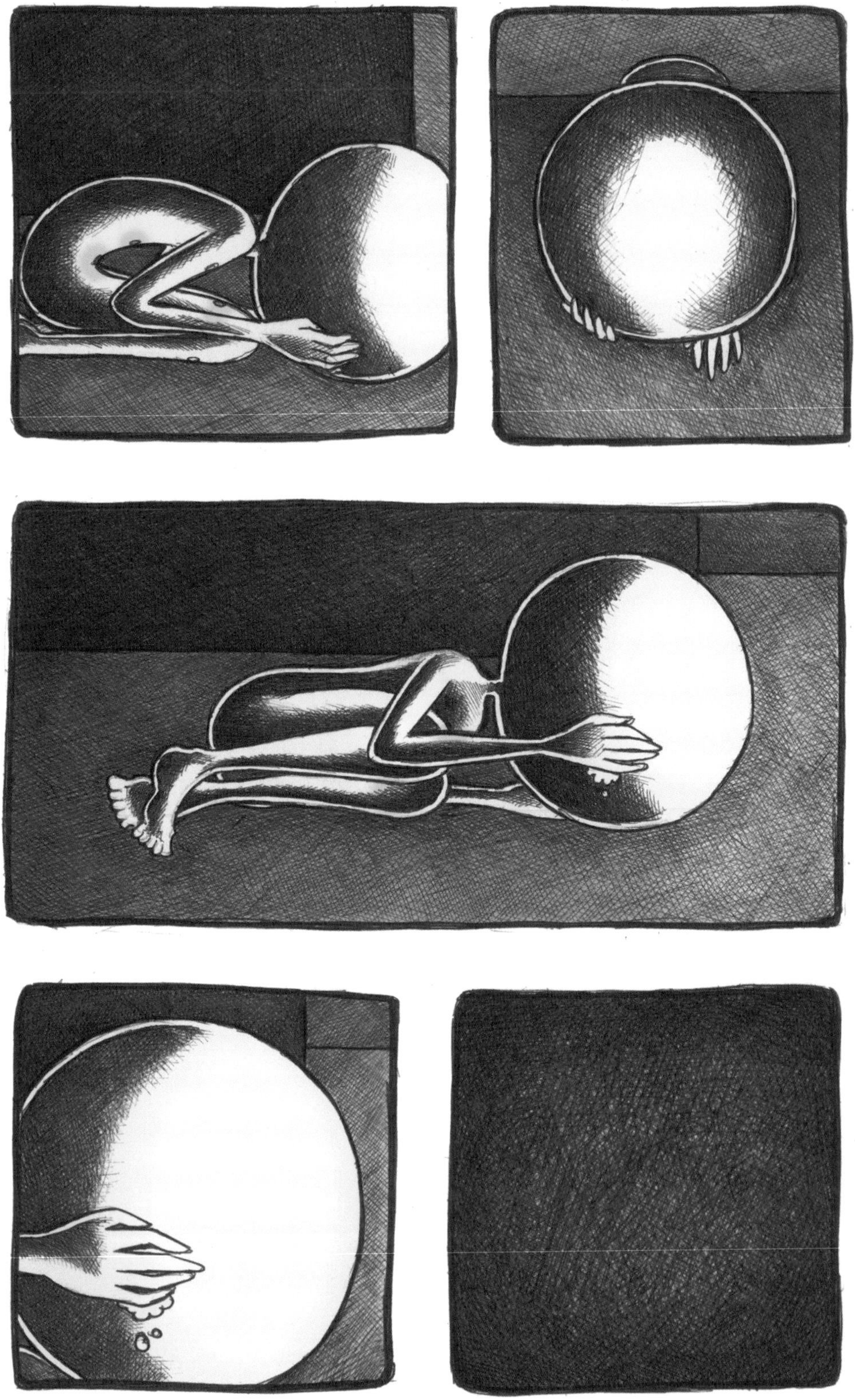

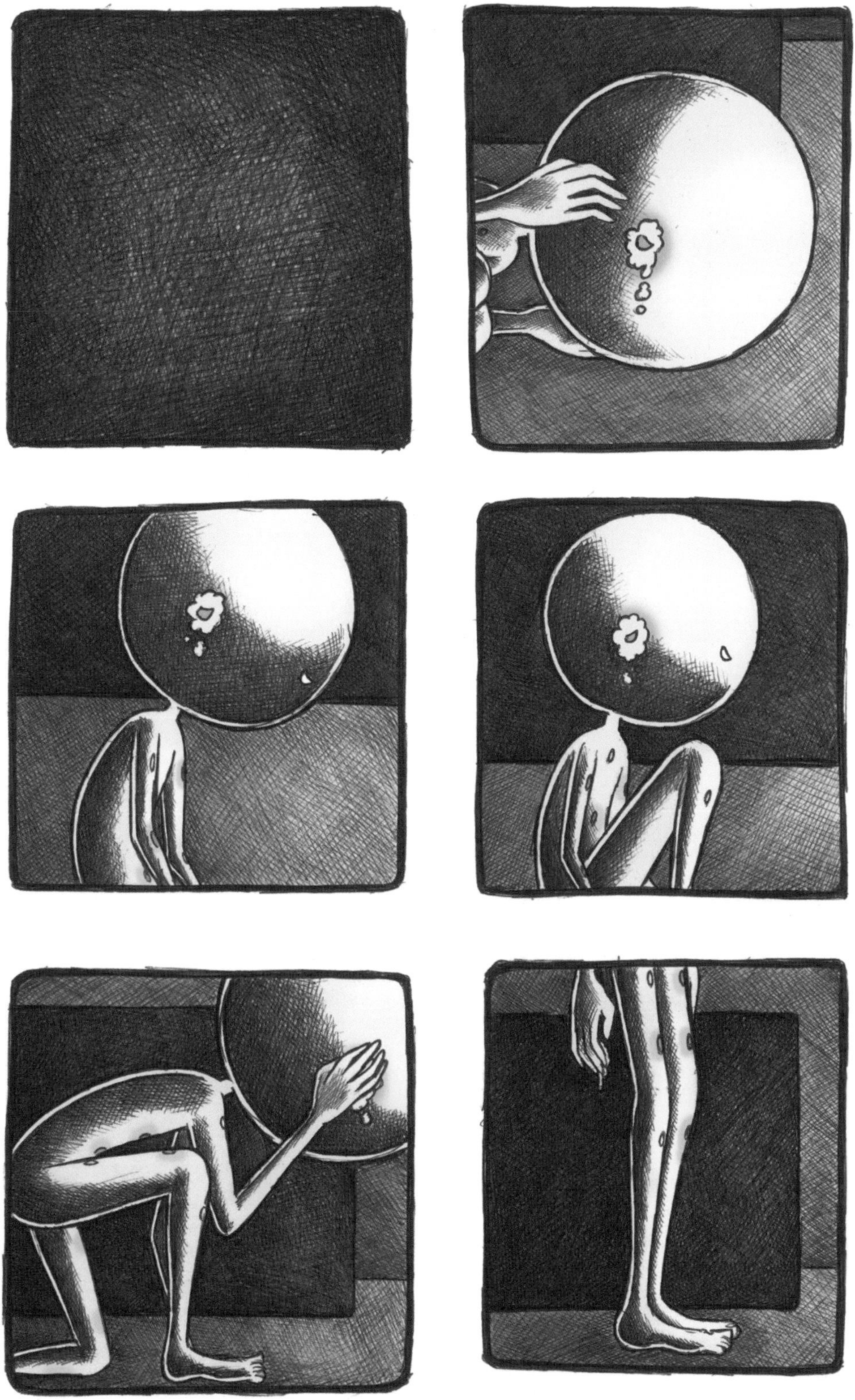

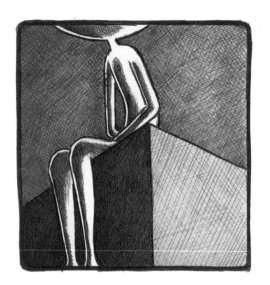

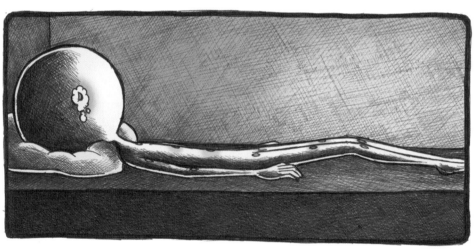
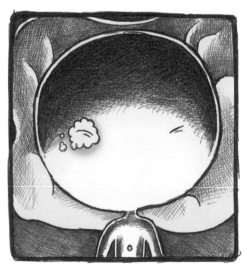
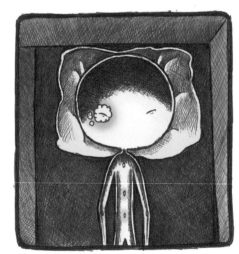

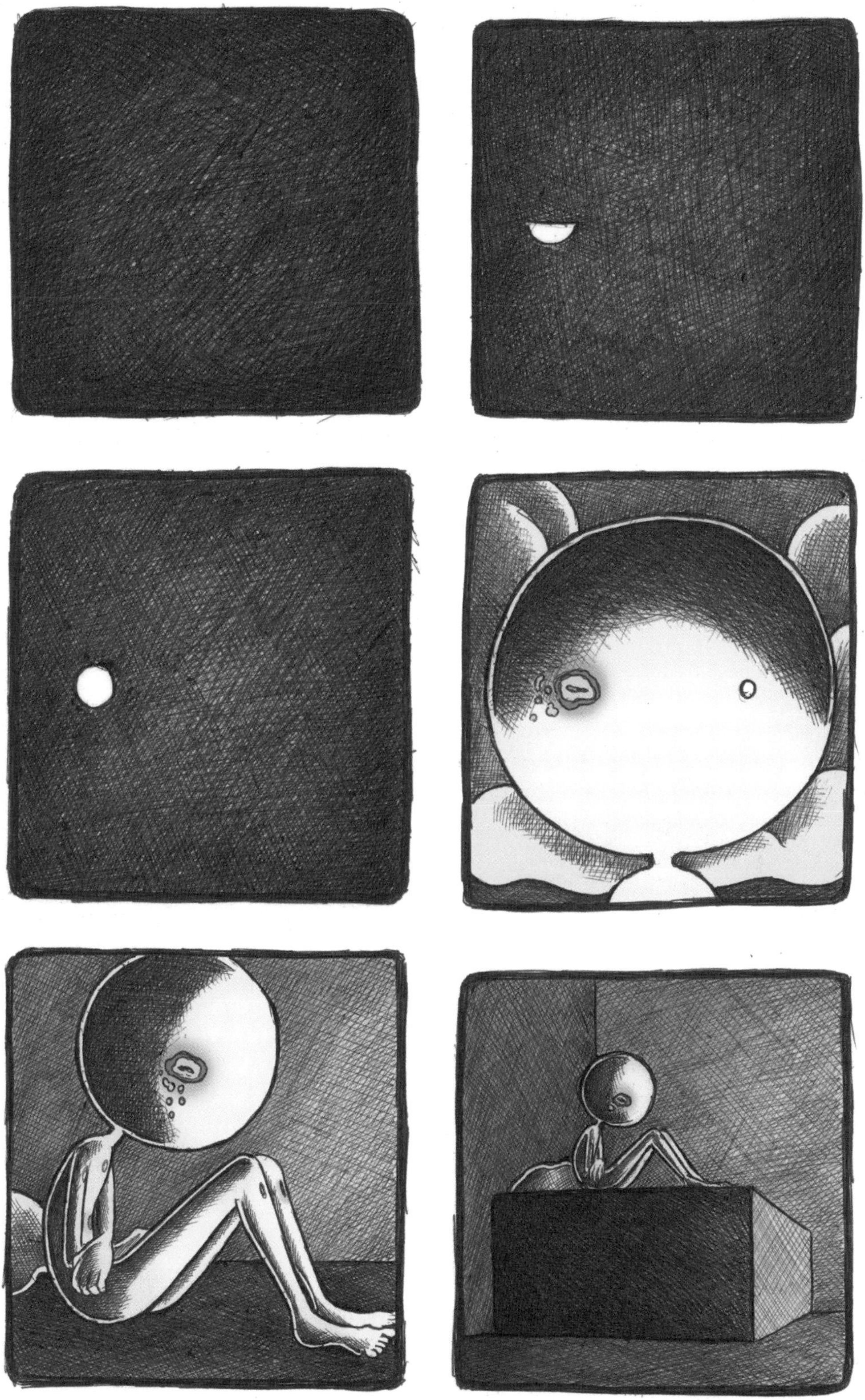

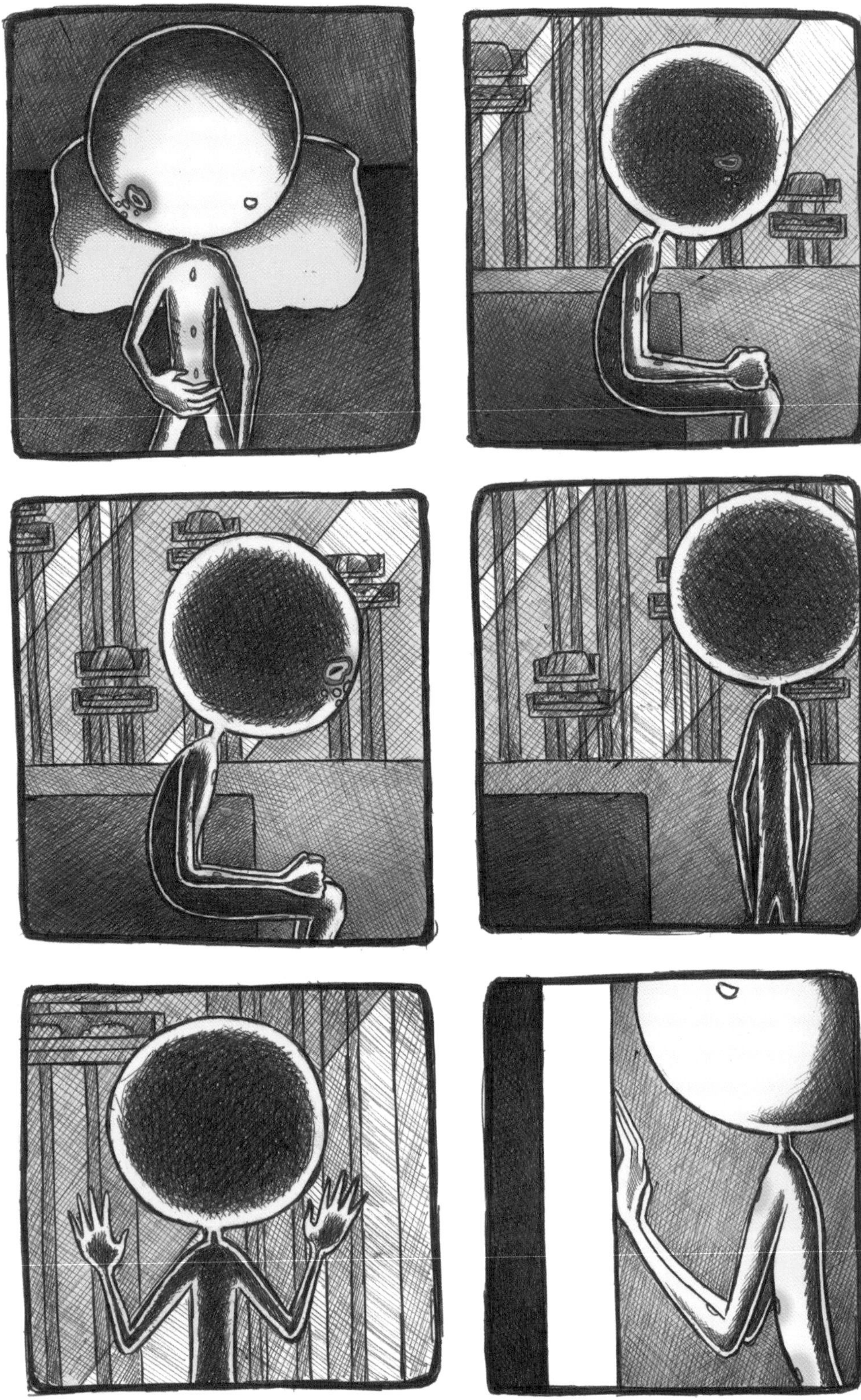

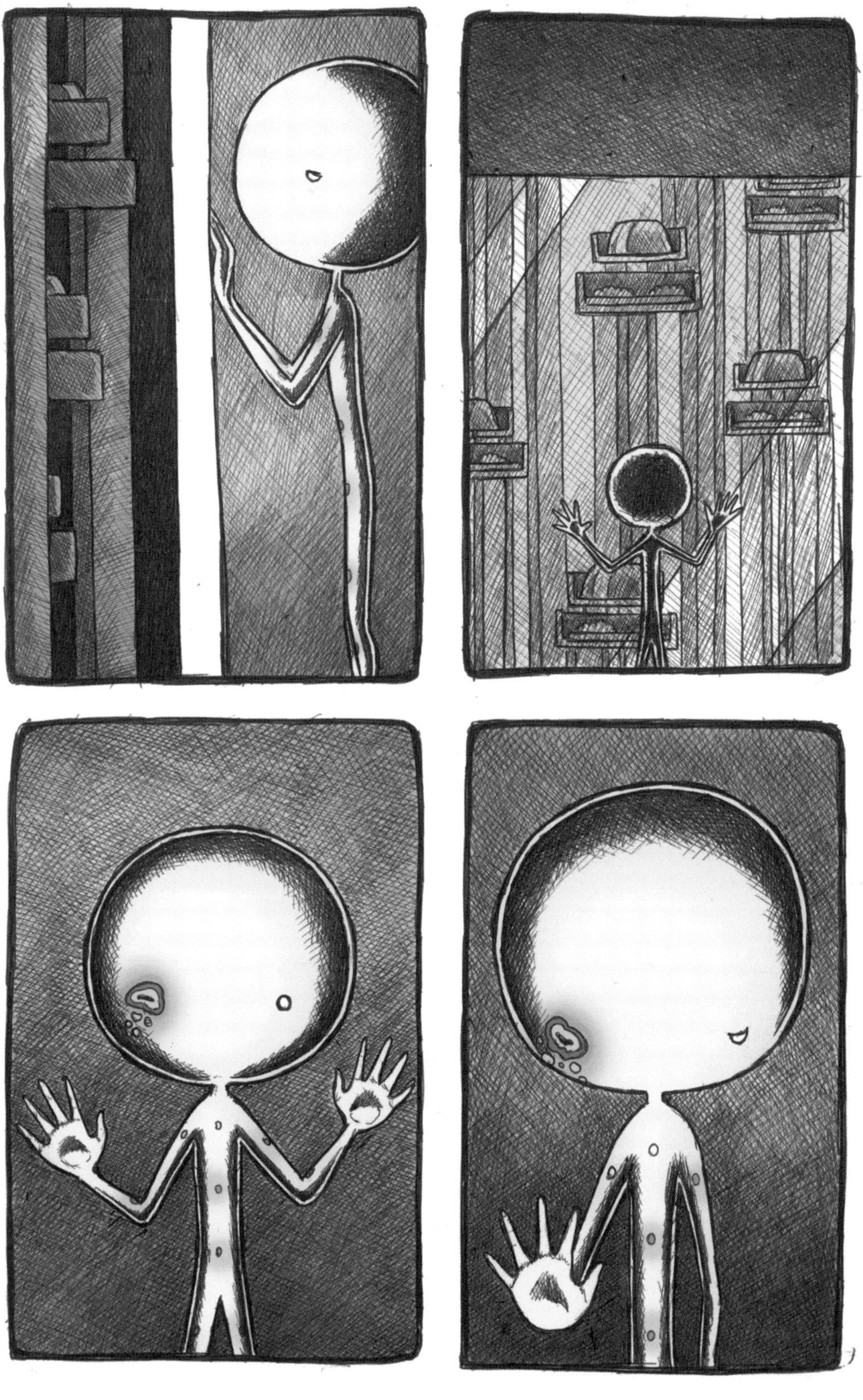

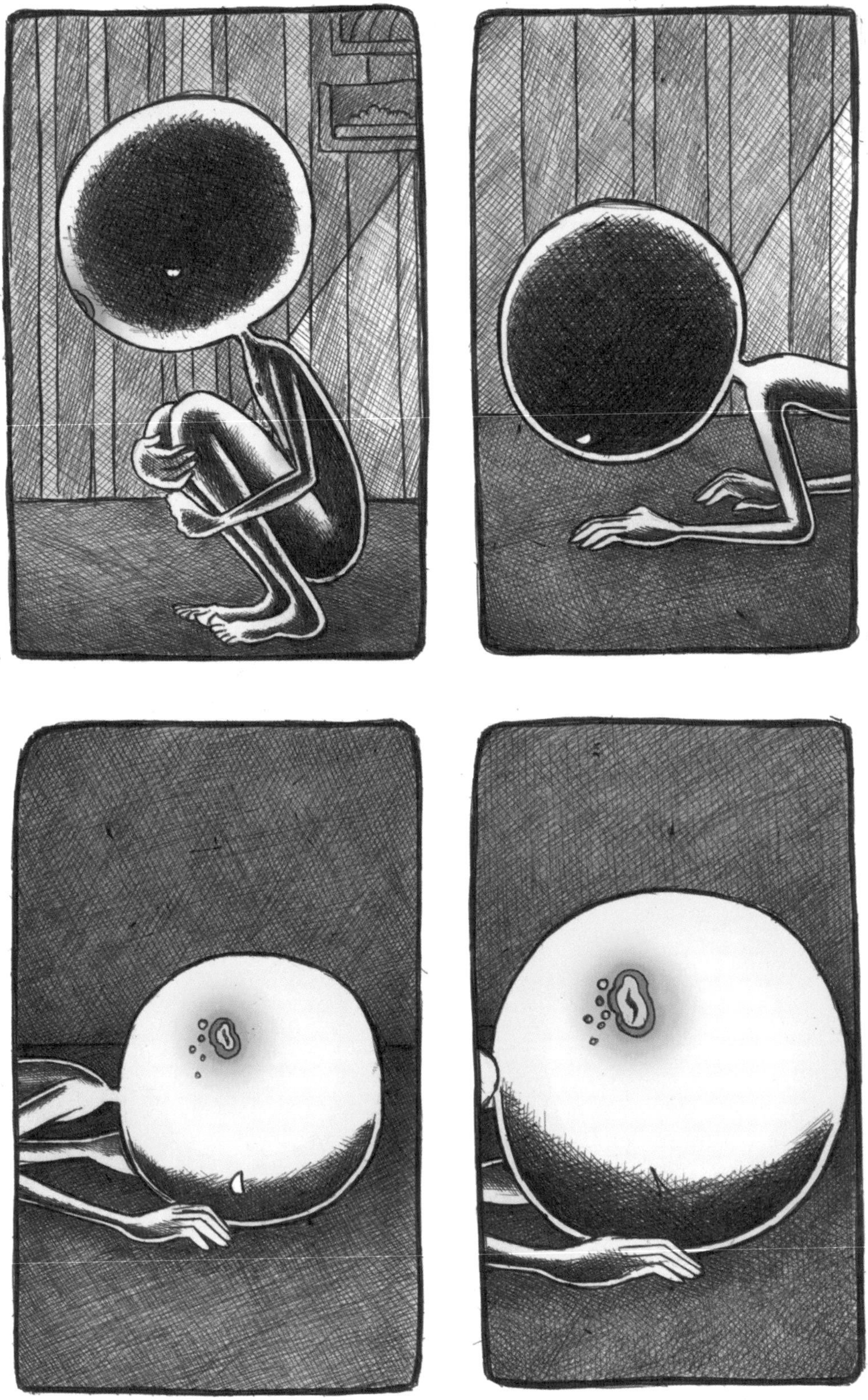

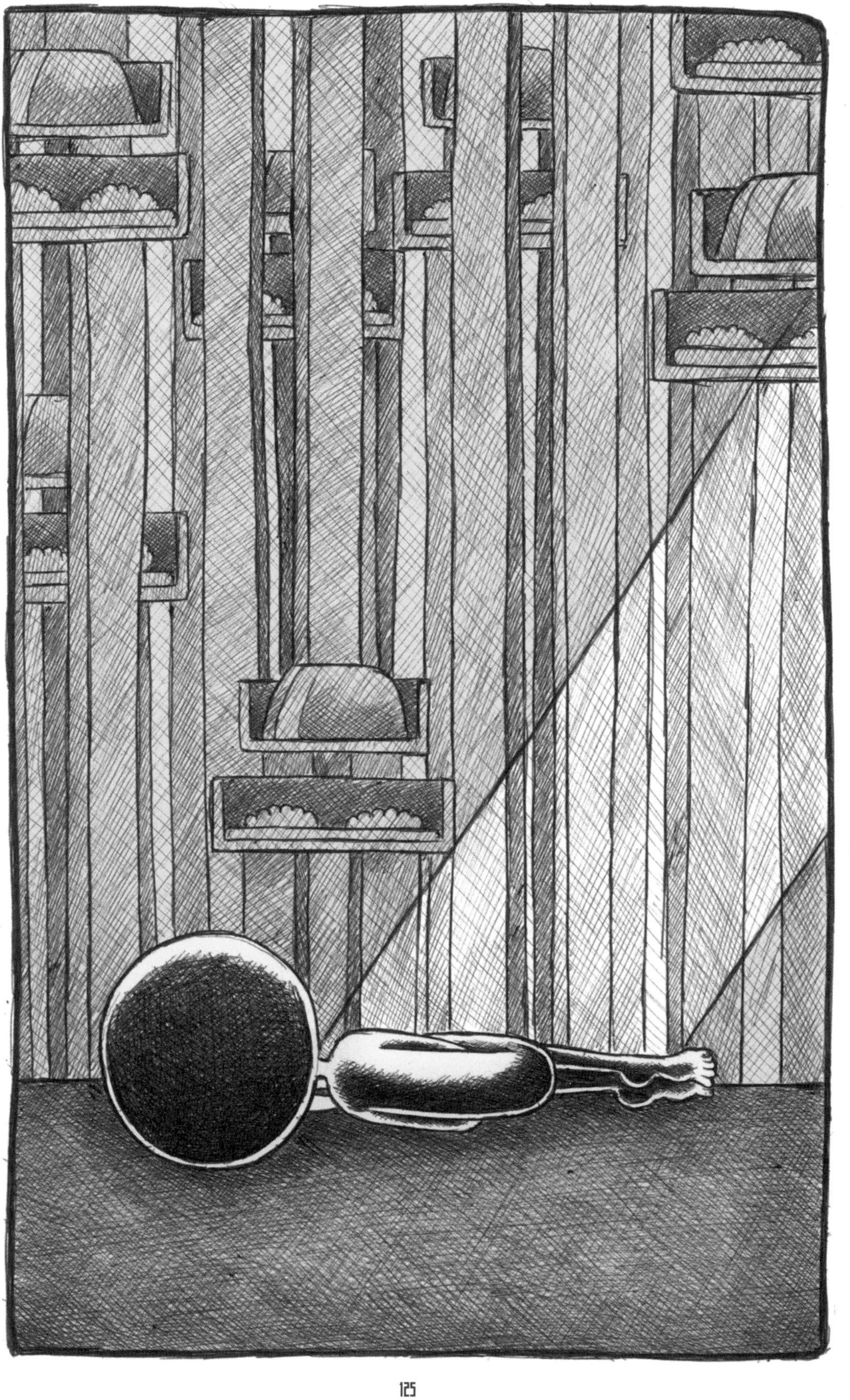

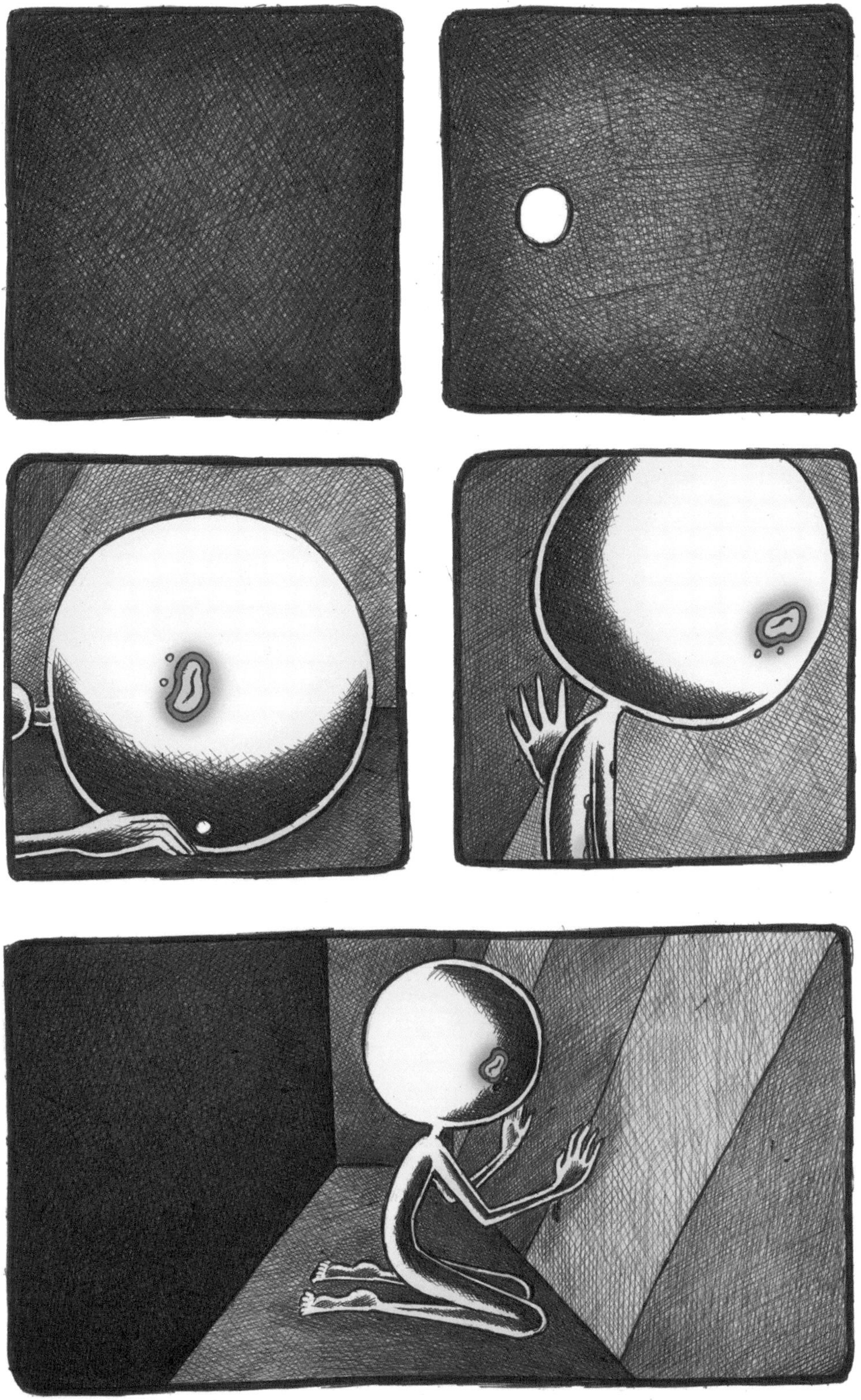

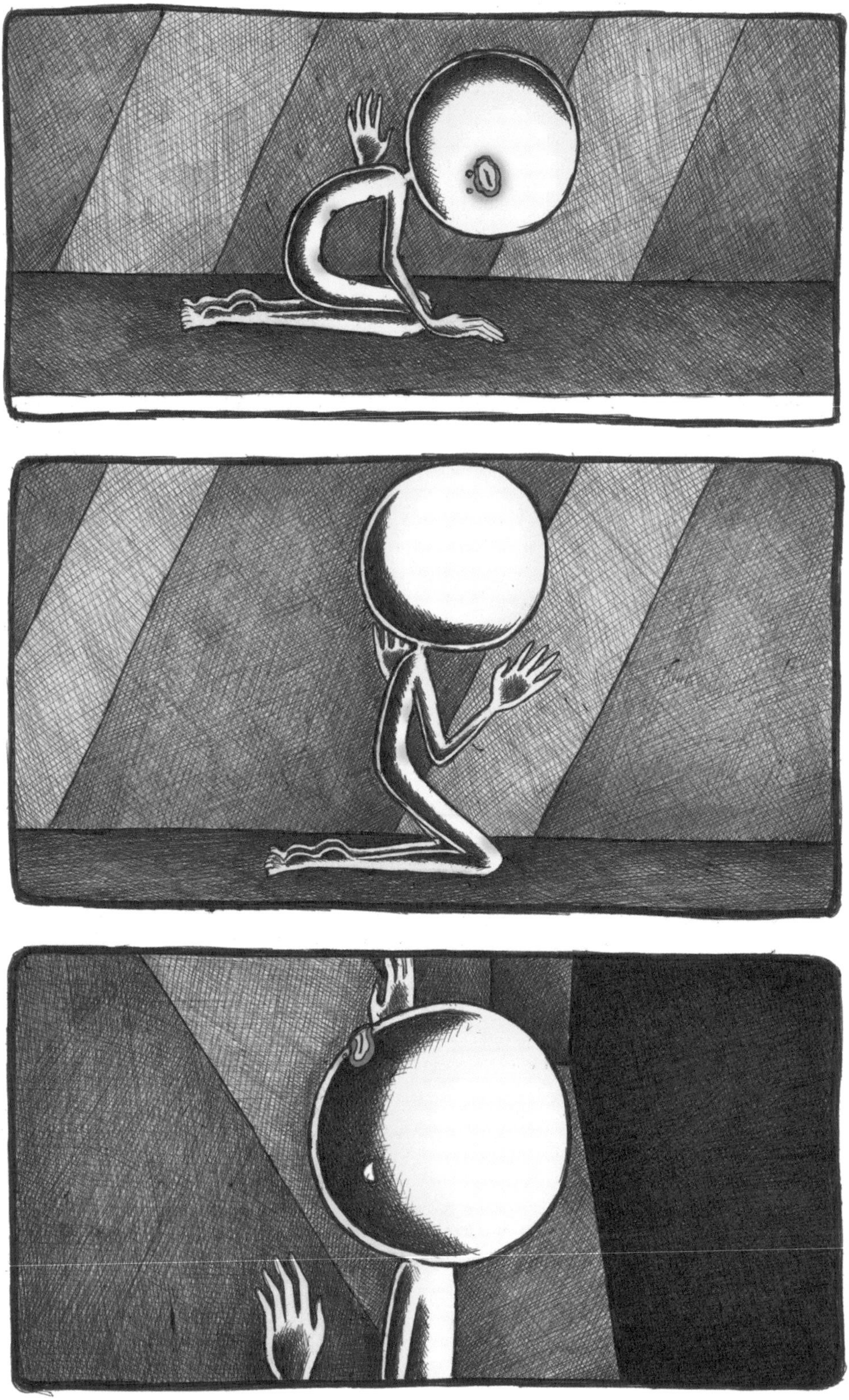

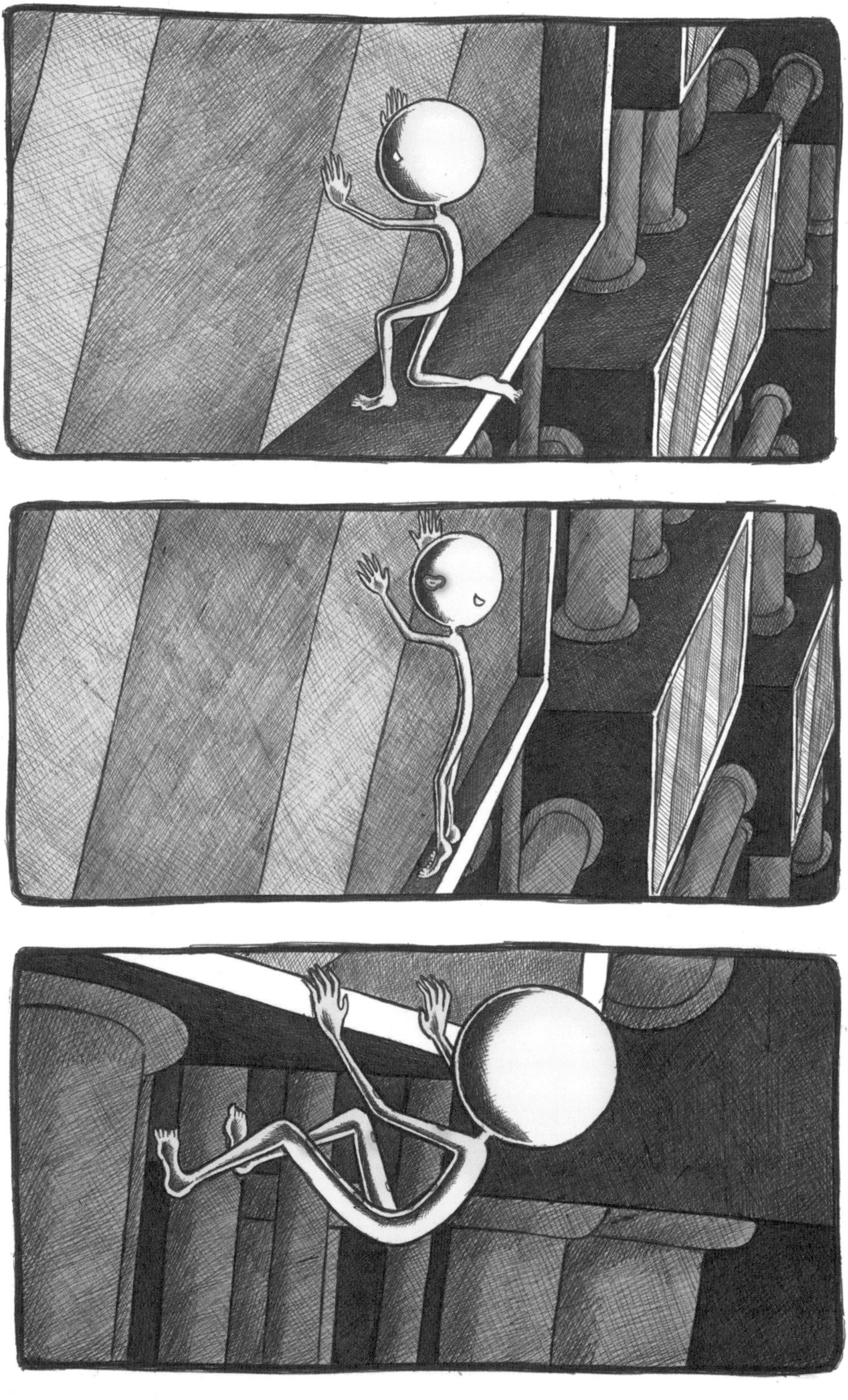

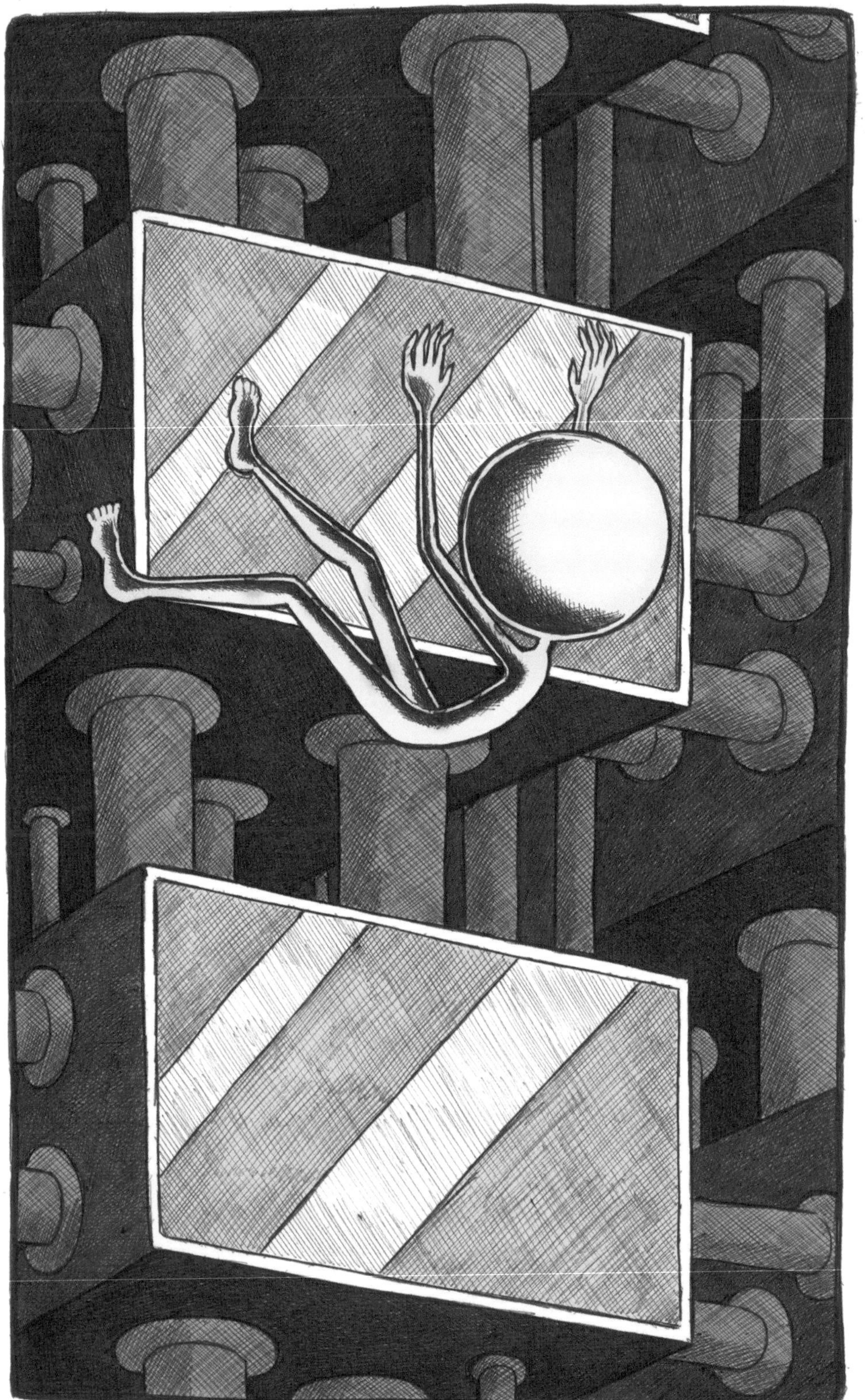

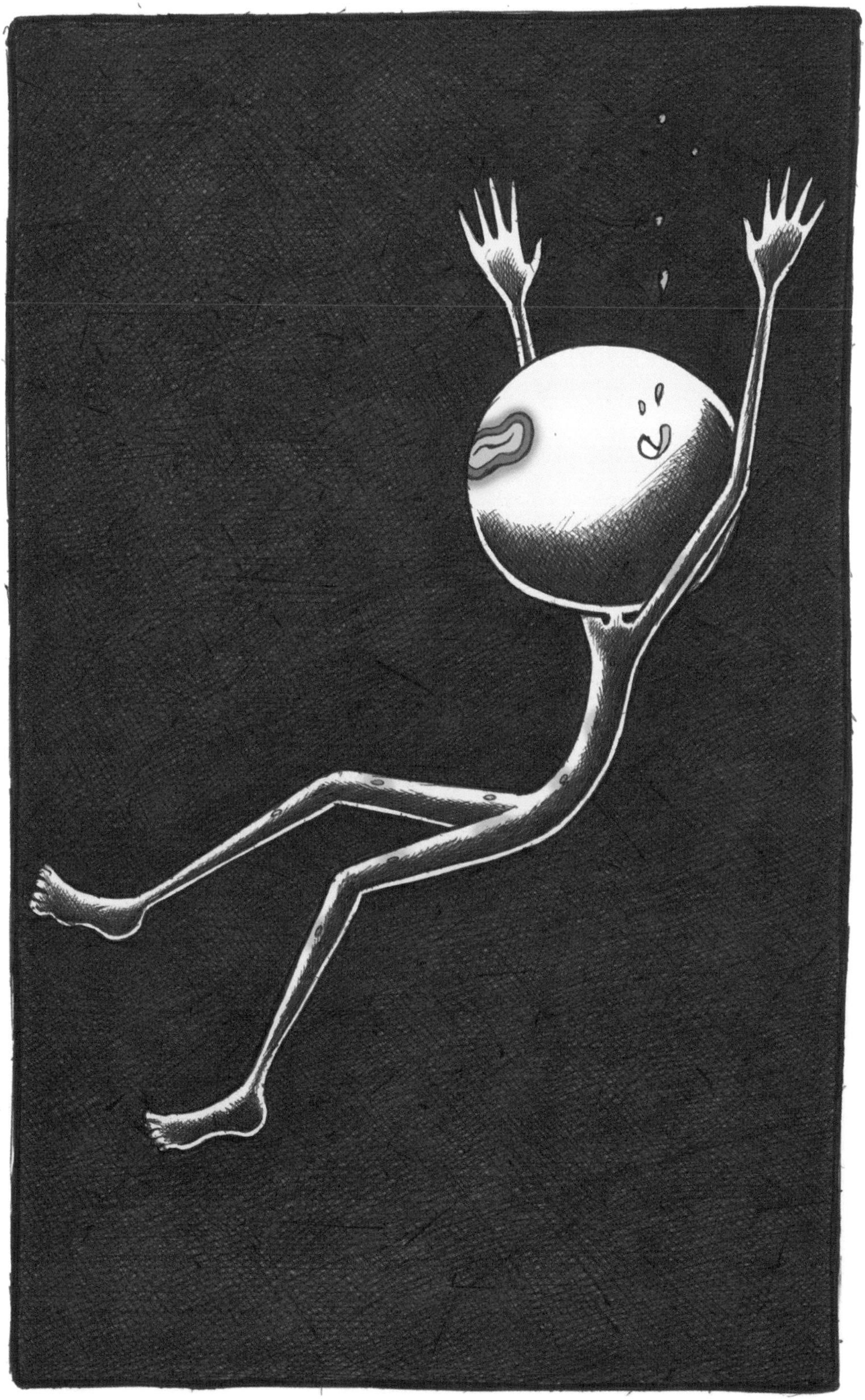

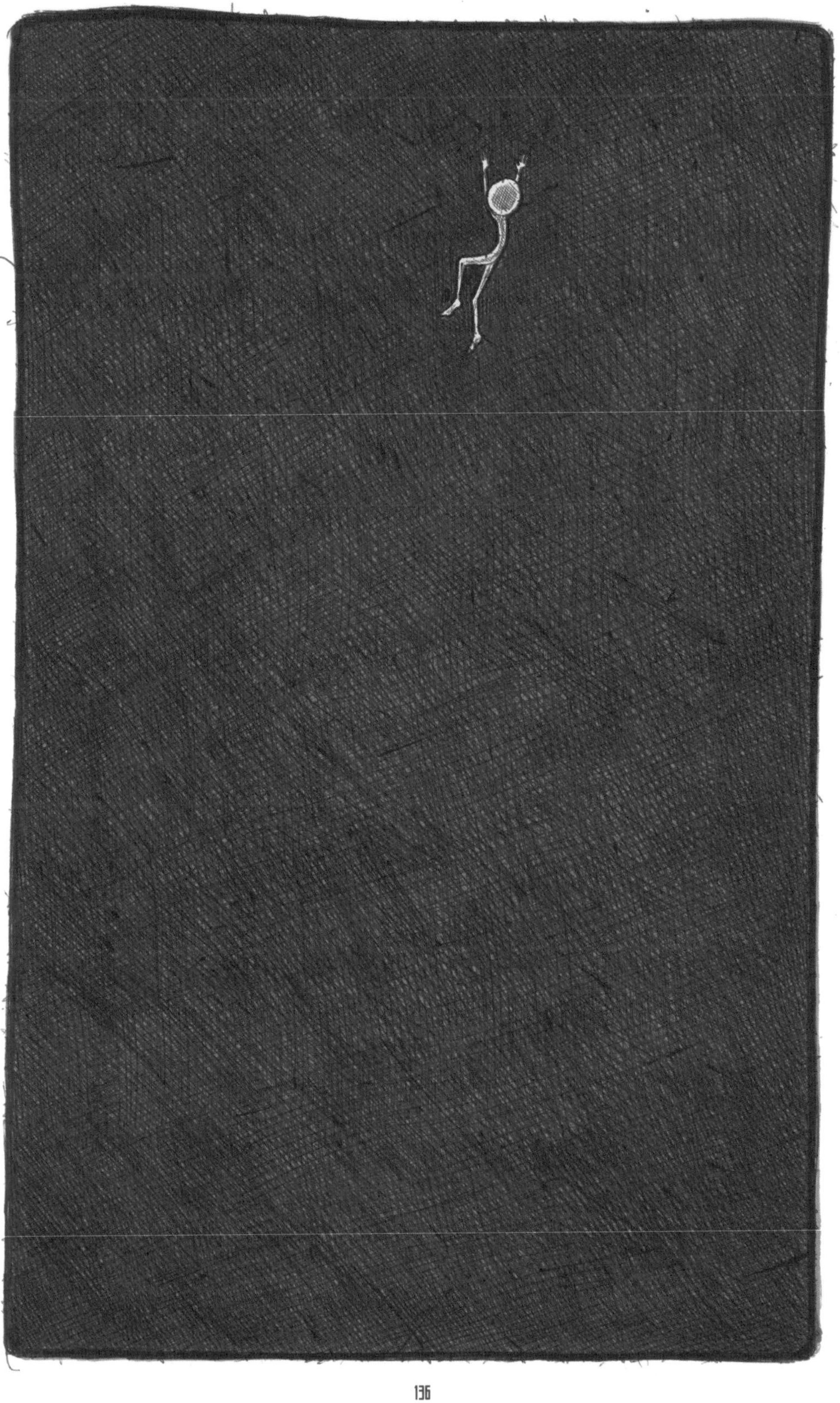

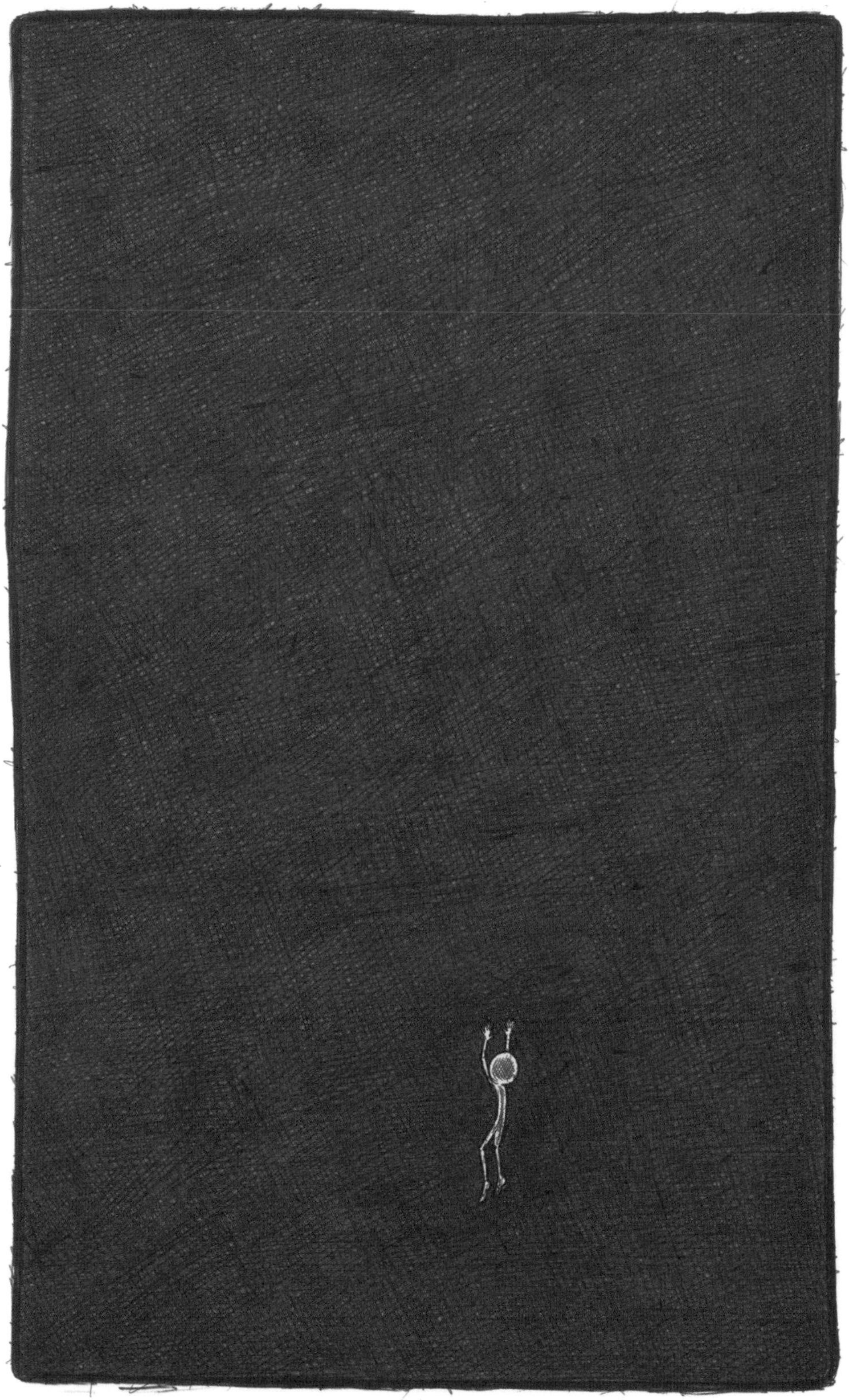

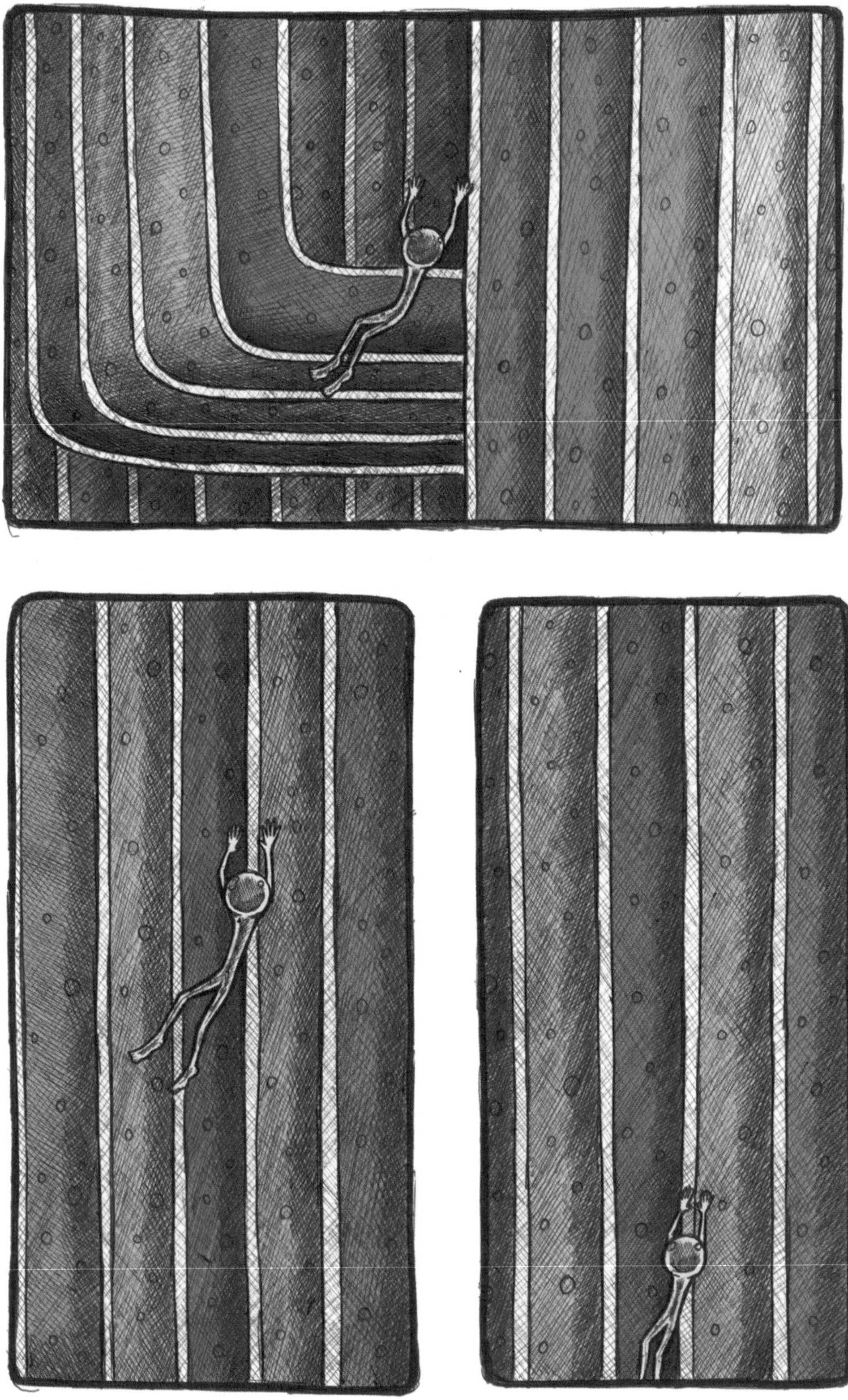

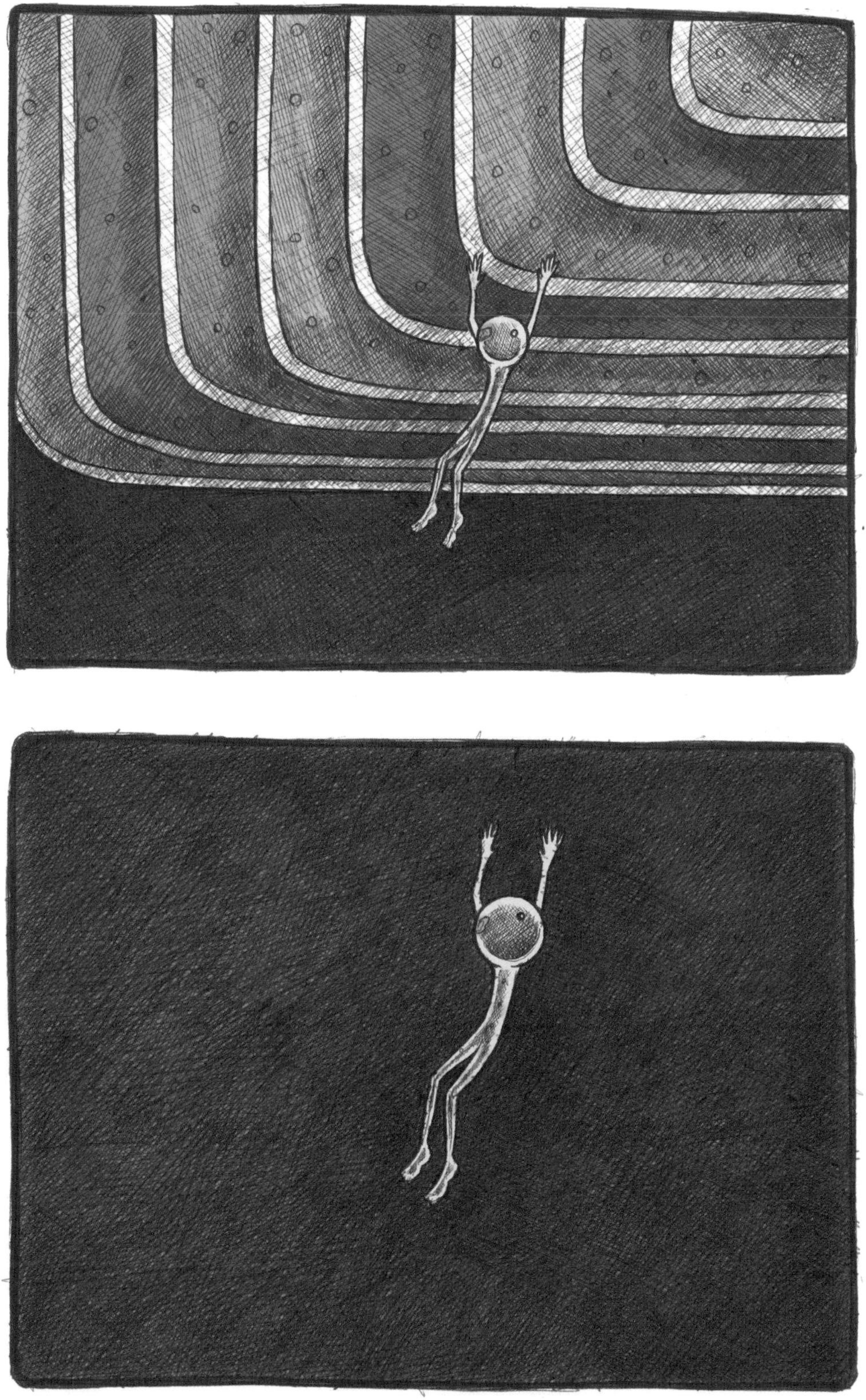

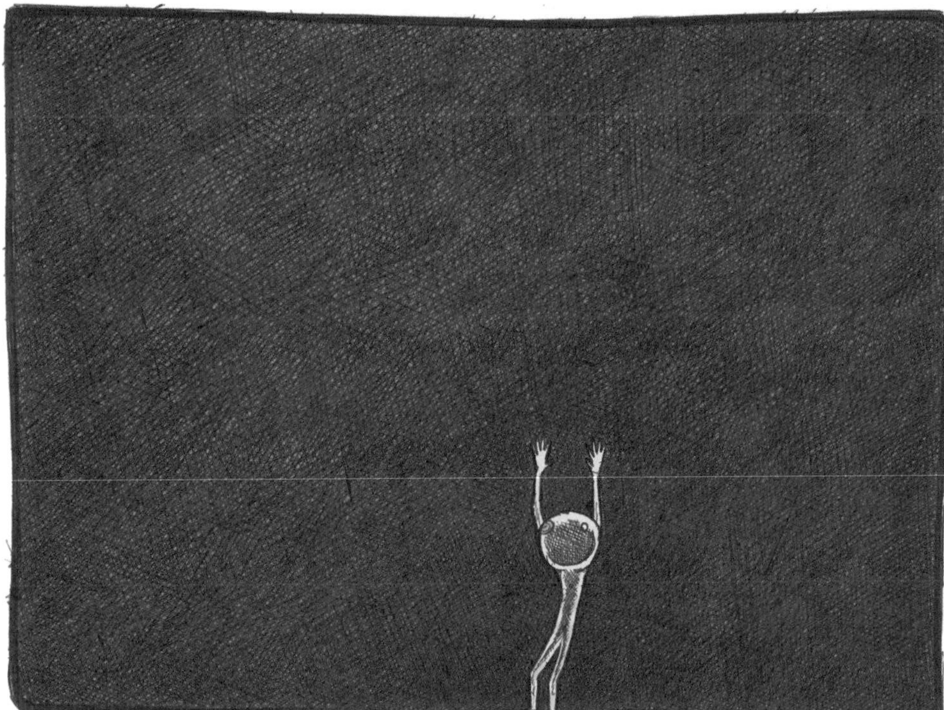

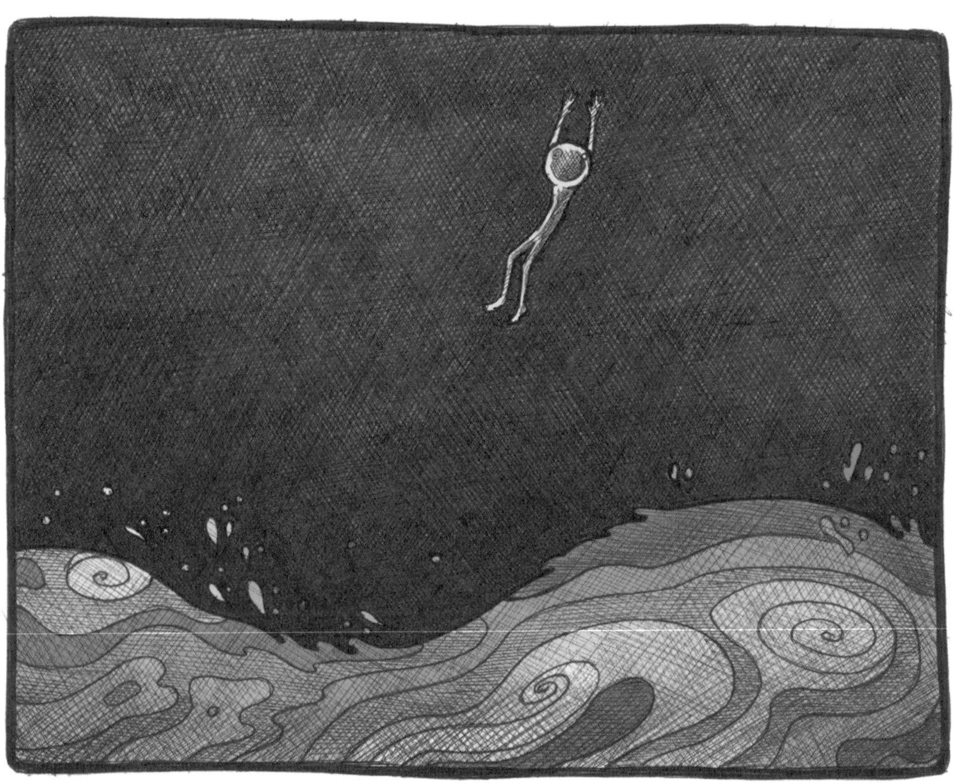

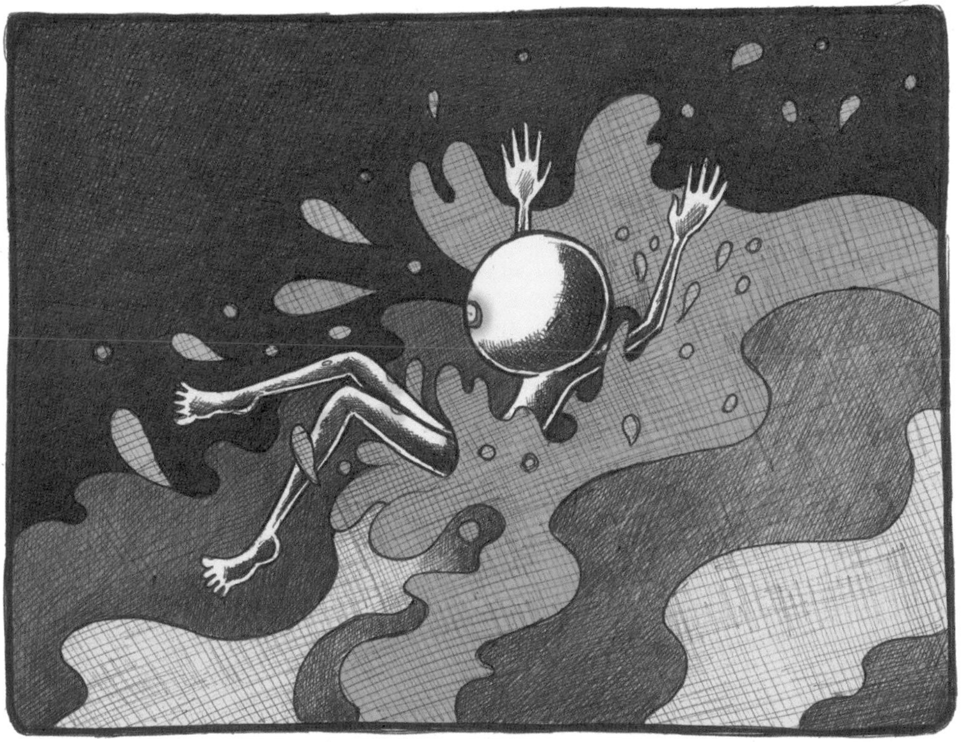

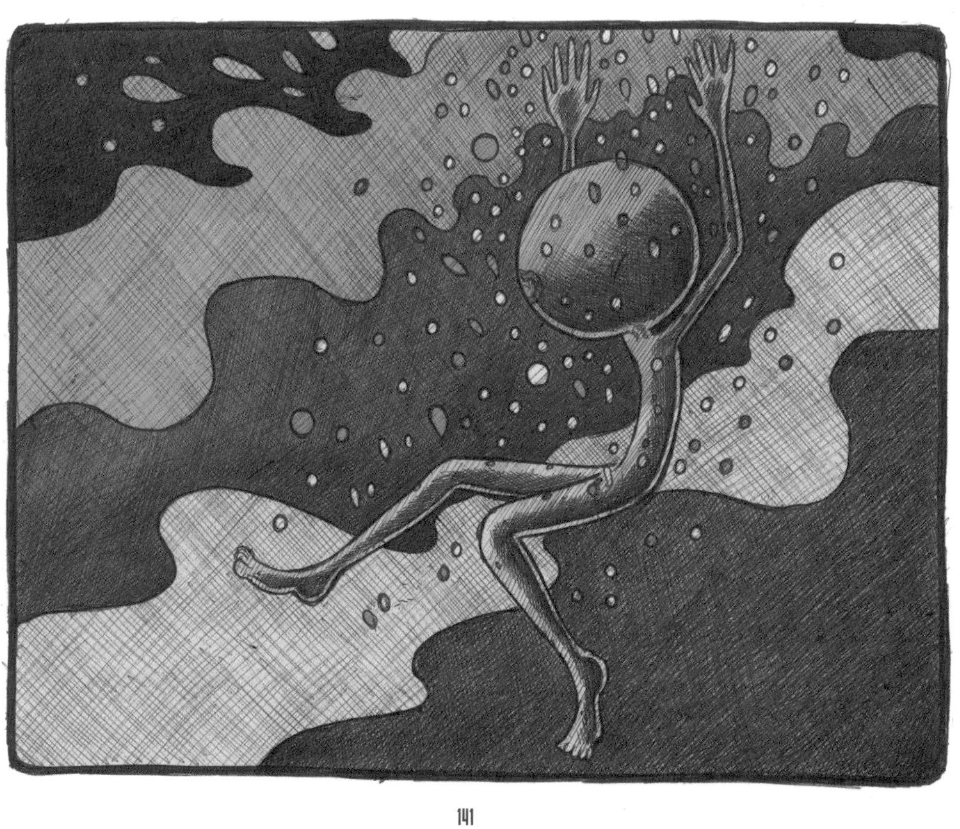

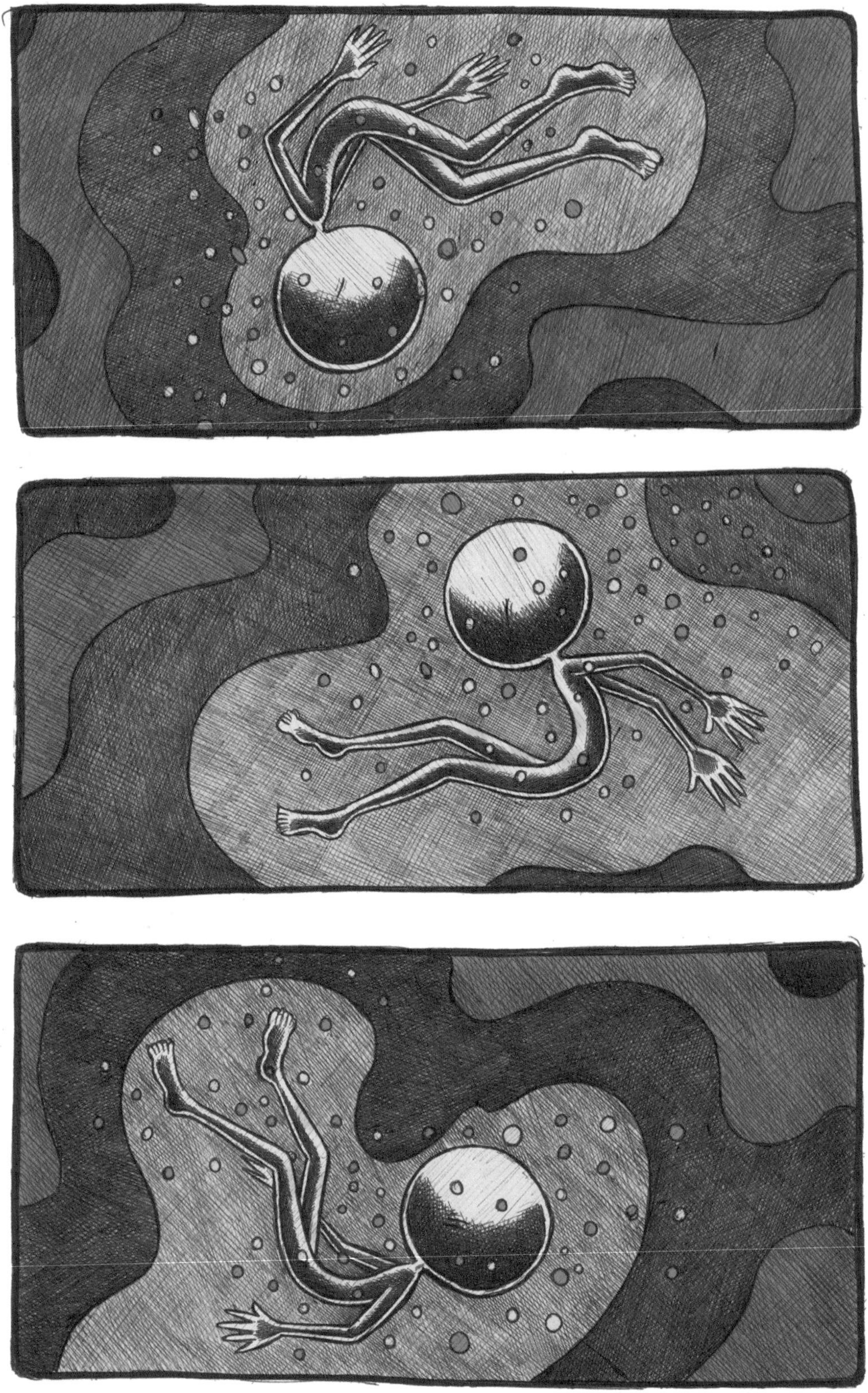

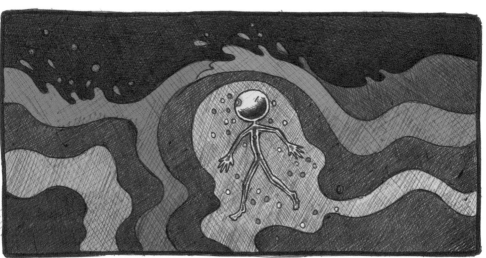

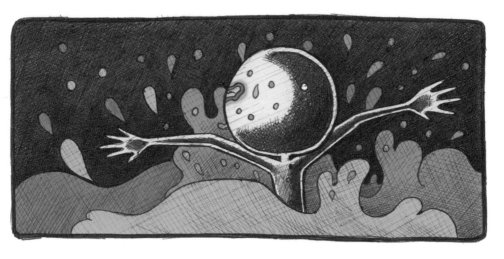

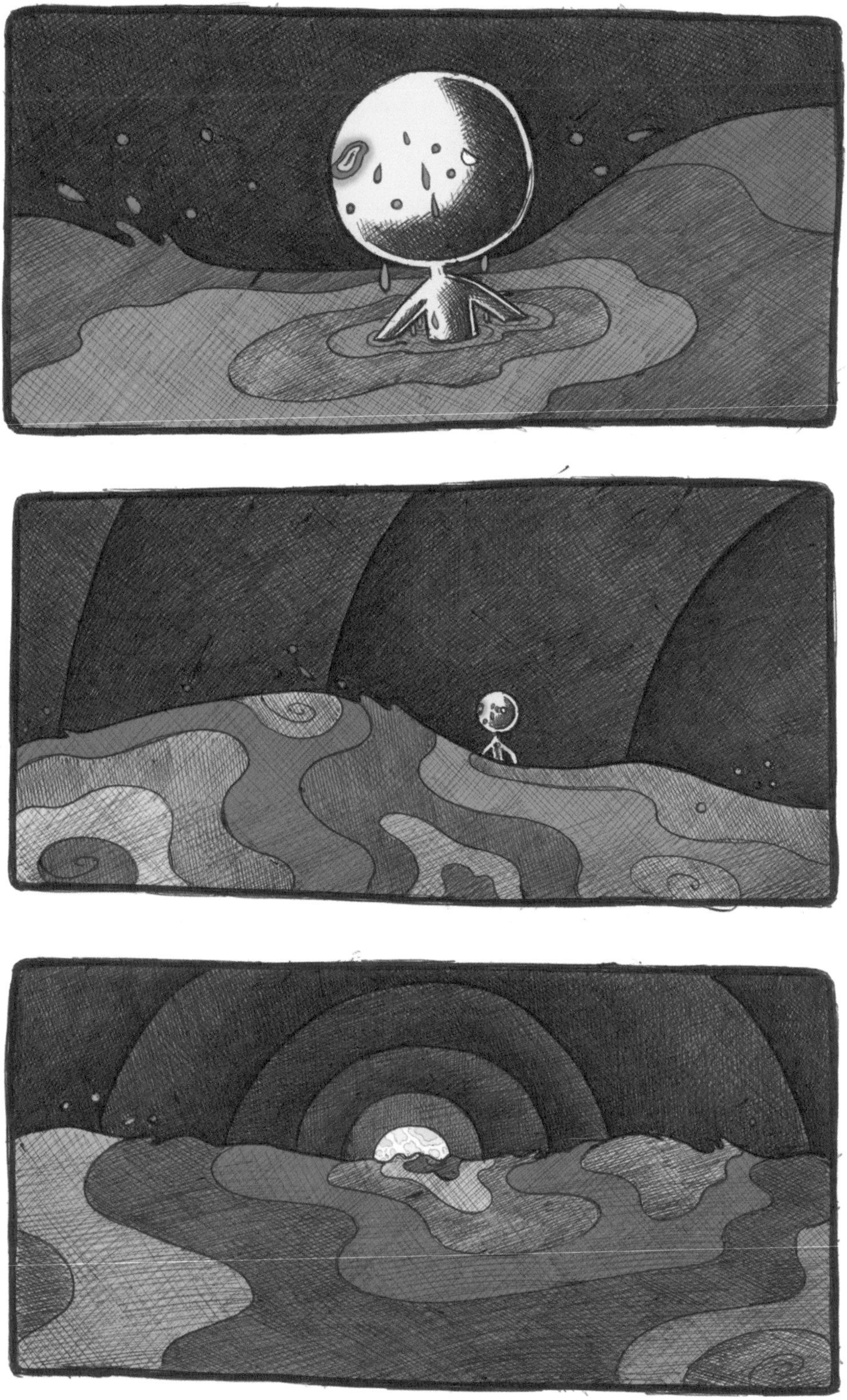

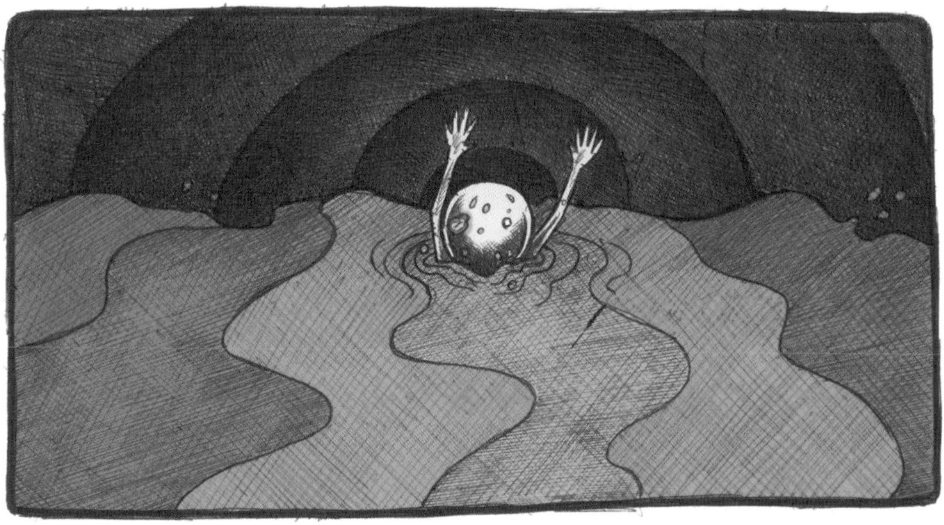

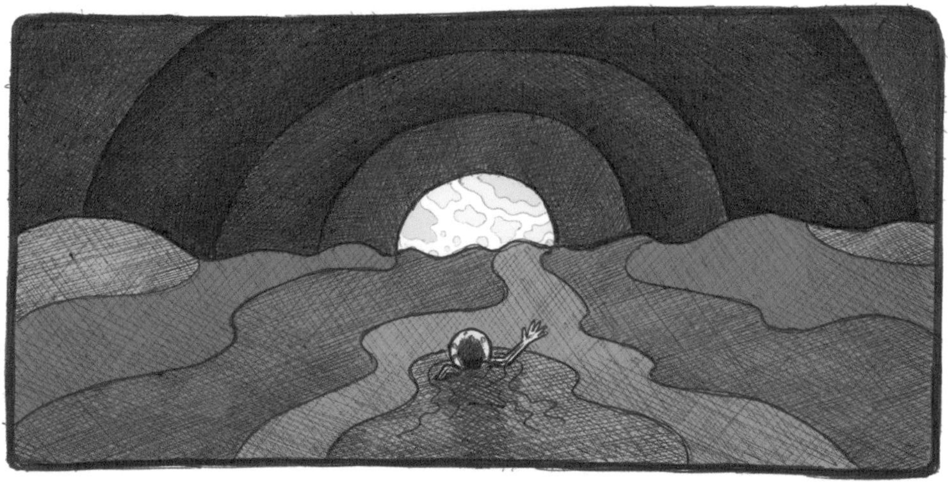

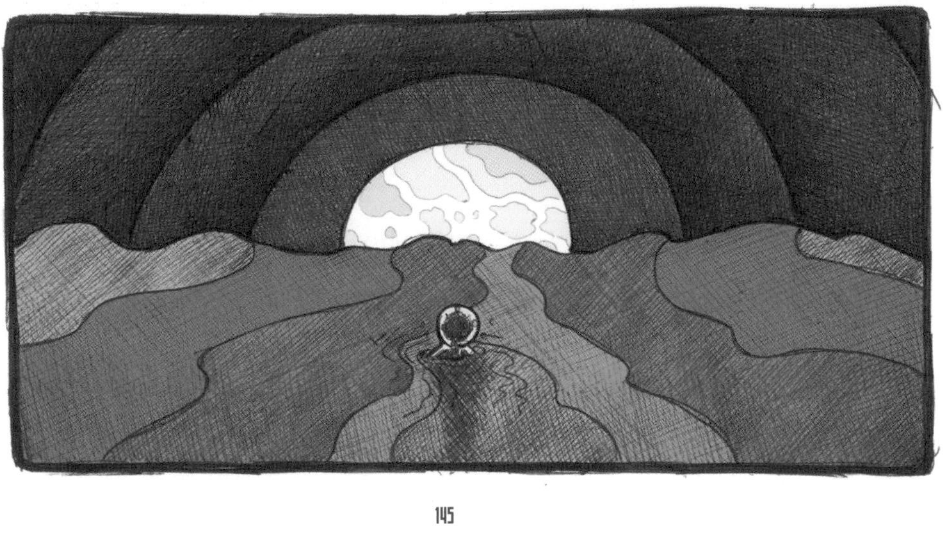

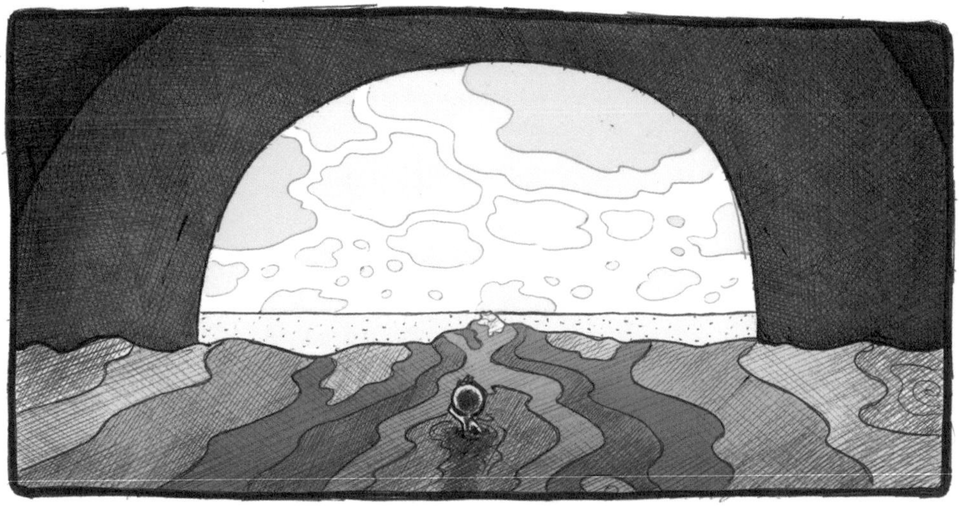
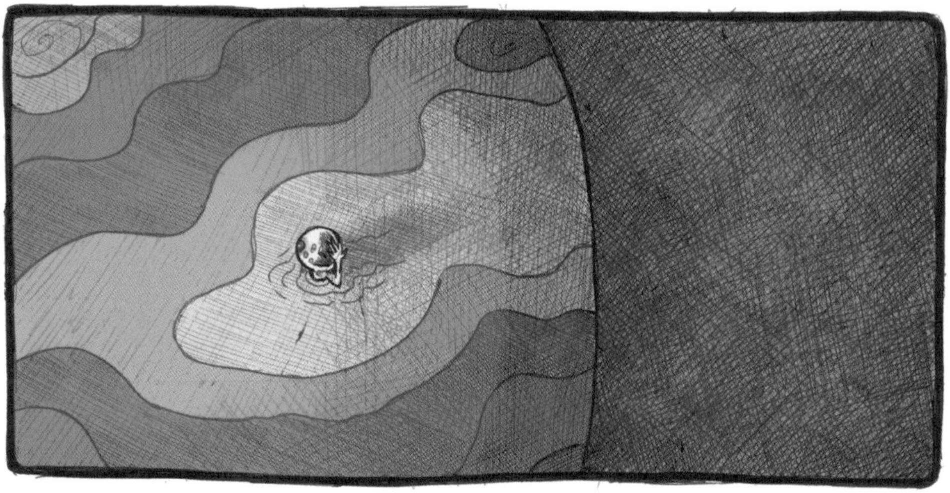
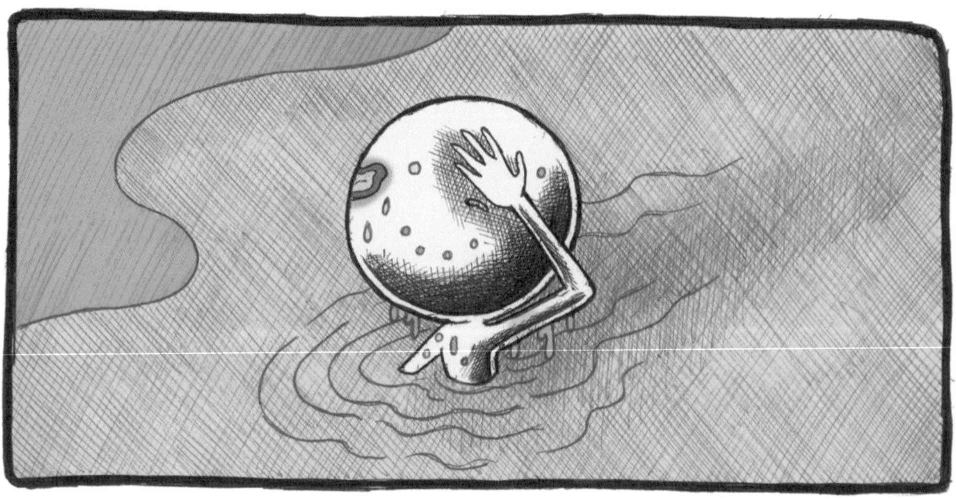

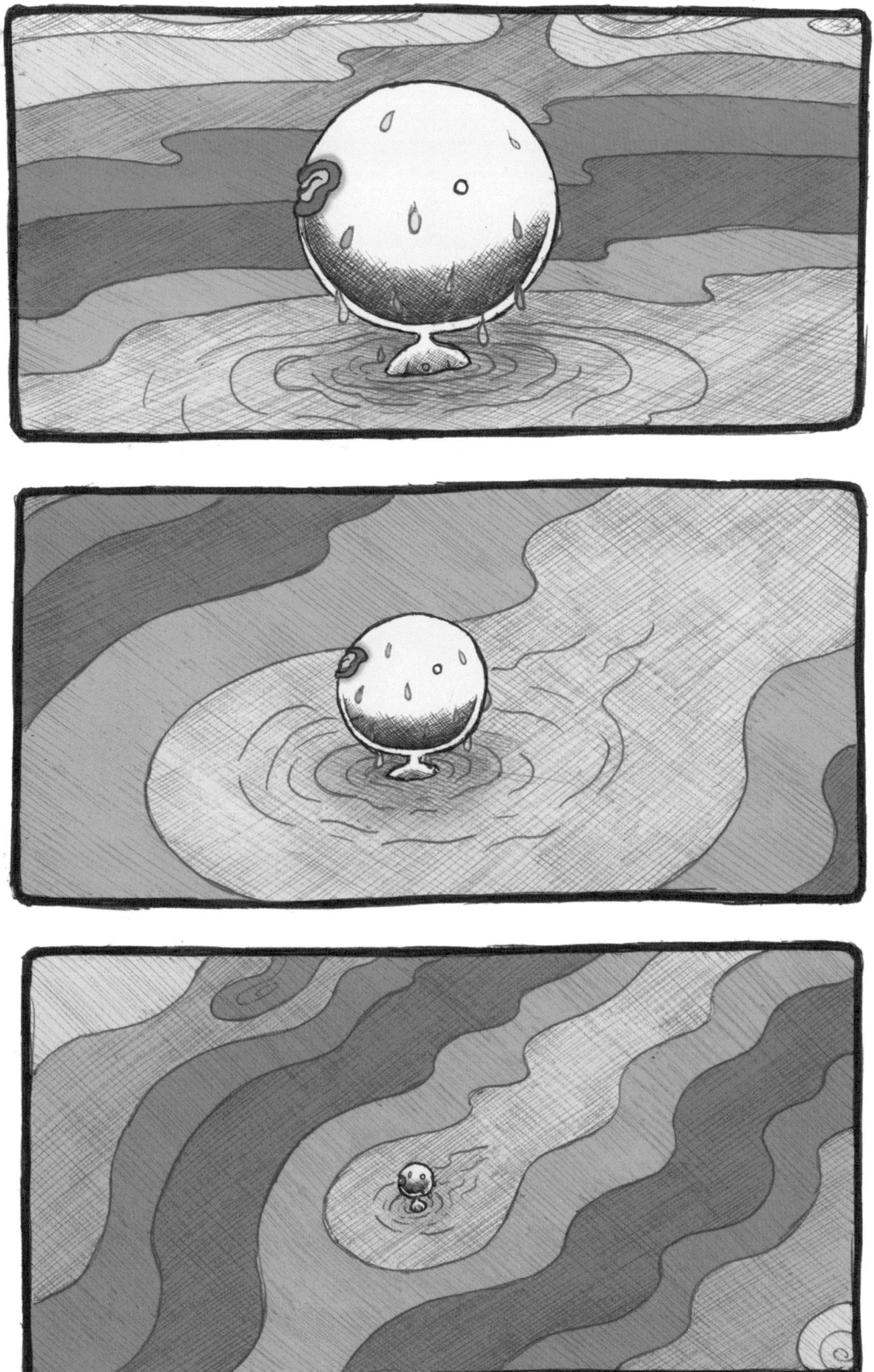

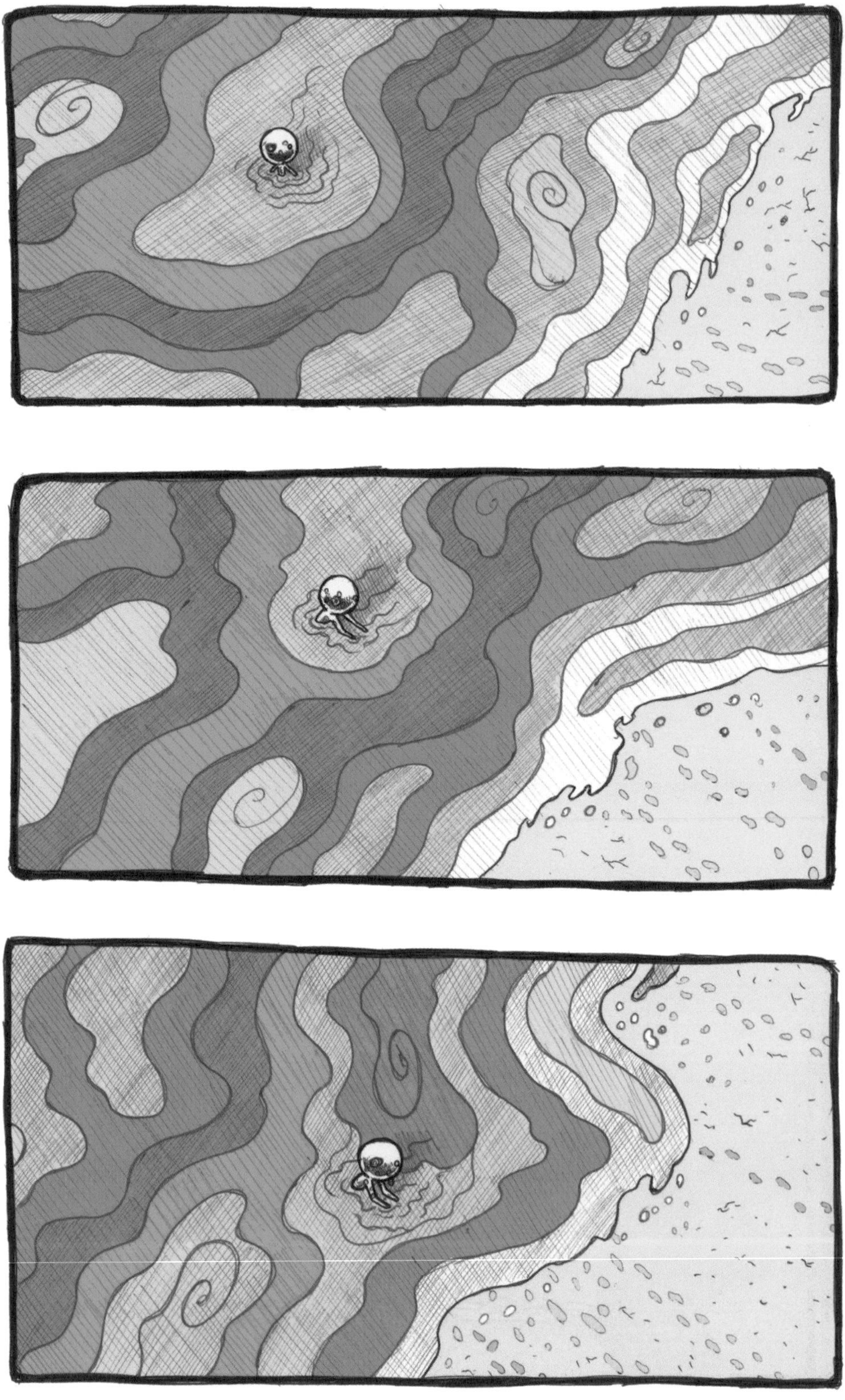

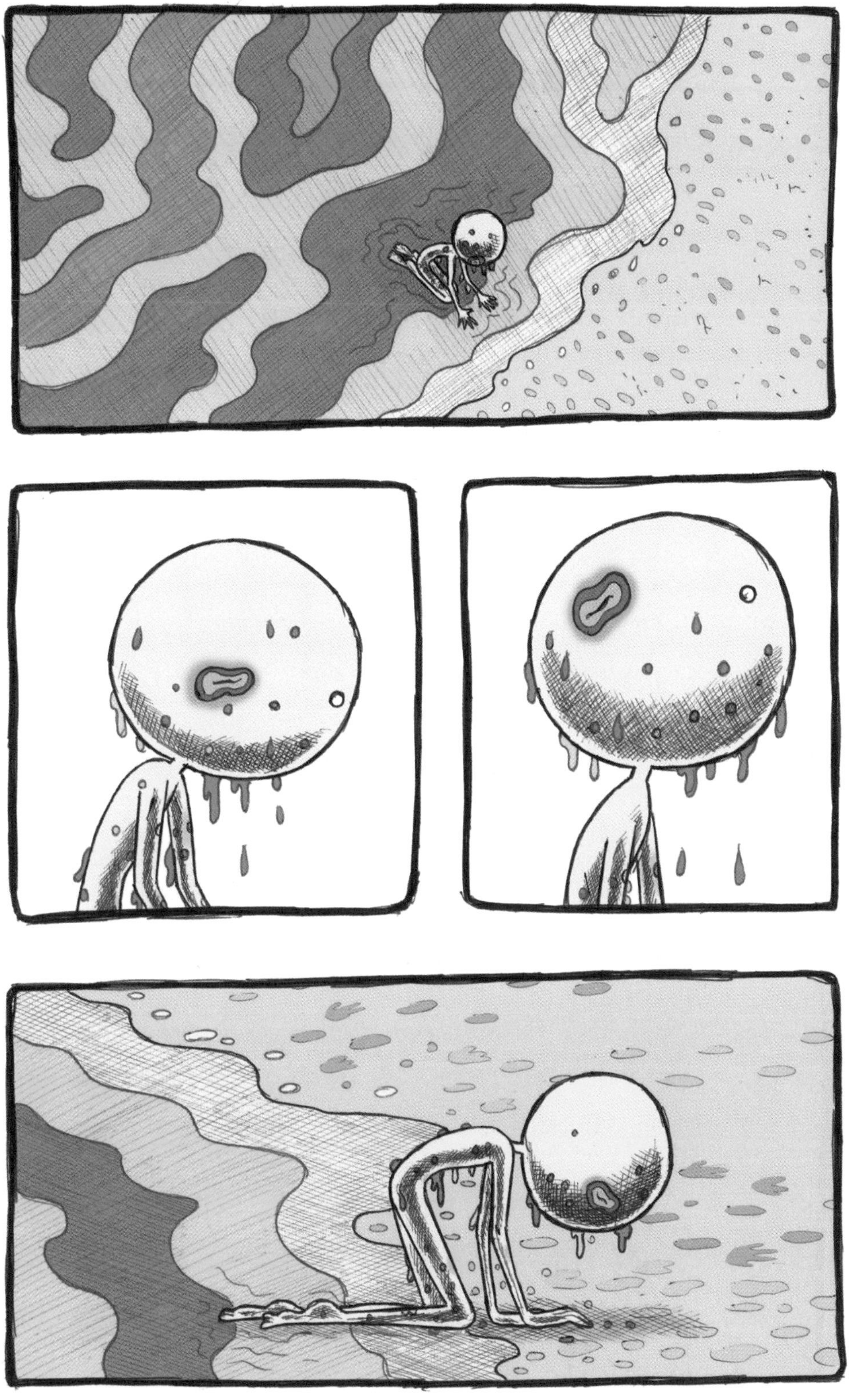

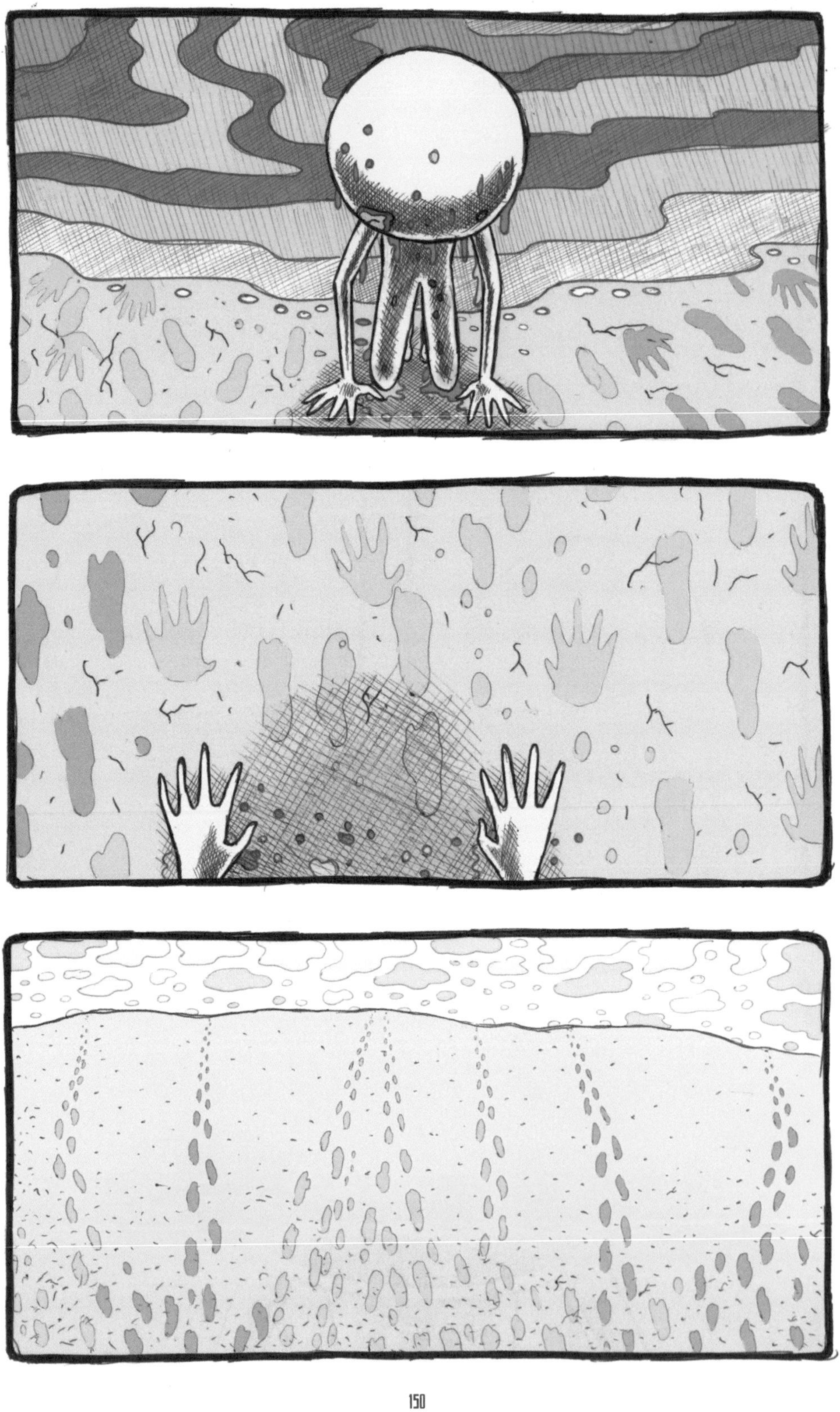

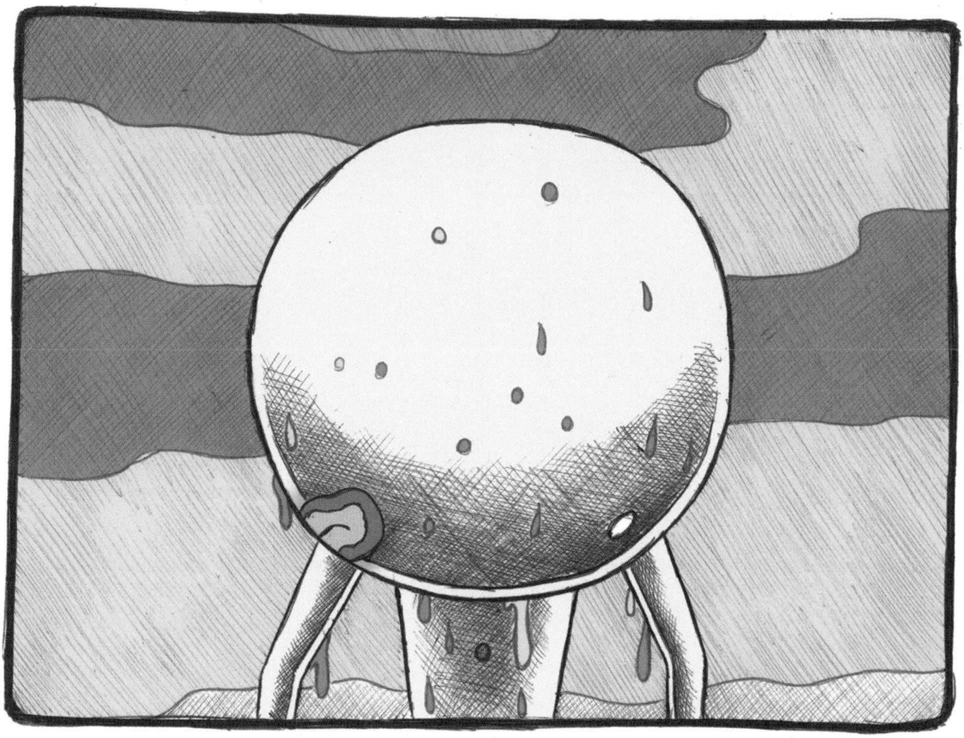

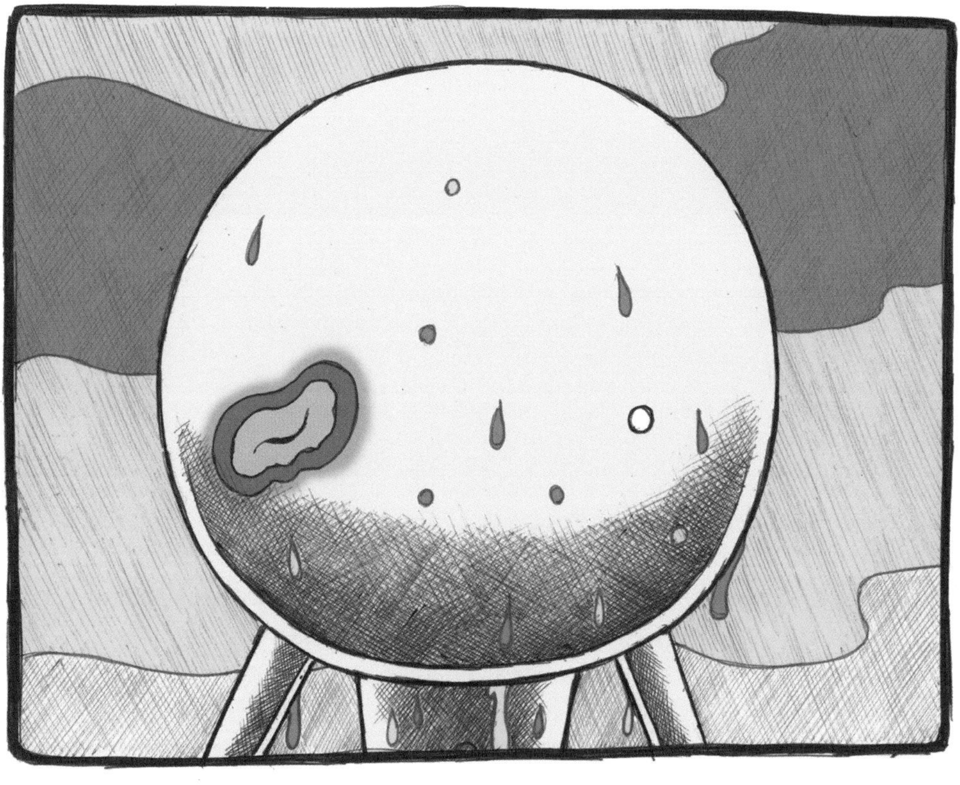

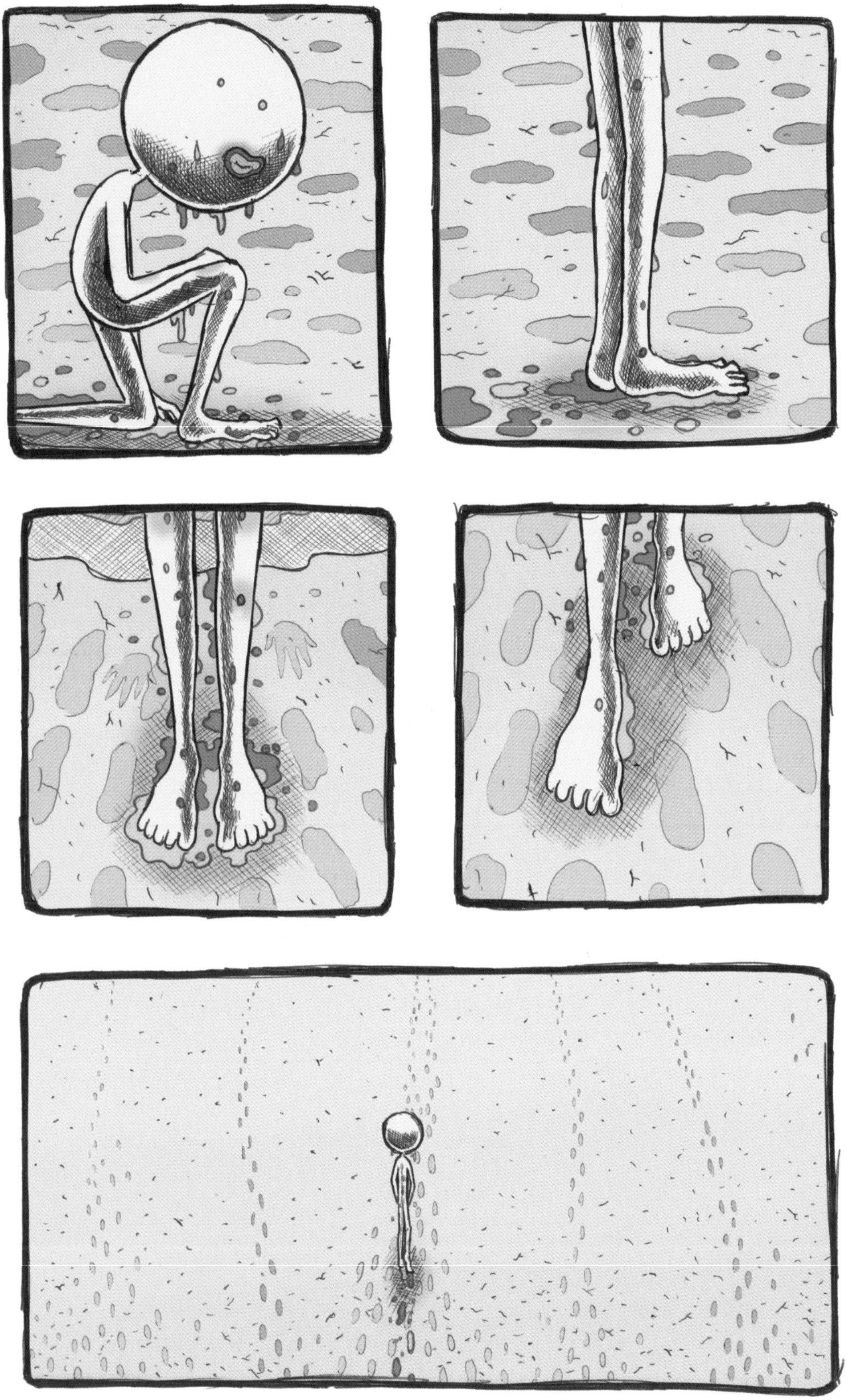

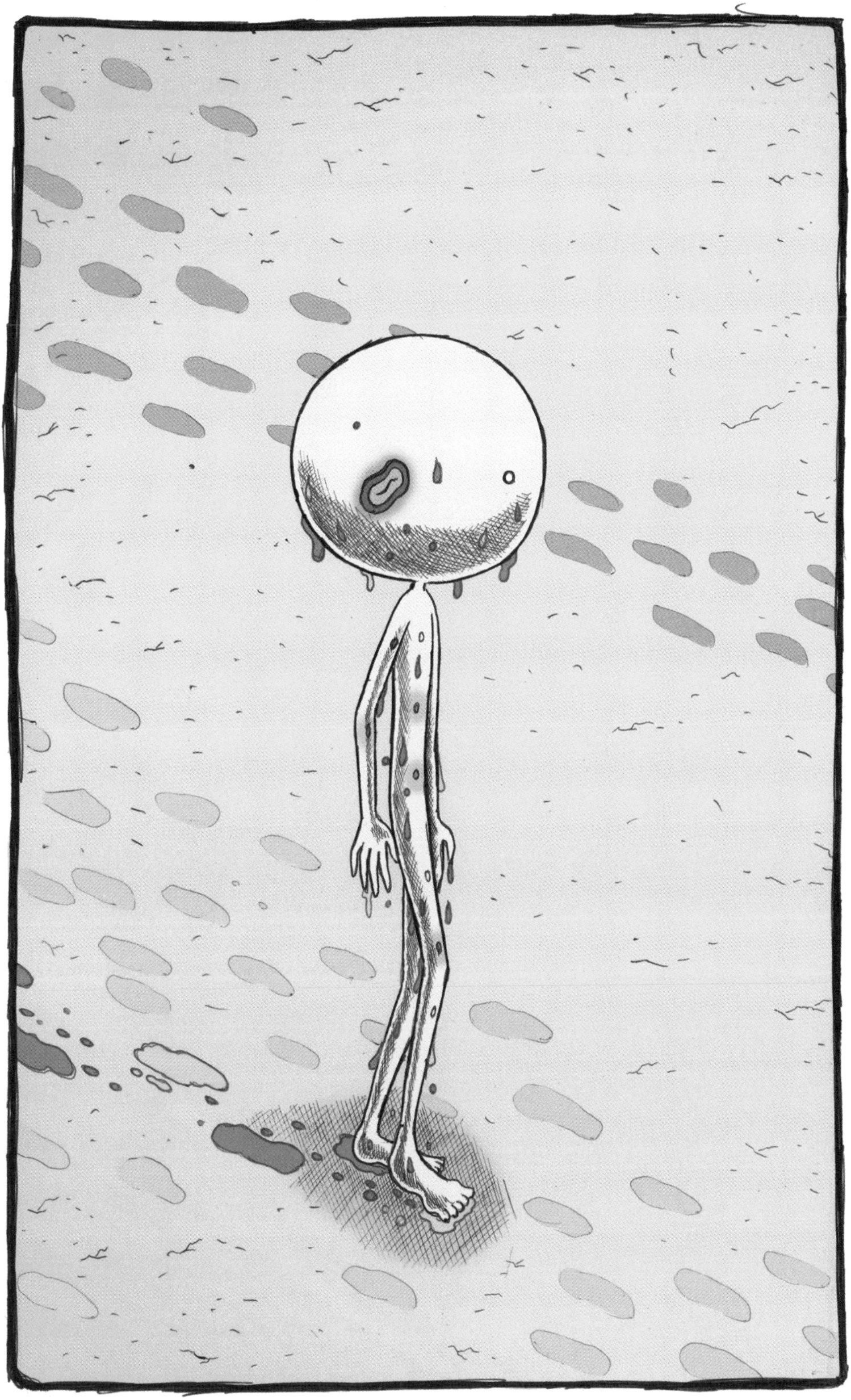

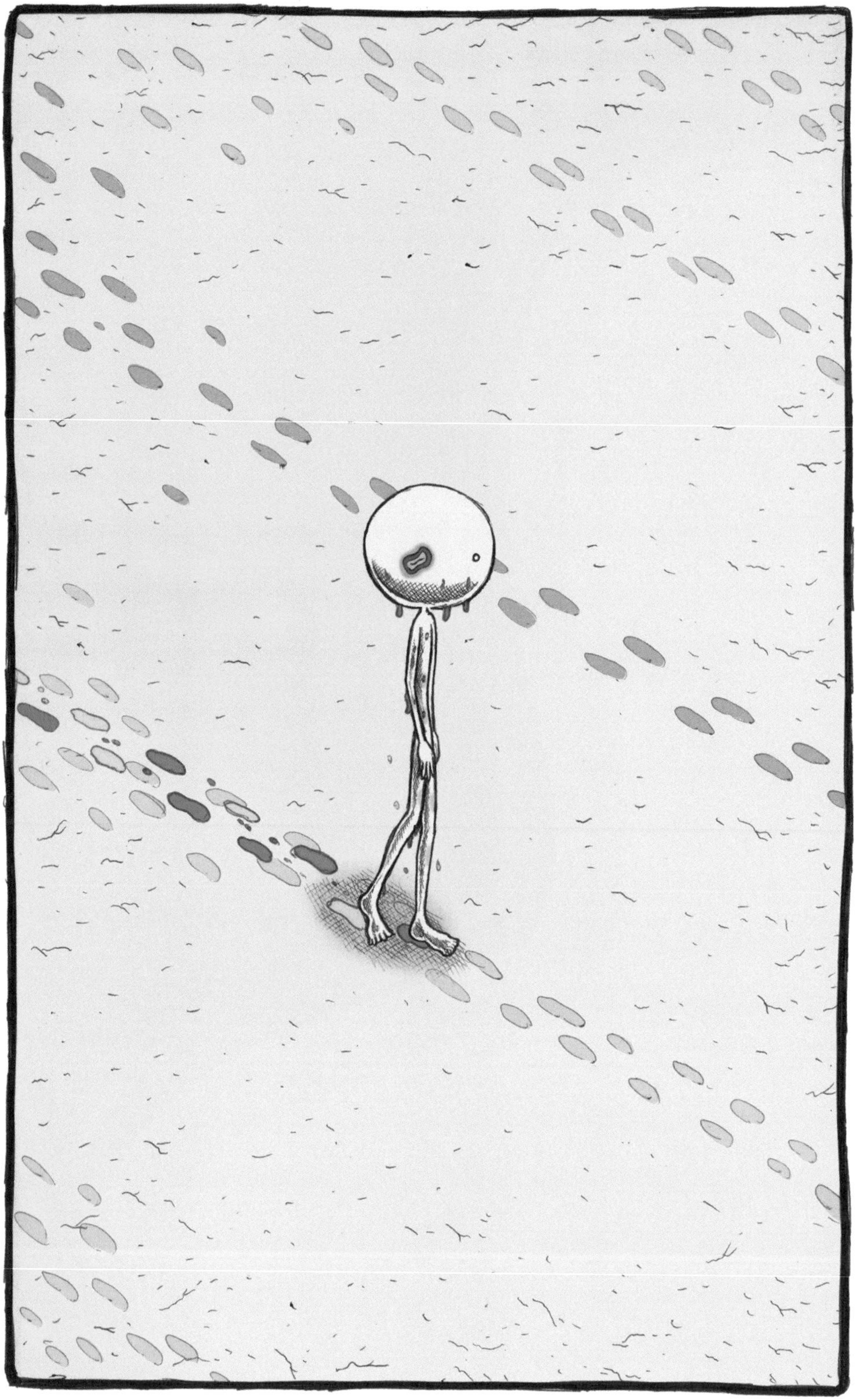

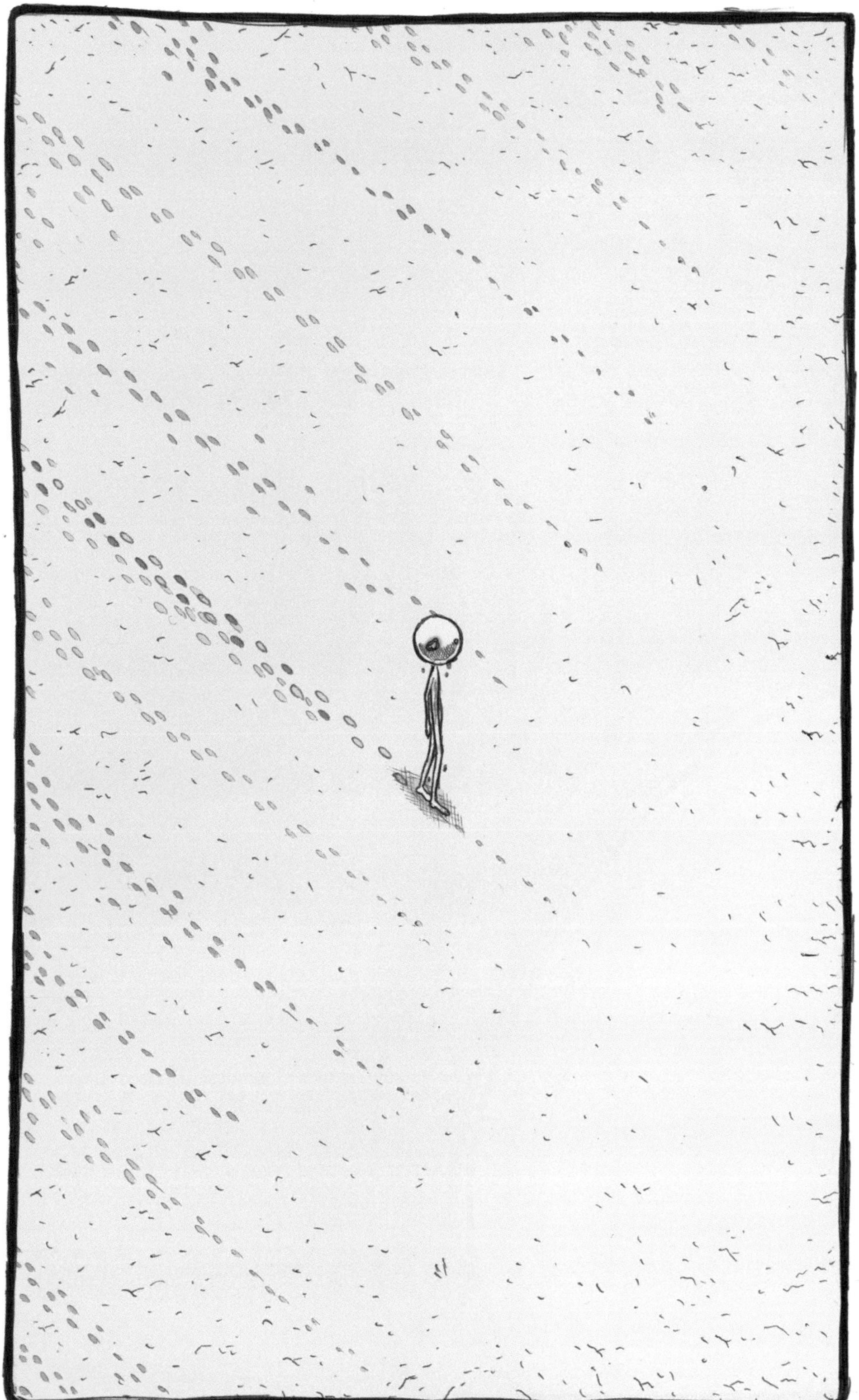

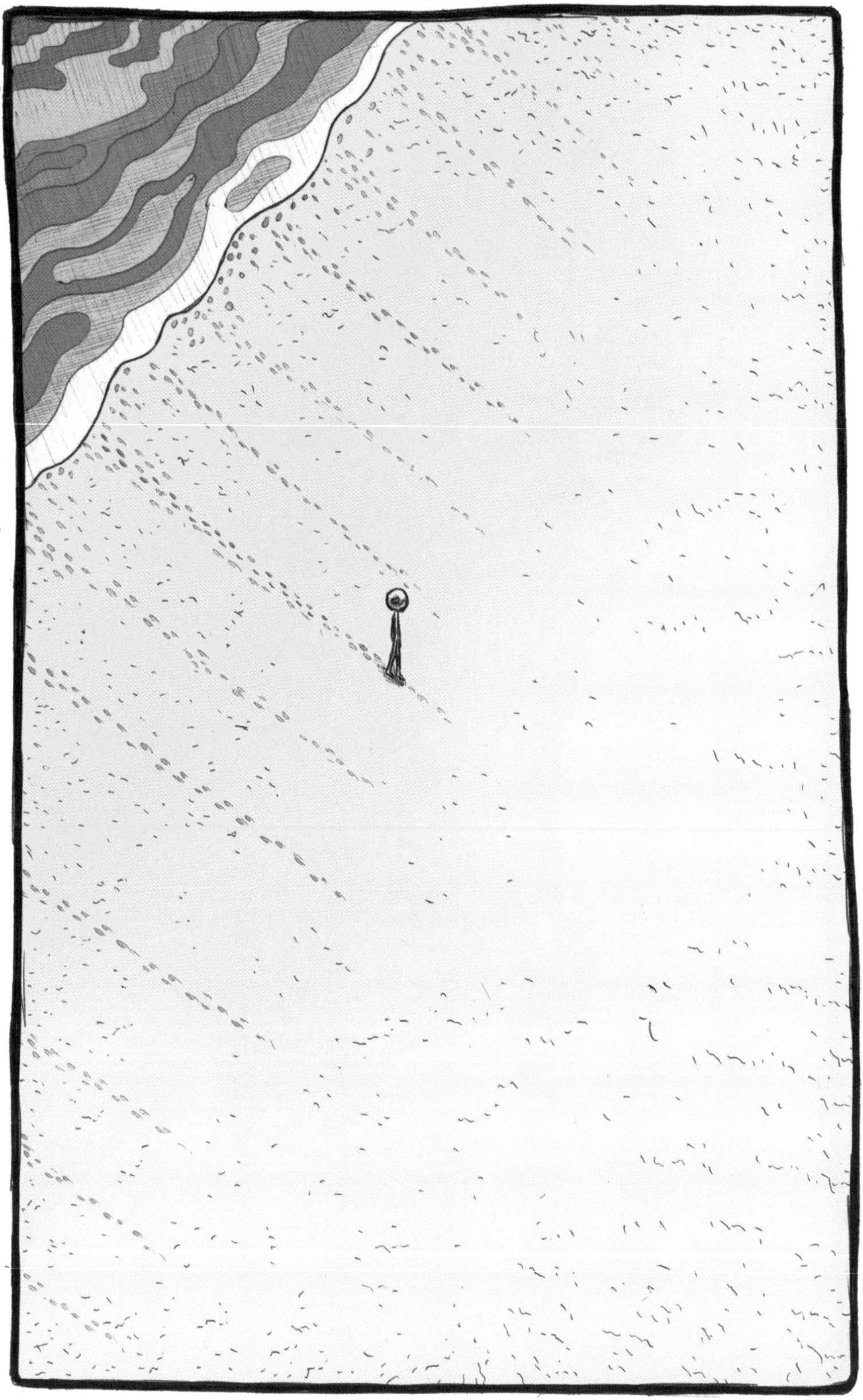

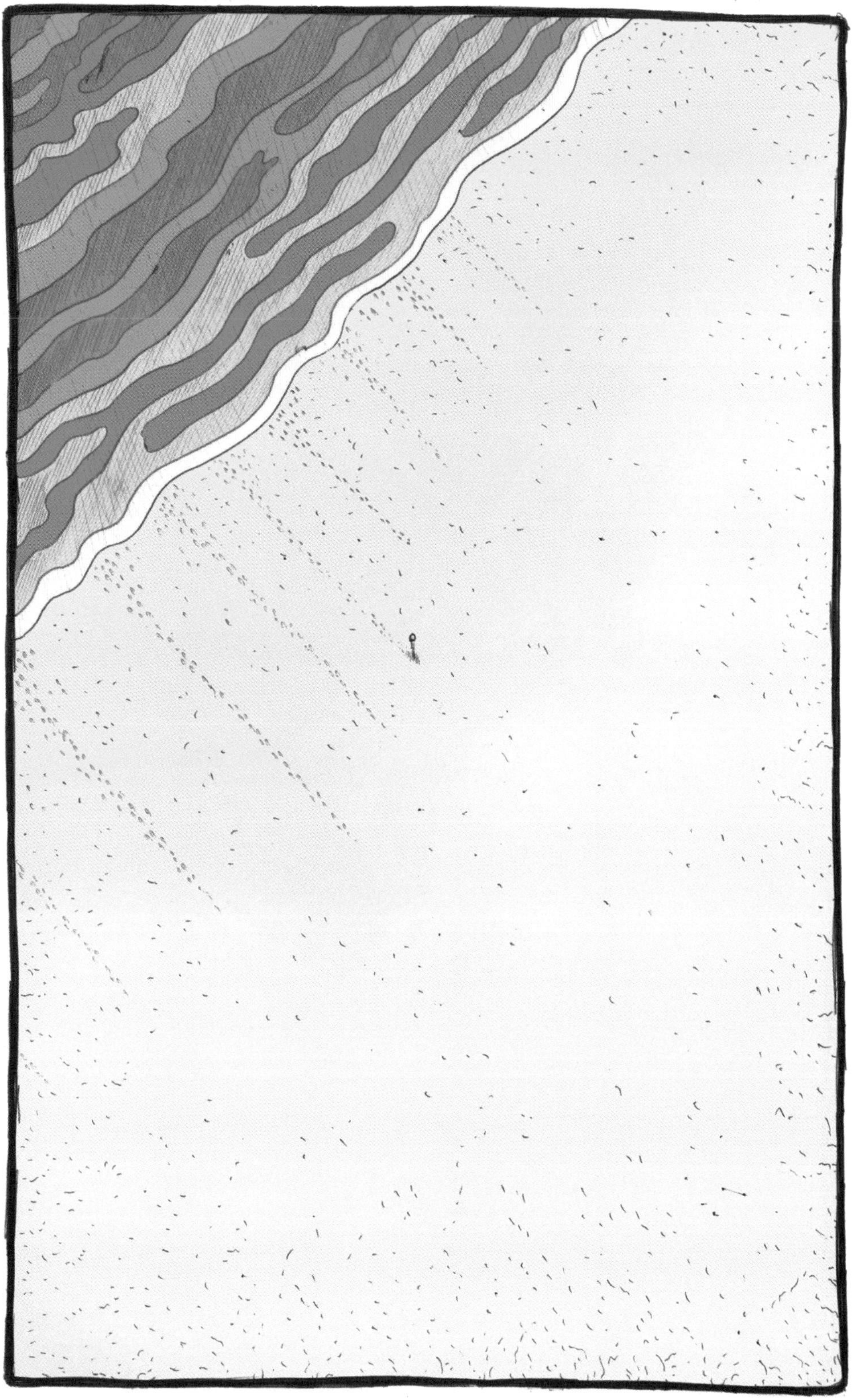

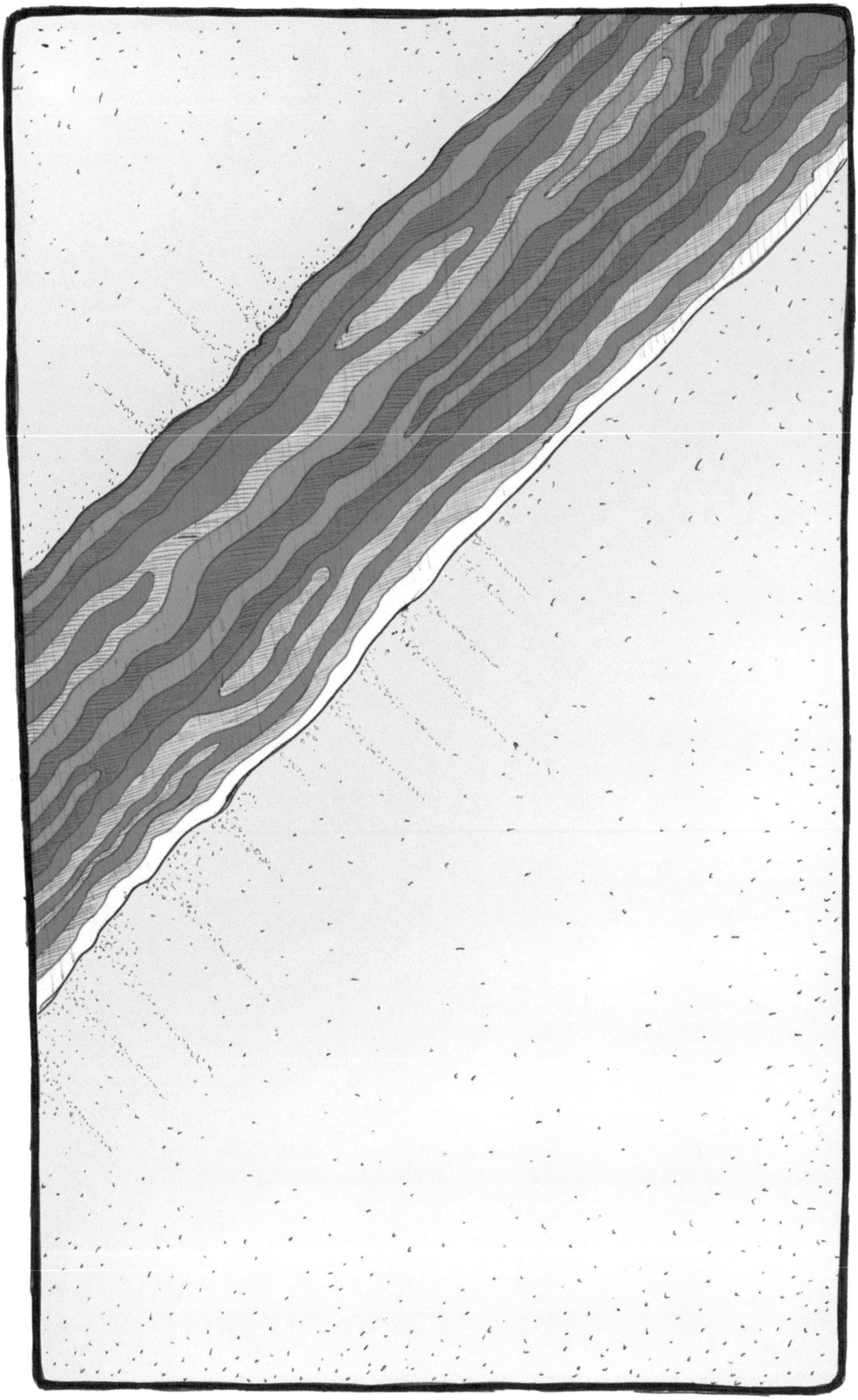

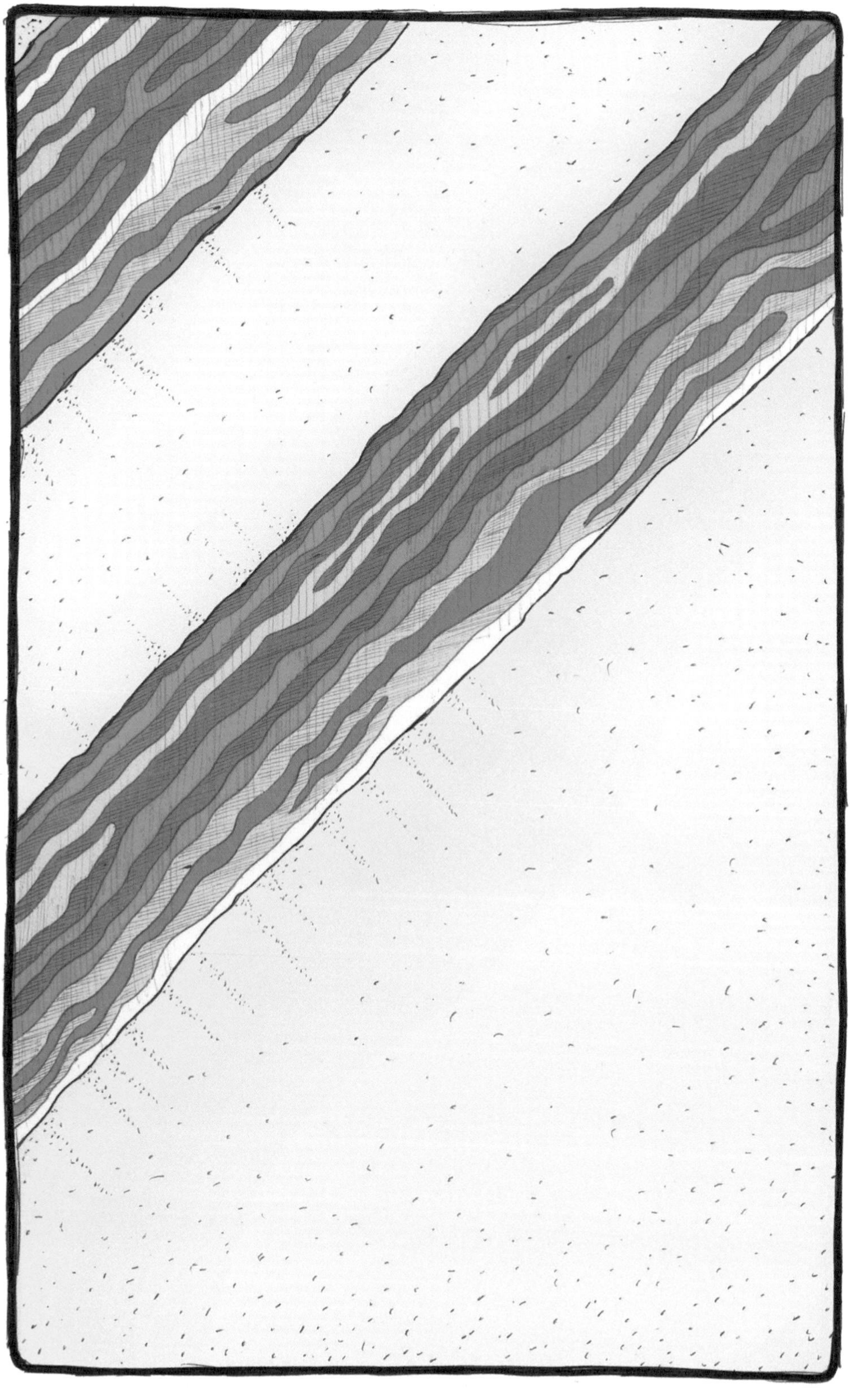

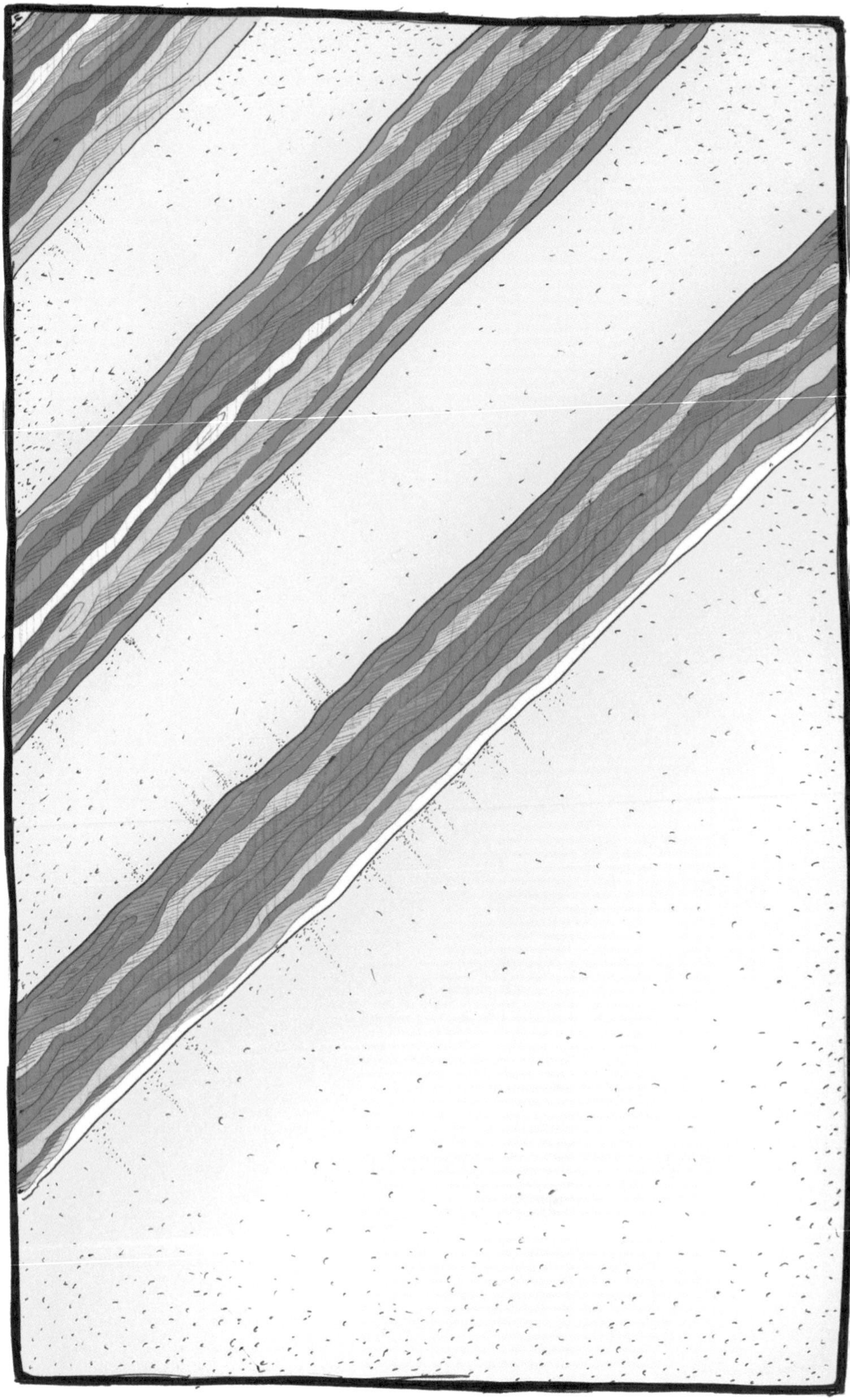

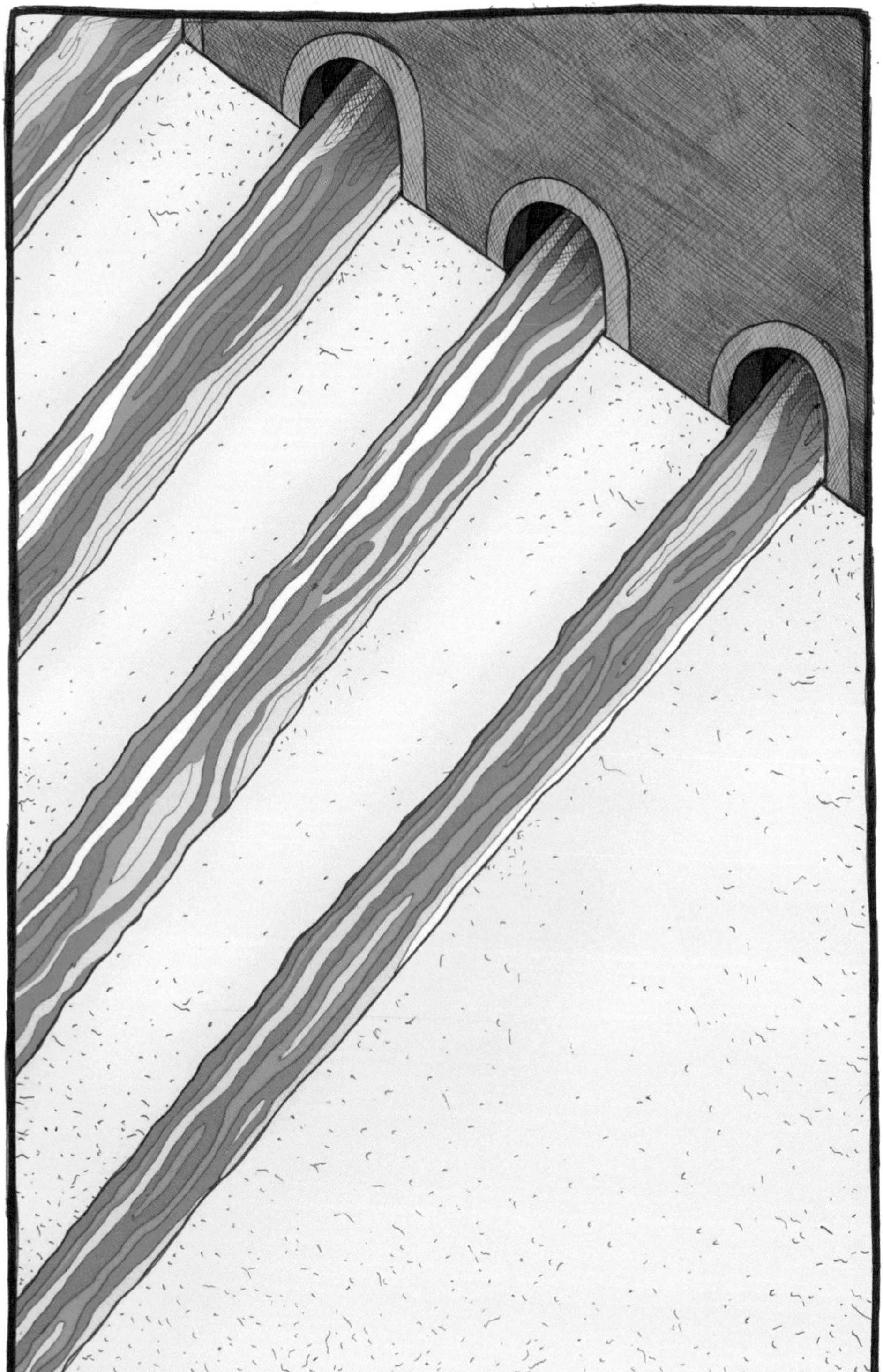

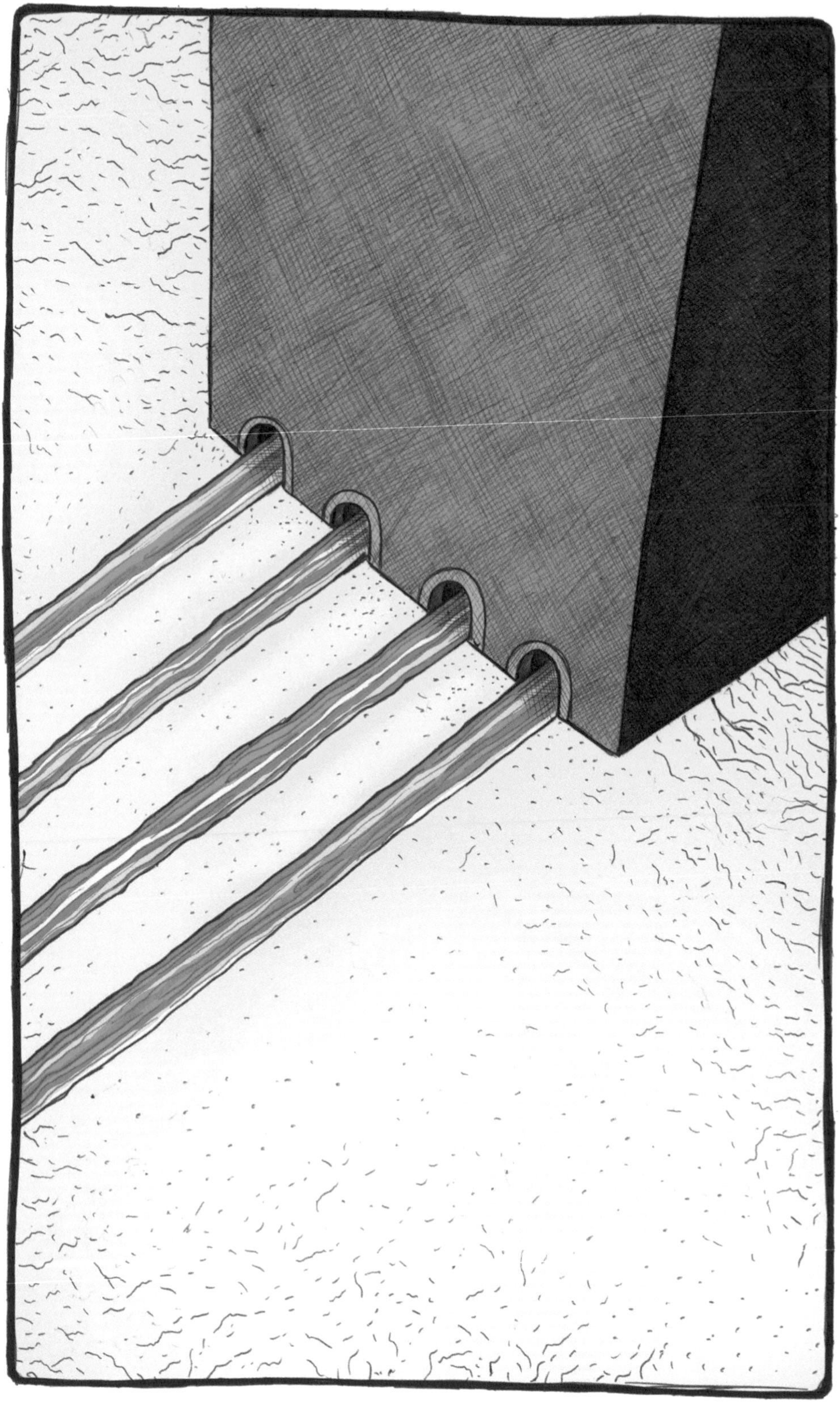

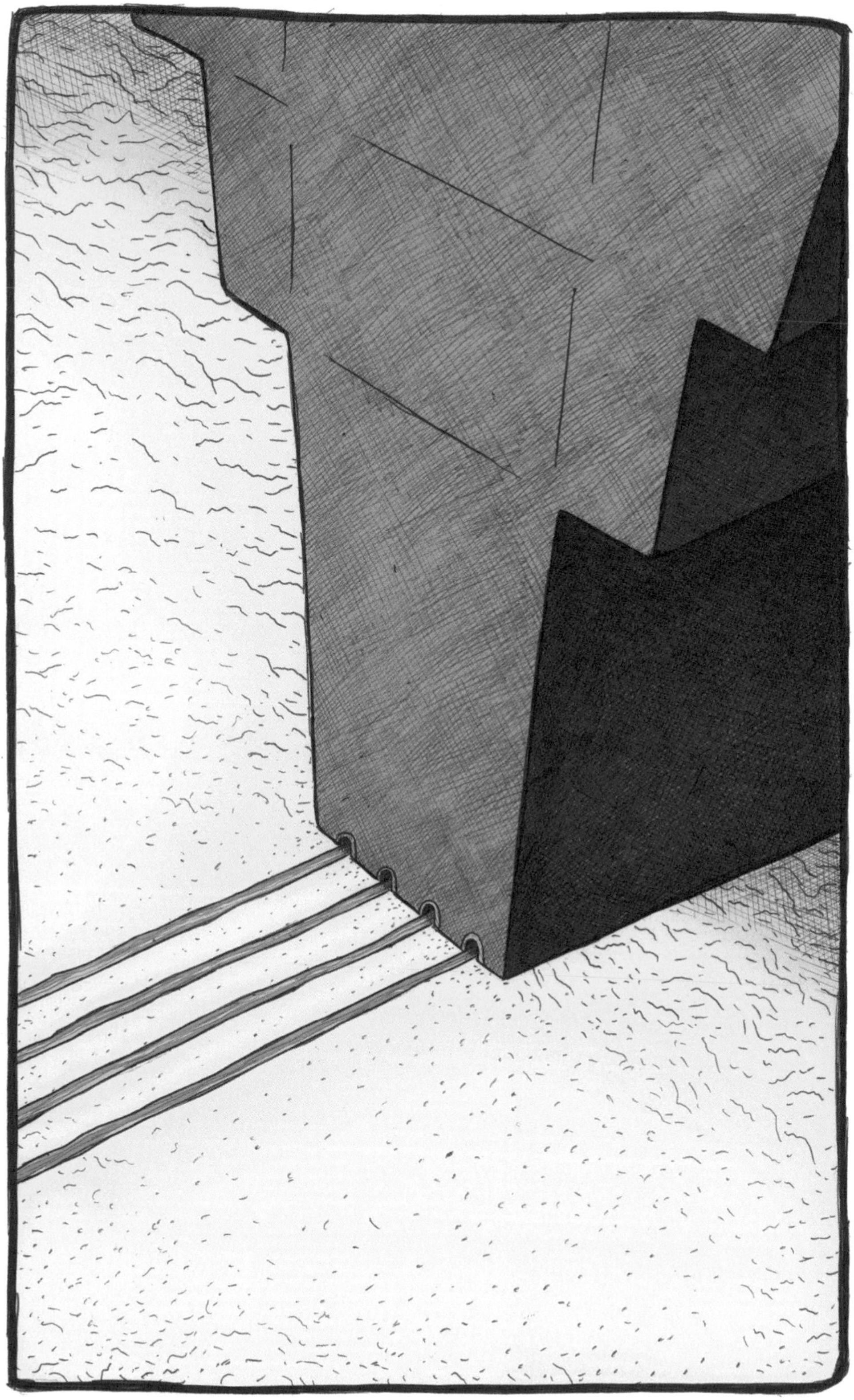

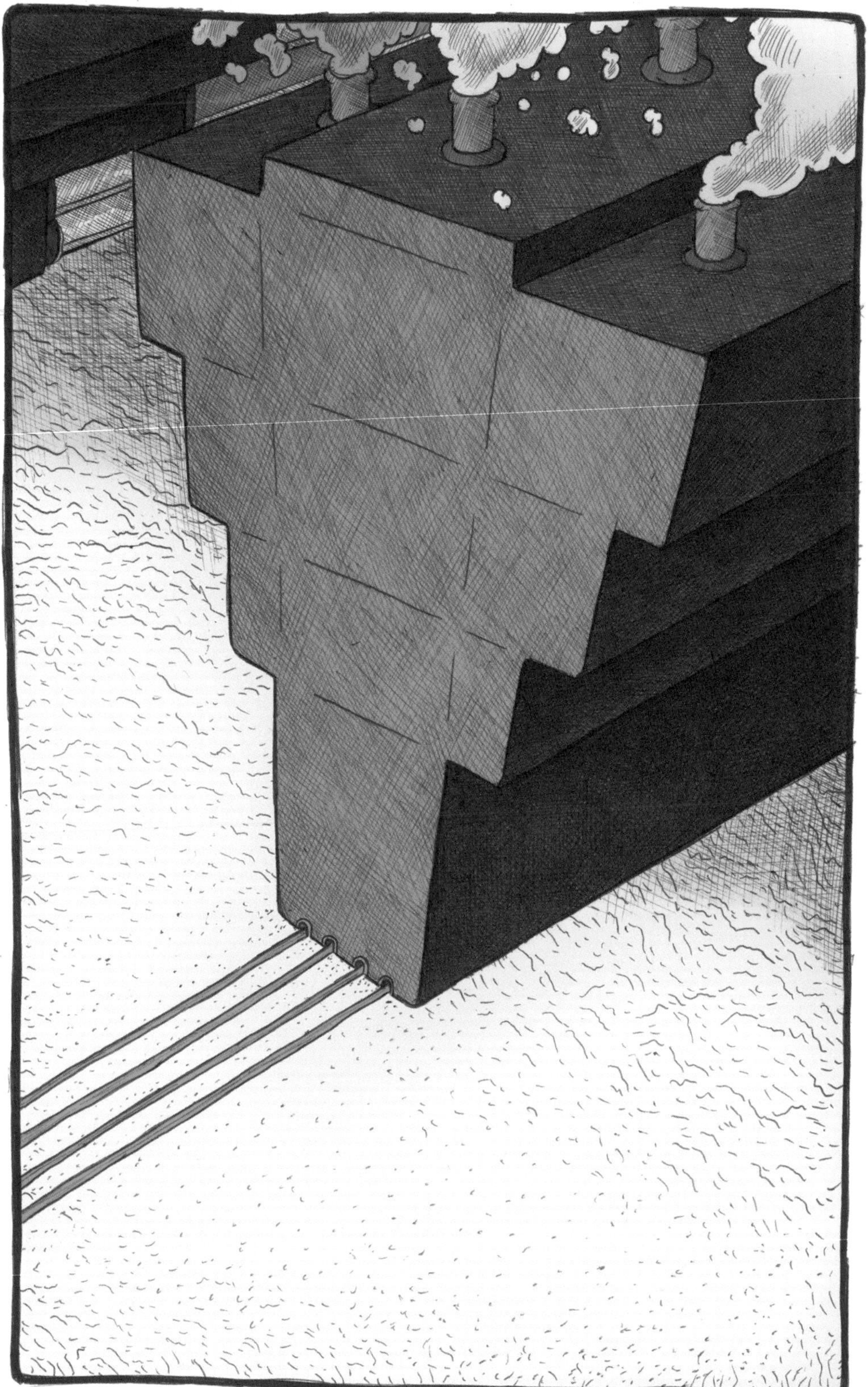

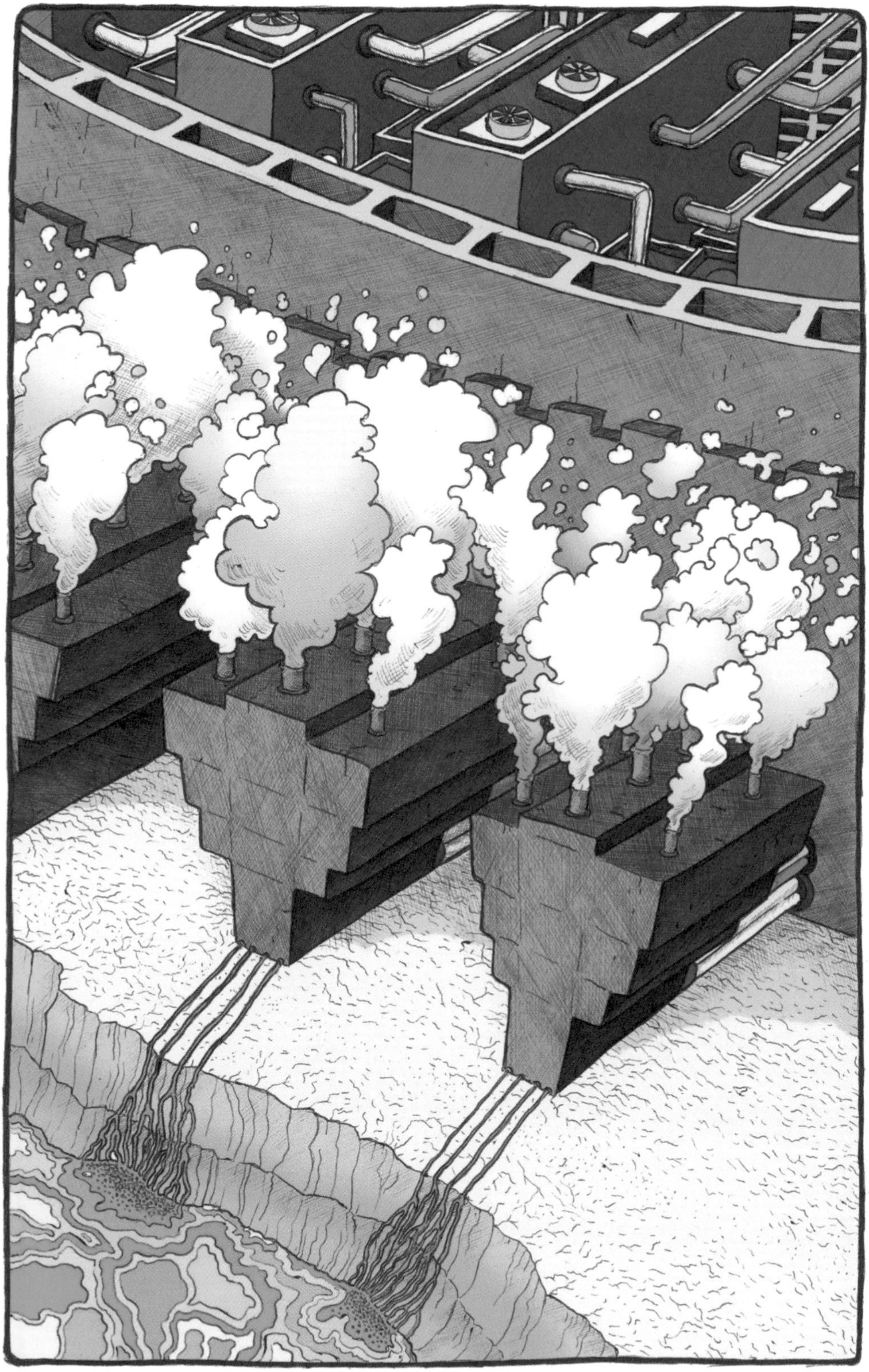

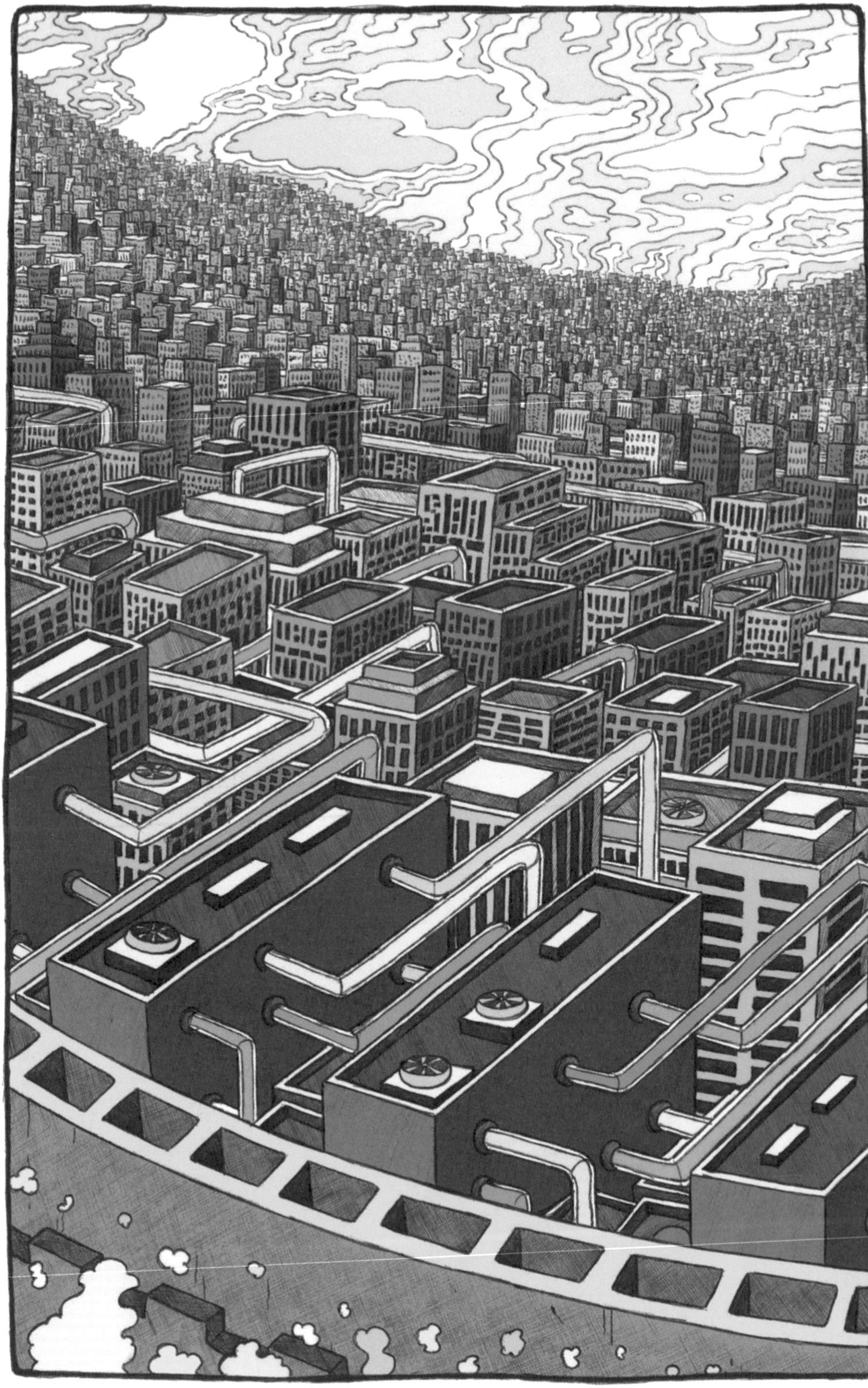

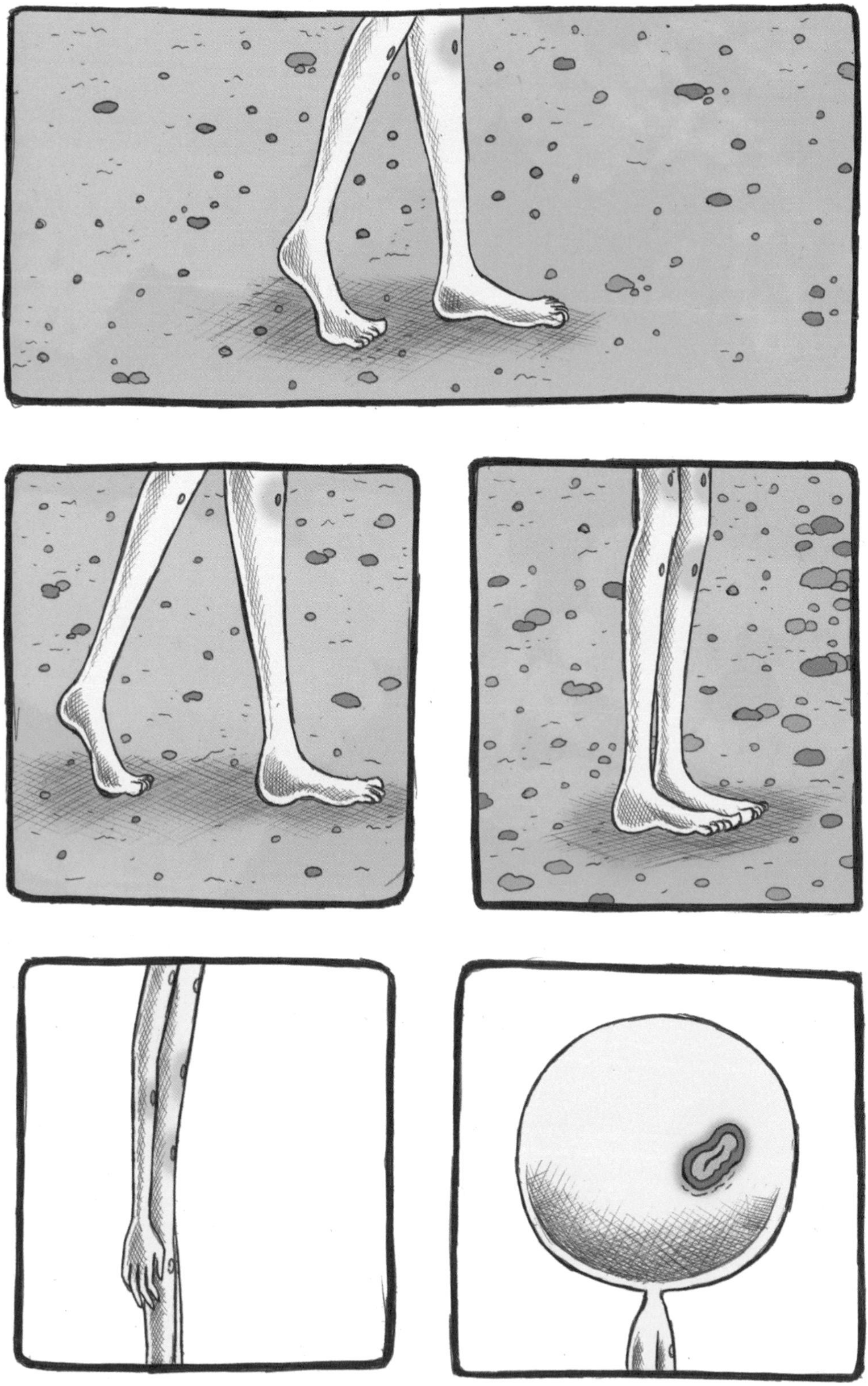

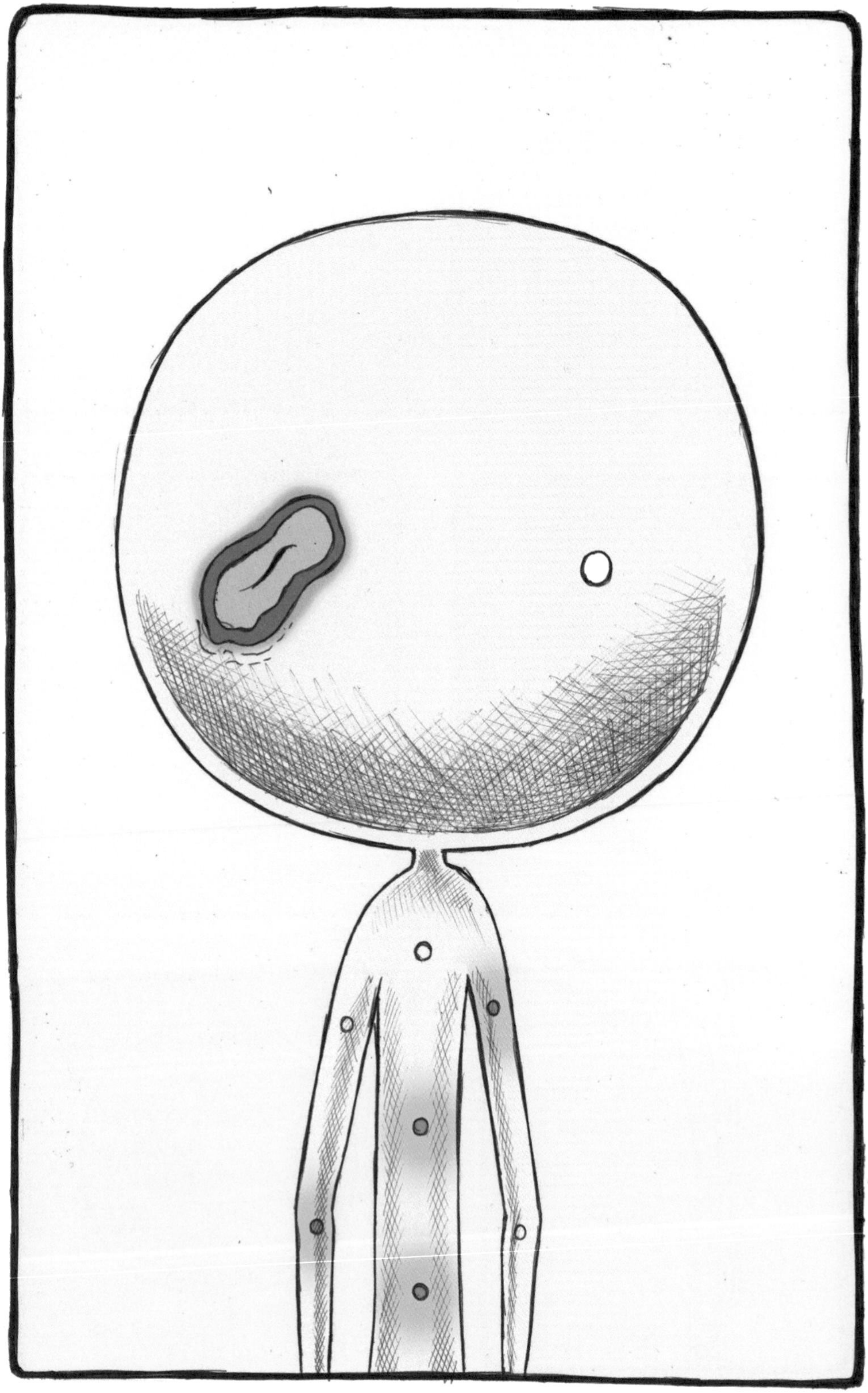

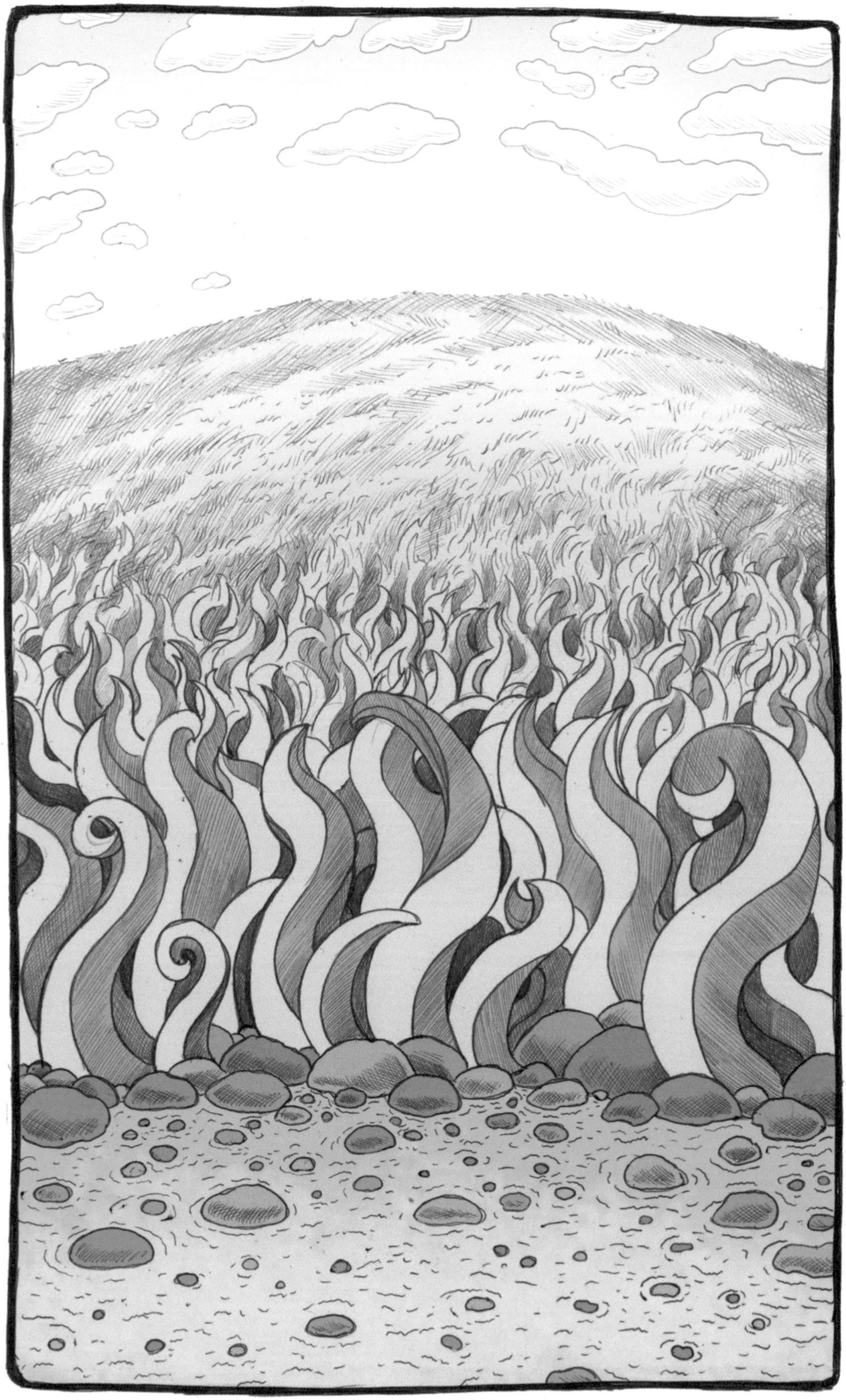

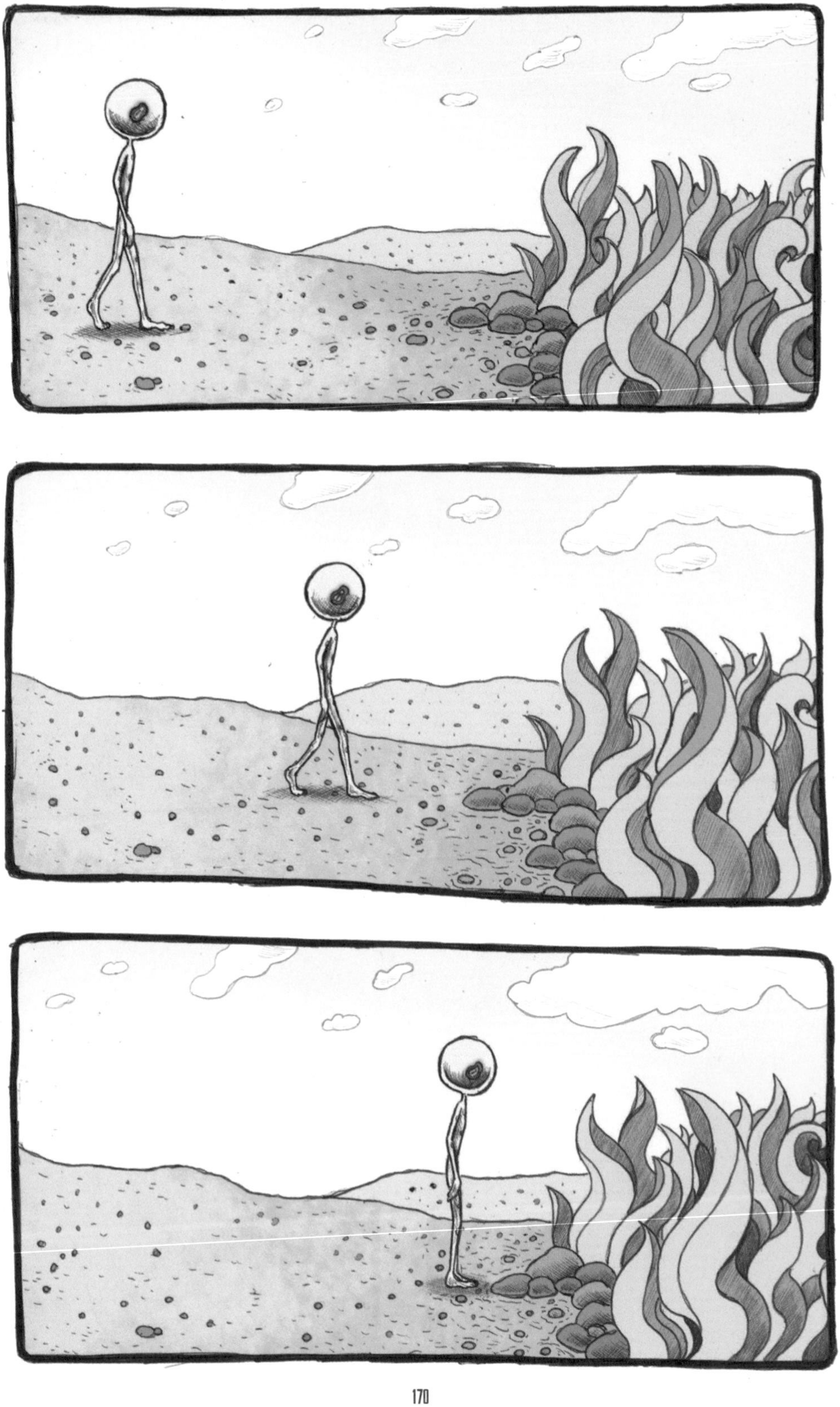

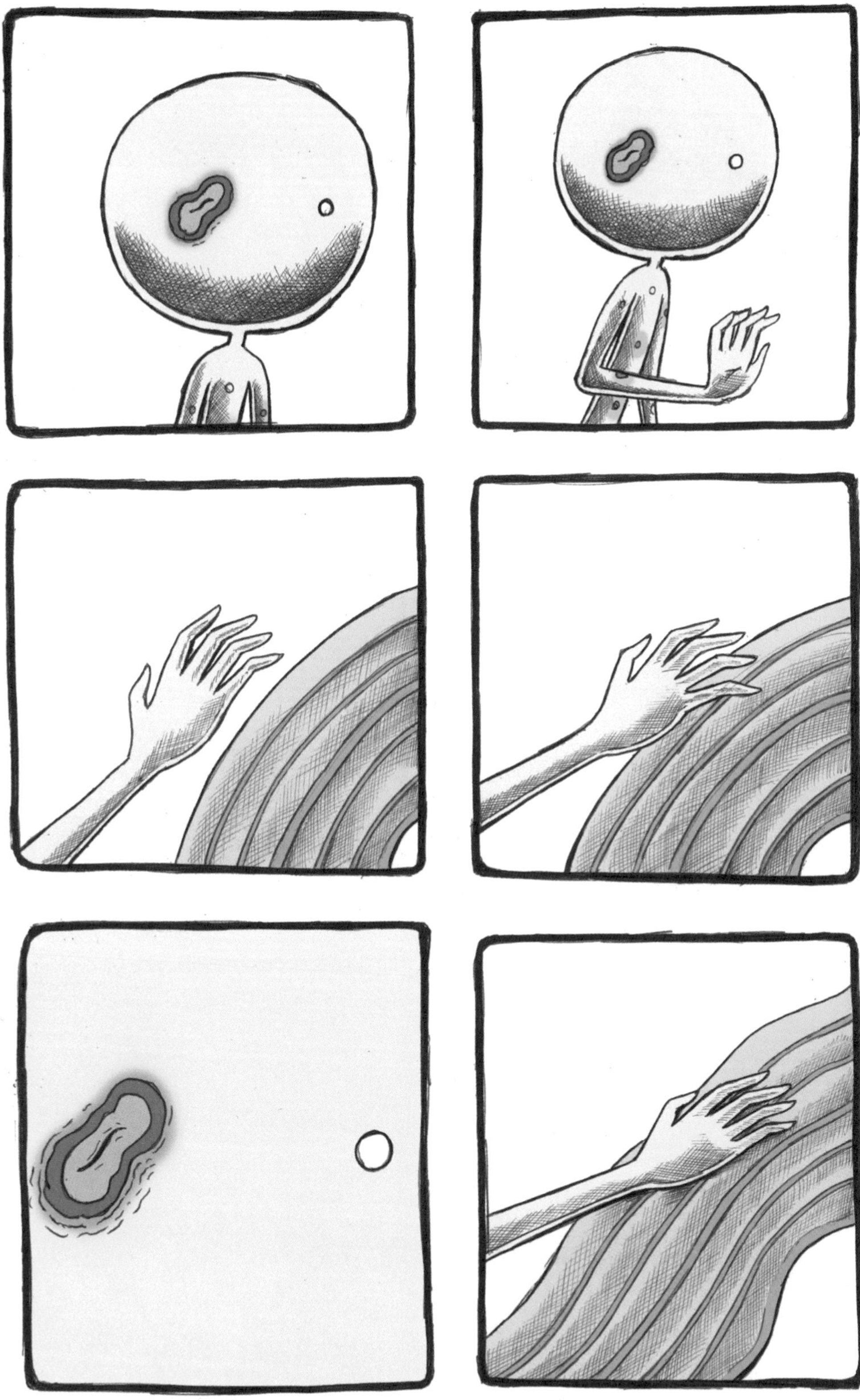

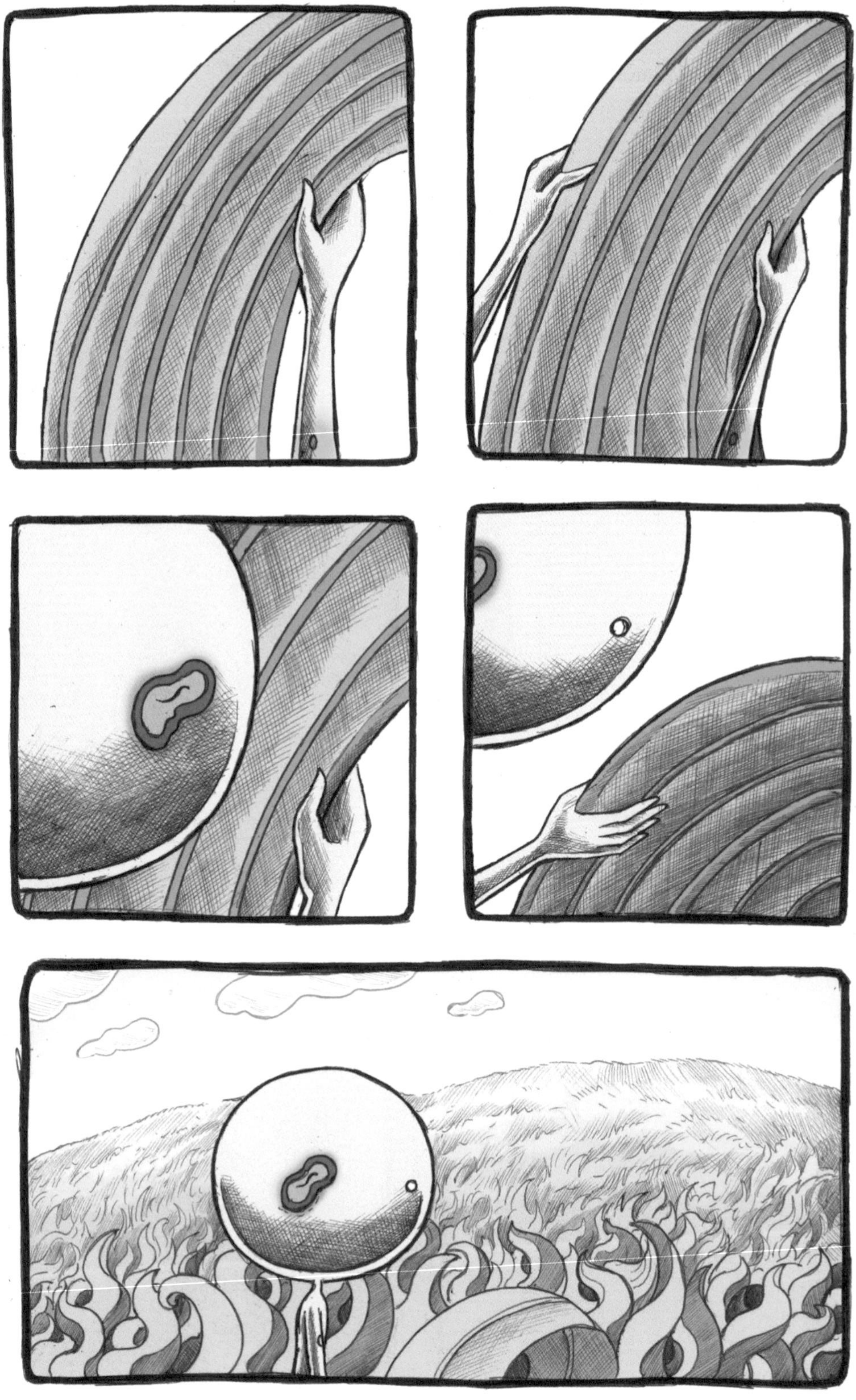

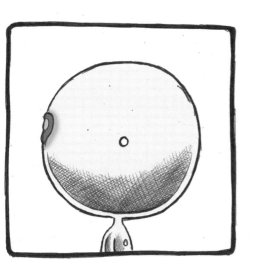
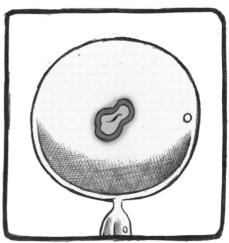

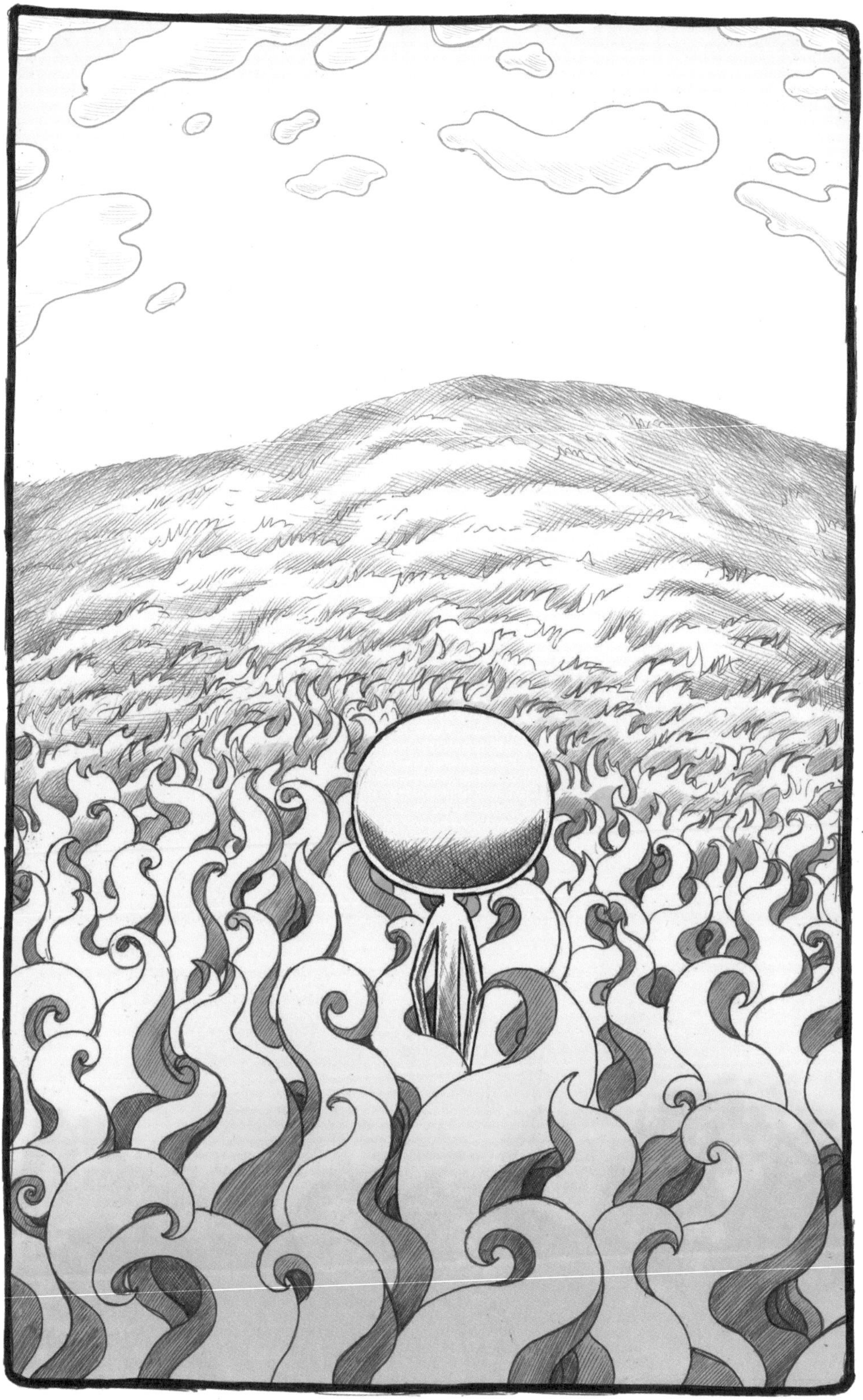

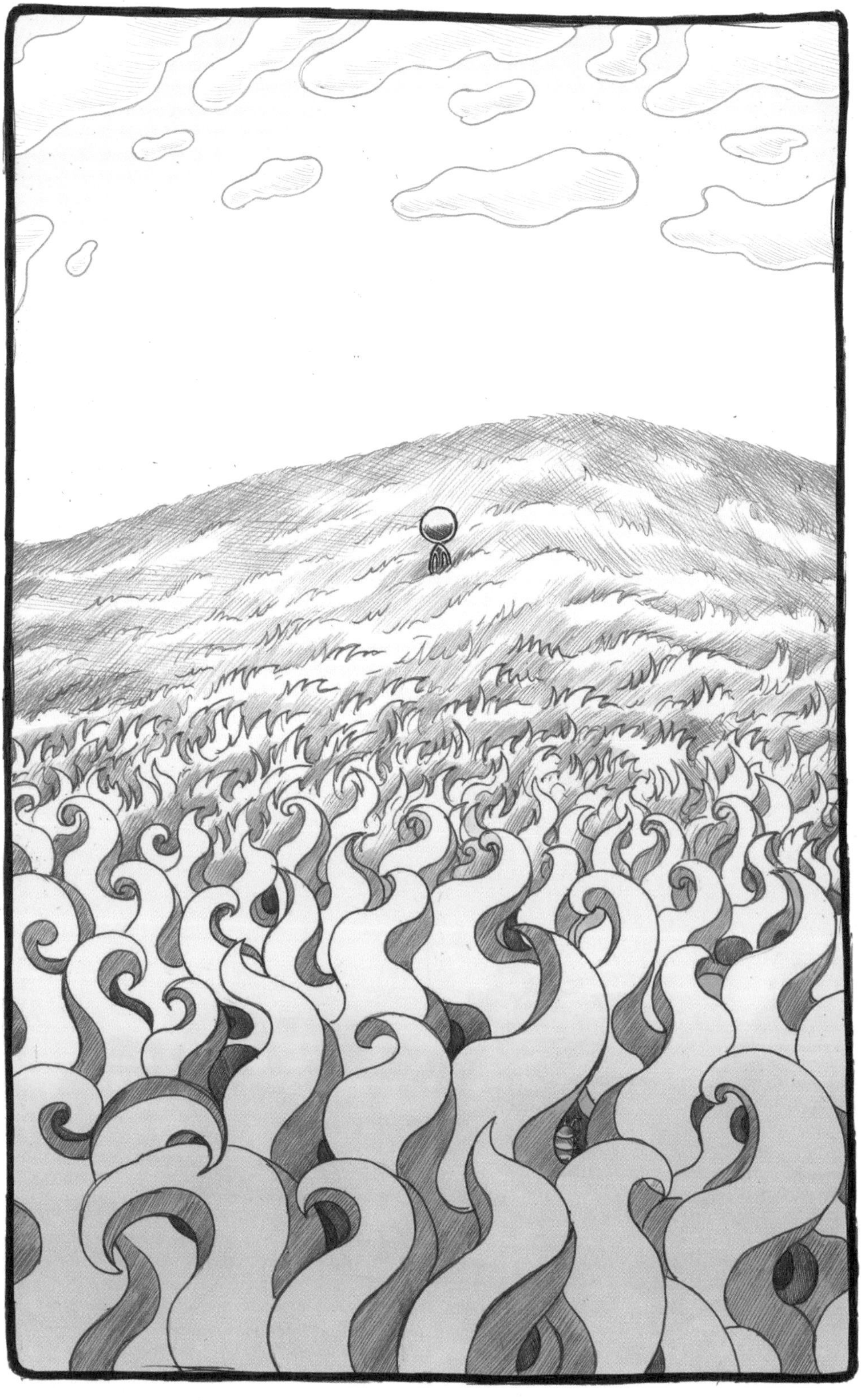

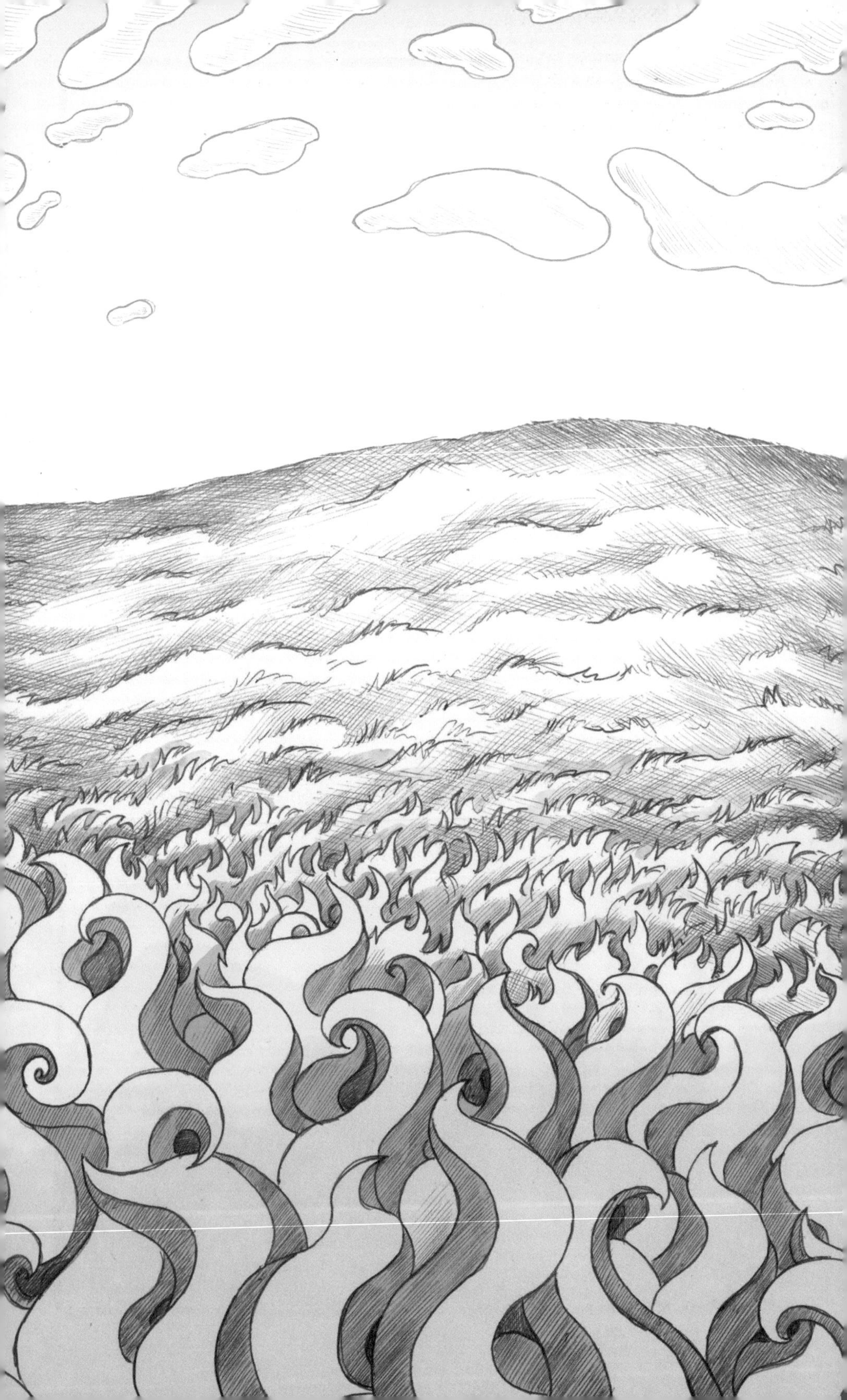